BENDIS◊OEMING
Takio

Created by:
Brian Michael Bendis,
Michael Avon Oeming & Olivia Bendis
Executed by:
Brian Michael Bendis & Michael Avon Oeming
Layout Assists: Taki Soma
Colors: Nick Filardi
Letters & Production: Chris Eliopoulos
Editor: Jennifer Grunwald
Book Design: Patrick McGrath
Cover Design: Tim Daniel
Business Affairs: Alisa Bendis

PREVIOUSLY

Two sisters in a multi-racial, adoptive family are driving each other insane! Their overprotective mother makes them do everything together. They can't get away from each other!

But when a one-of-a-kind, once-in-a-lifetime accident gives them real-life superpowers, these two sisters become the first actual superheroes in the entire world. And it is awesome! Now the sisters have to get along, save the world and get home by six...or they are so grounded!

TAKIO 2. First printing 2013. Contains material originally published in magazine form as TAKIO VOL. 2 #1-4. ISBN# 978-0-7851-6553-8. Published by MARVEL WORLDWIDE, INC., a subsidiary of MARVEL ENTERTAINMENT, LLC. OFFICE OF PUBLICATION: 417 5th Avenue, New York, NY 10016. Copyright © 2012 and 2013 Jinxworld, Inc. All rights reserved. Takio, its logo design, and all characters featured in or on this issue and the distinctive names and likenesses thereof, and all related indicia are trademarks of Jinxworld, Inc. ICON and its logos are TM & © Marvel Characters, Inc. No similarity between any of the names, characters, persons, and/or institutions in this magazine with those of any living or dead person or institution is intended, and any such similarity that may exist is purely coincidental. $16.99 per copy in the U.S. and $18.99 in Canada (GST #R127032852); Canadian Agreement #40668537. **Printed in the U.S.A. Manufactured between 9/23/2013 and 11/4/2013 by R.R. DONNELLEY, INC., SALEM, VA, USA. by SHERIDAN BOOKS, INC., CHELSEA, MI, USA.**

10 9 8 7 6 5 4 3 2 1

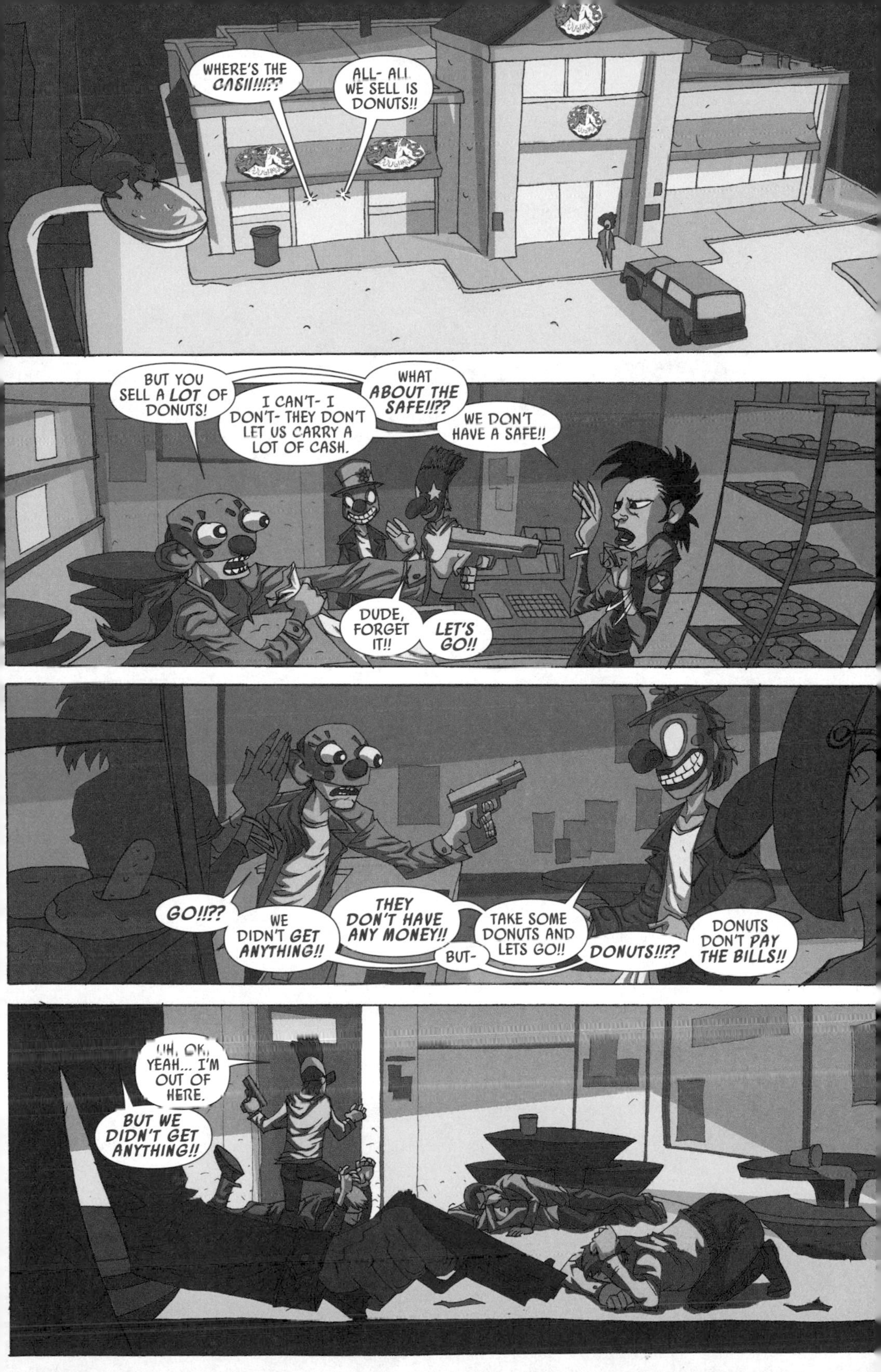
WHERE'S THE CASH!!!??
ALL- ALL WE SELL IS DONUTS!!
BUT YOU SELL A LOT OF DONUTS!
I CAN'T- I DON'T- THEY DON'T LET US CARRY A LOT OF CASH.
WHAT ABOUT THE SAFE!!??
WE DON'T HAVE A SAFE!!
DUDE, FORGET IT!!
LET'S GO!!
GO!!??
WE DIDN'T GET ANYTHING!!
THEY DON'T HAVE ANY MONEY!!
BUT-
TAKE SOME DONUTS AND LETS GO!!
DONUTS!!??
DONUTS DON'T PAY THE BILLS!!
UH, OK, YEAH... I'M OUT OF HERE.
BUT WE DIDN'T GET ANYTHING!!

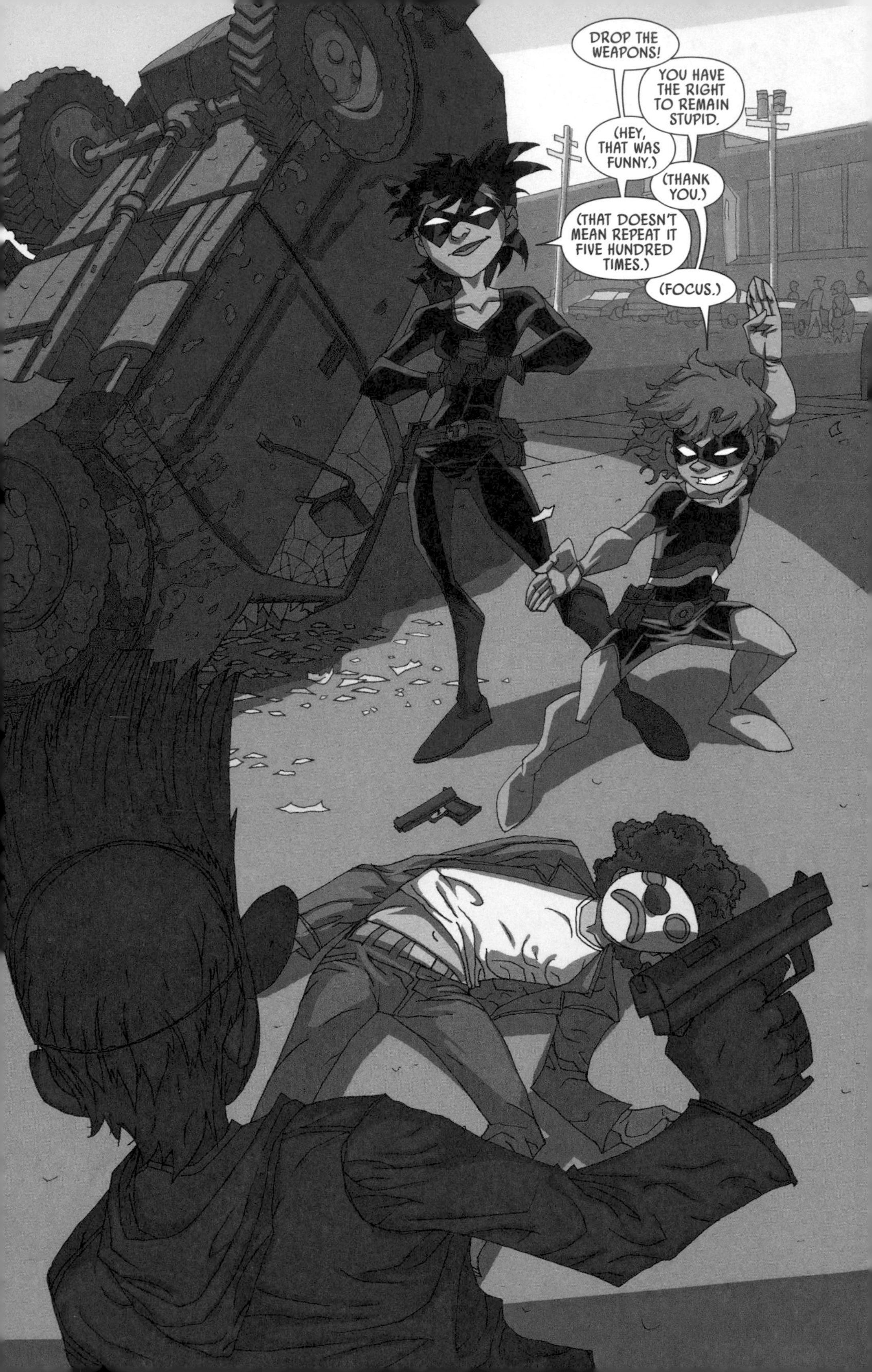
DROP THE WEAPONS!
YOU HAVE THE RIGHT TO REMAIN STUPID.
(HEY, THAT WAS FUNNY.)
(THANK YOU.)
(THAT DOESN'T MEAN REPEAT IT FIVE HUNDRED TIMES.)
(FOCUS.)

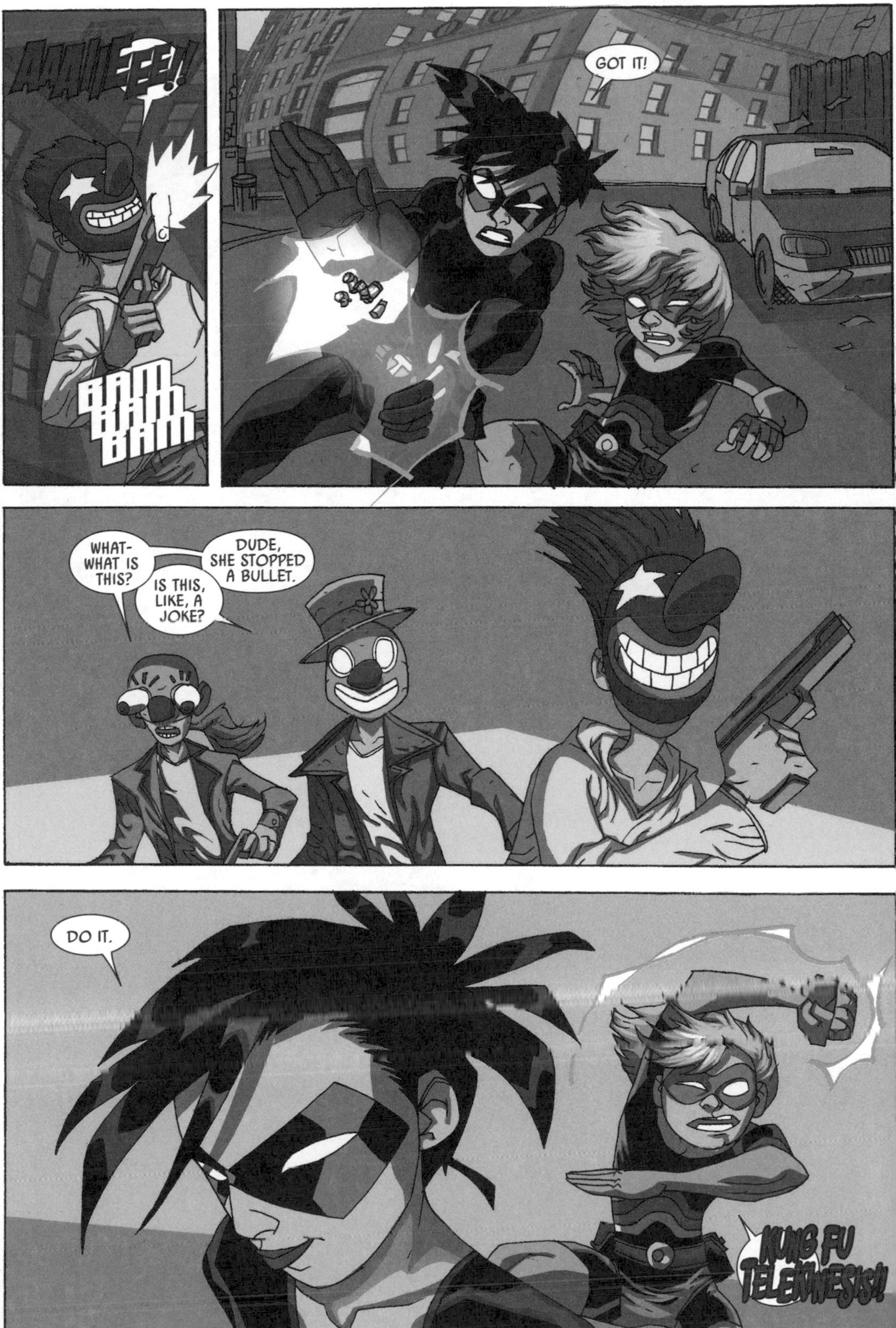

AAAIIEEE!!
BAM BAM BAM
GOT IT!
WHAT- WHAT IS THIS?
DUDE, SHE STOPPED A BULLET.
IS THIS, LIKE, A JOKE?
DO IT.
KUNG FU TELEKINESIS!!

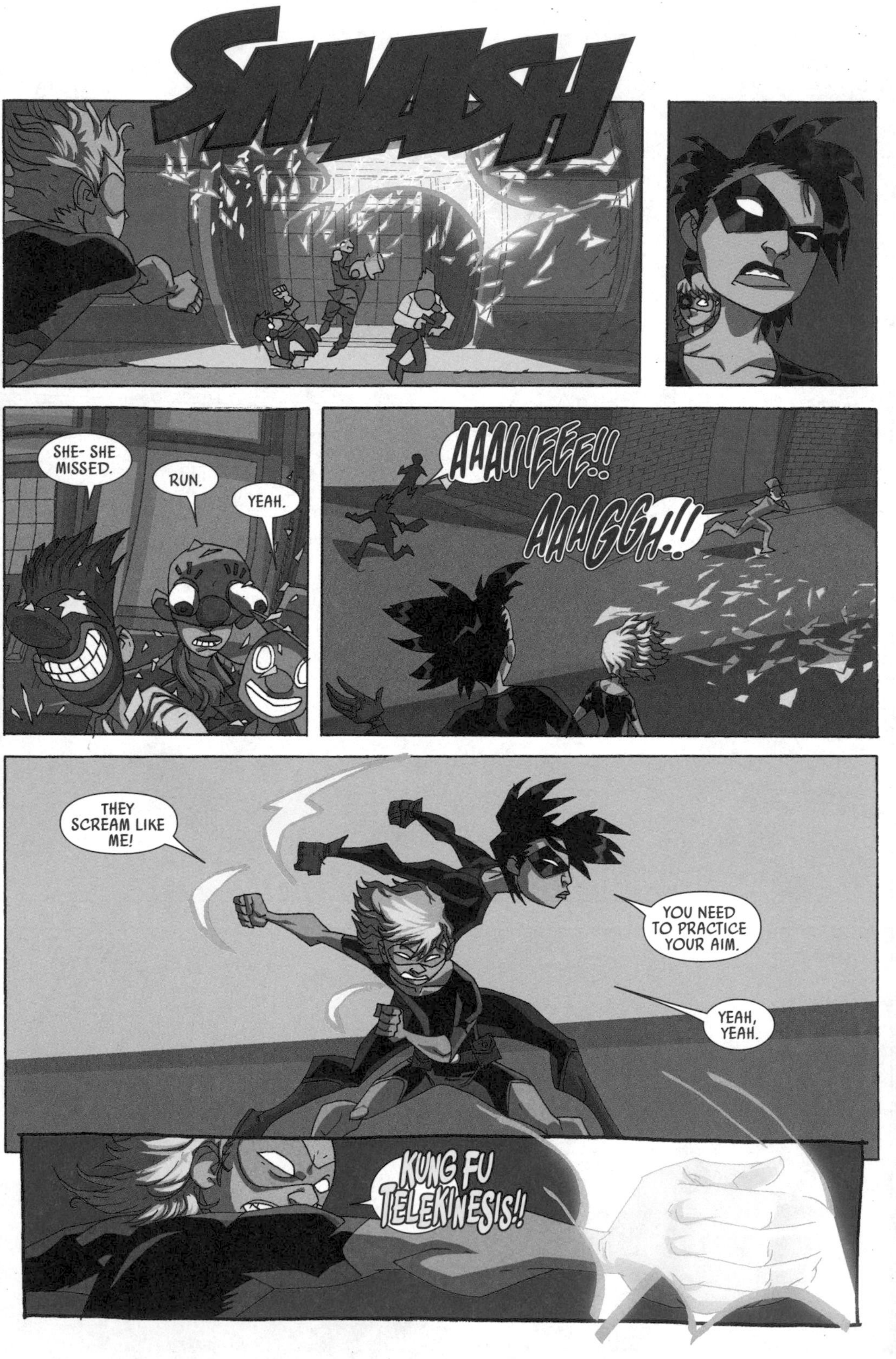
SMASH
SHE- SHE MISSED.
RUN.
YEAH.
AAAIIIEEE!!
AAAGGH!!
THEY SCREAM LIKE ME!
YOU NEED TO PRACTICE YOUR AIM.
YEAH, YEAH.
KUNG FU TELEKINESIS!!

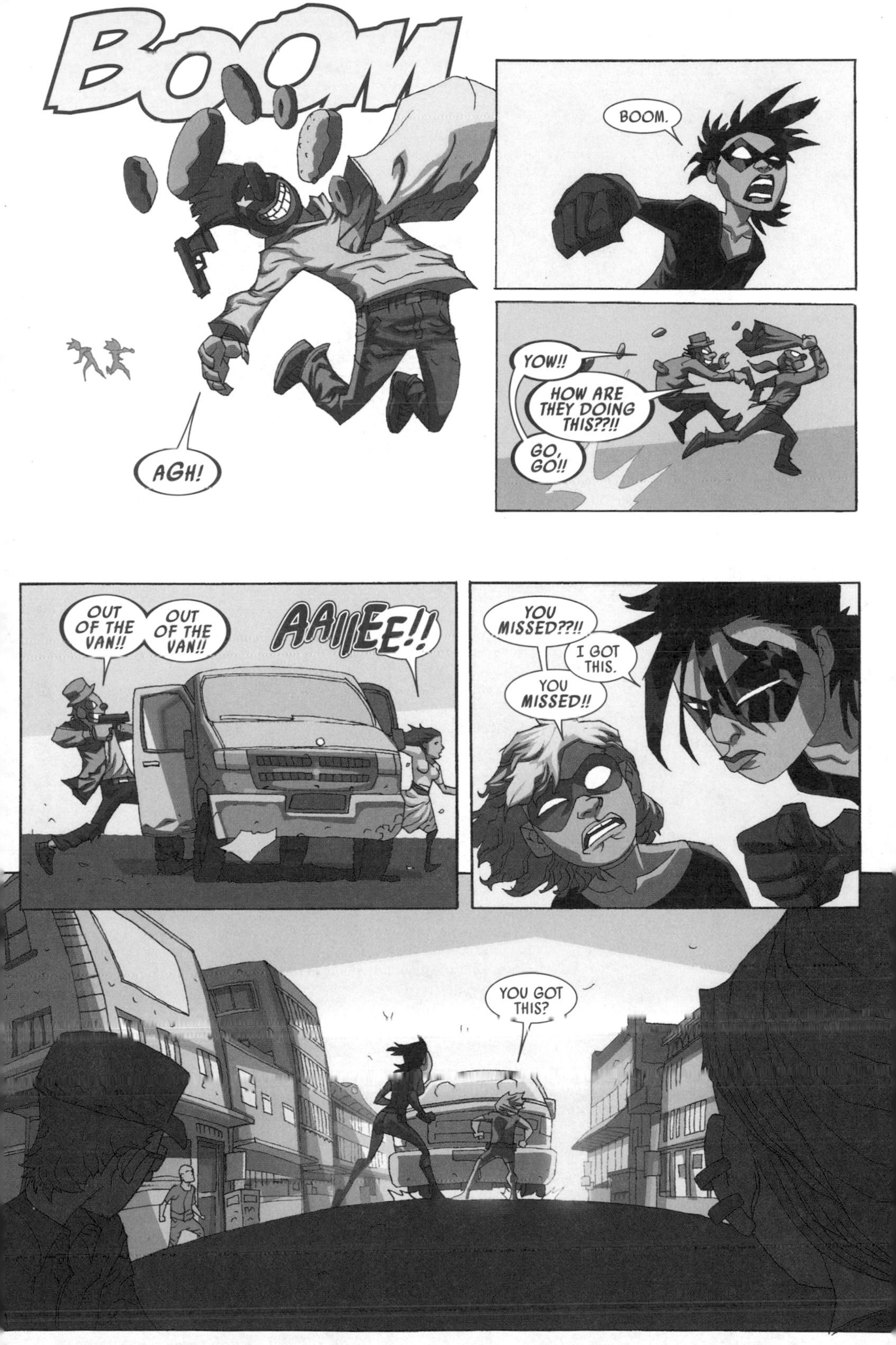
BOOM
AGH!
BOOM.
YOW!!
HOW ARE THEY DOING THIS??!!
GO, GO!!
OUT OF THE VAN!!
OUT OF THE VAN!!
AAIIEE!!
YOU MISSED??!!
I GOT THIS.
YOU MISSED!!
YOU GOT THIS?

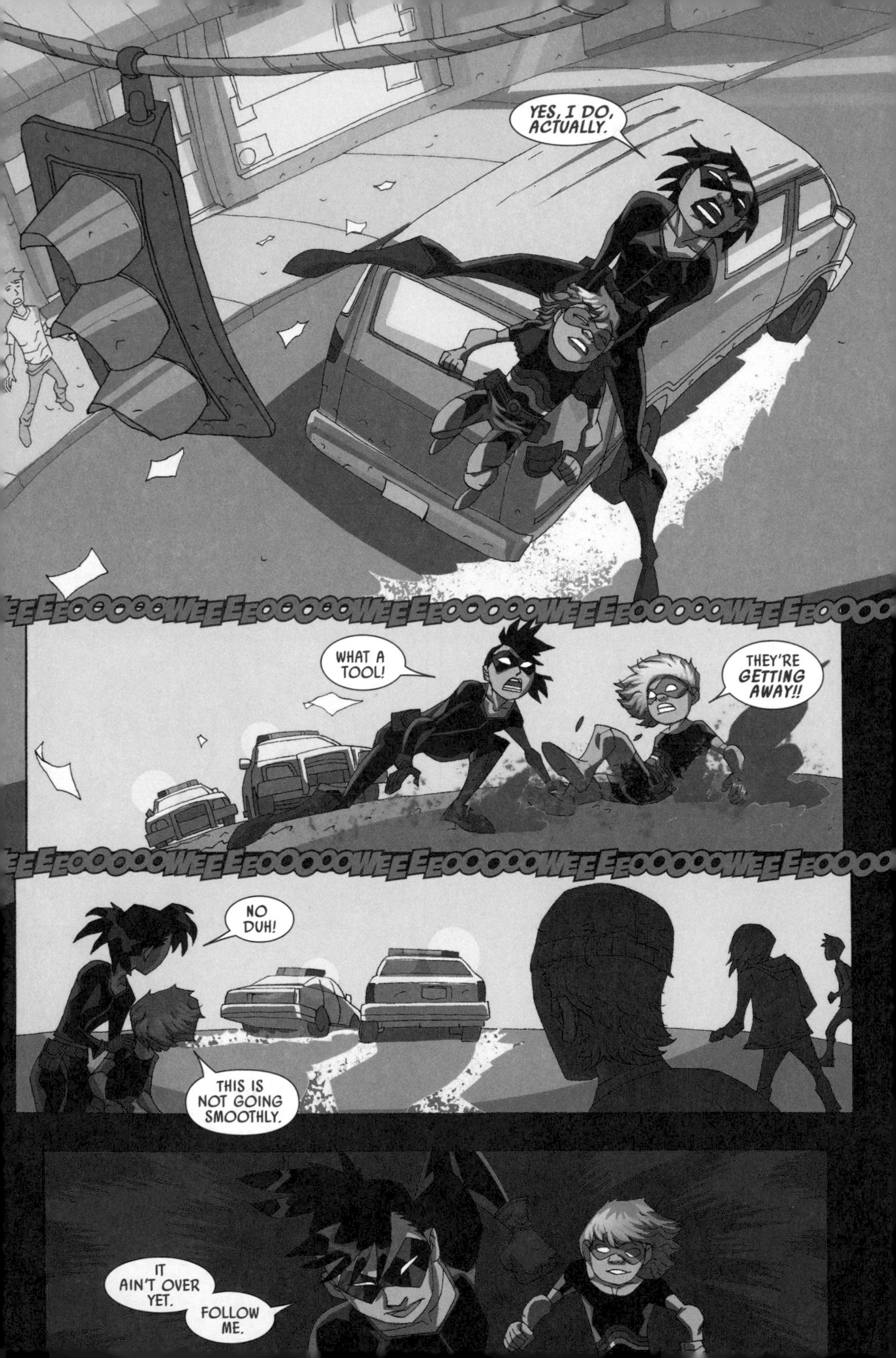
YES, I DO, ACTUALLY.
EEEEOOOOOOWEEEEOOOOOOWEEEEOOOOOOWEEEEOOOOOOWEEEEOOOOO
WHAT A TOOL!
THEY'RE GETTING AWAY!!
EEEEOOOOOOWEEEEOOOOOOWEEEEOOOOOOWEEEEOOOOOOWEEEEOOOOO
NO DUH!
THIS IS NOT GOING SMOOTHLY.
IT AIN'T OVER YET.
FOLLOW ME.

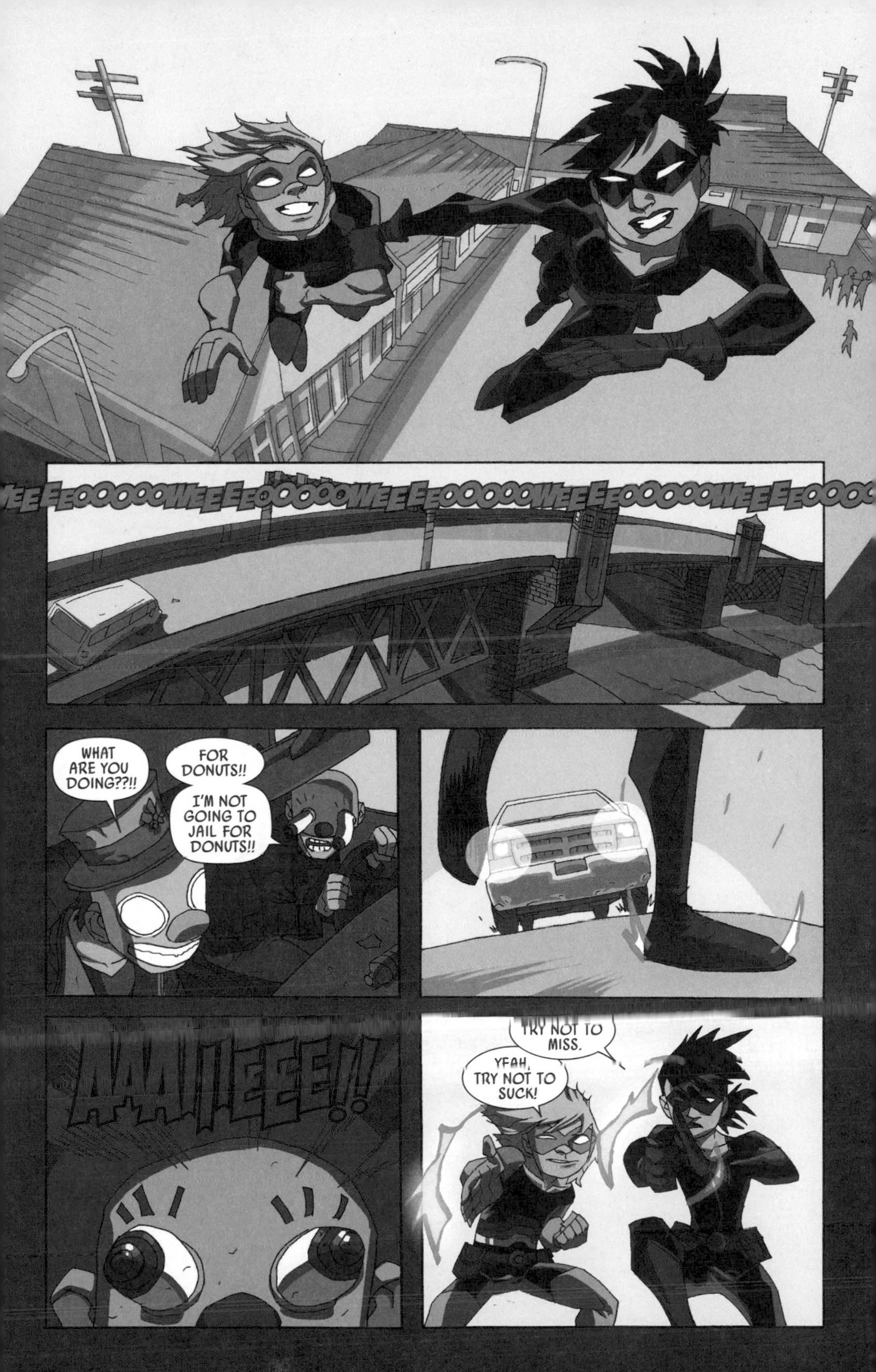
WEEEEOOOOOOWEEEEOOOOOOWEEEEOOOOOOWEEEEOOOO
WHAT ARE YOU DOING??!!
FOR DONUTS!!
I'M NOT GOING TO JAIL FOR DONUTS!!
AAAIEEEE!!
TRY NOT TO MISS.
YEAH, TRY NOT TO SUCK!

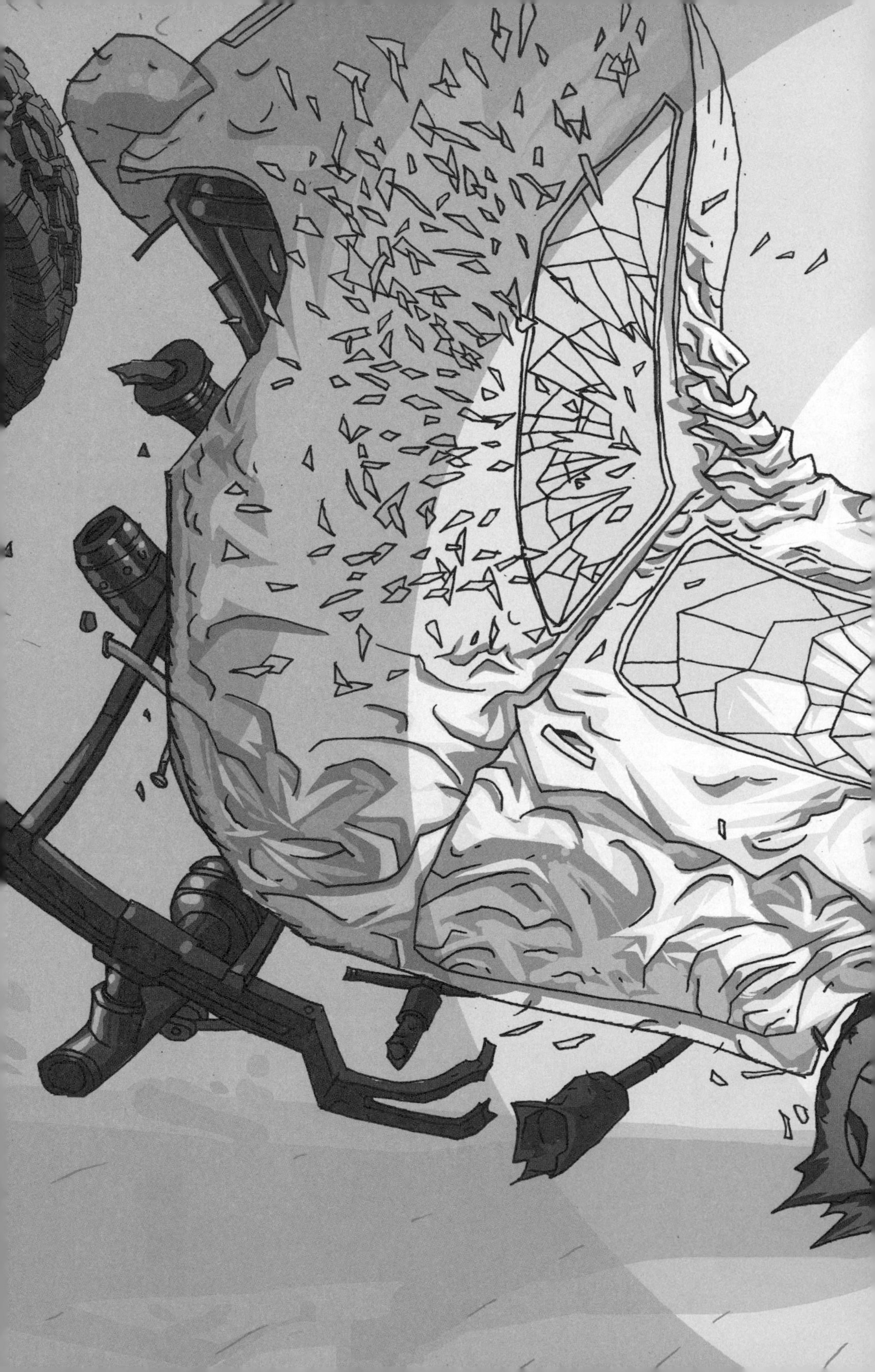

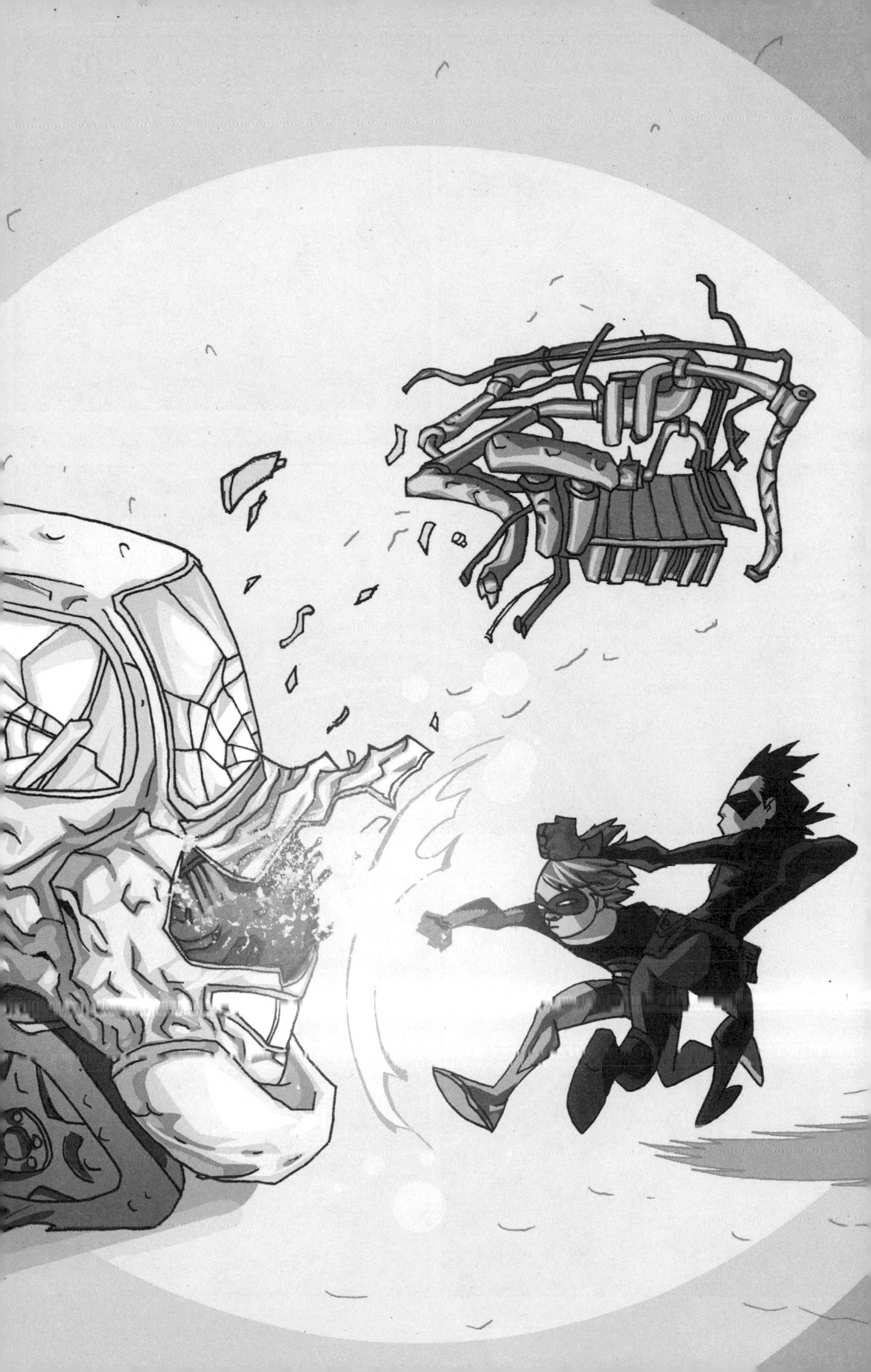

WHOAWAZAKI!

THIS IS— THIS IS EMBARRASSING.

I TOLD YOU!

TOLD ME WHAT??

EEEEOOOOOWEEEEOOOOOWEEEEOOOOOWEEEEOOOOOWEEEEOOOOOWEEEEOOOOO

GET YOUR HANDS ON YOUR HEADS!!

EVERYONE ON THE GROUND.

WE SHOULD STAY AND TAKE A BOW.

WE SHOULD GET OUT OF HERE BEFORE WE GET ARRESTED, UNMASKED AND GROUNDED.

OR THAT.

WHAT WAS THAT??

HOW SHOULD I KNOW??

"LADIES AND GENTLEMEN, OUR FIRST GUEST IS THE CUTE HALF OF THE SUPERHERO DUO TAKIO...

"MAKING HER TALK SHOW DEBUT..."

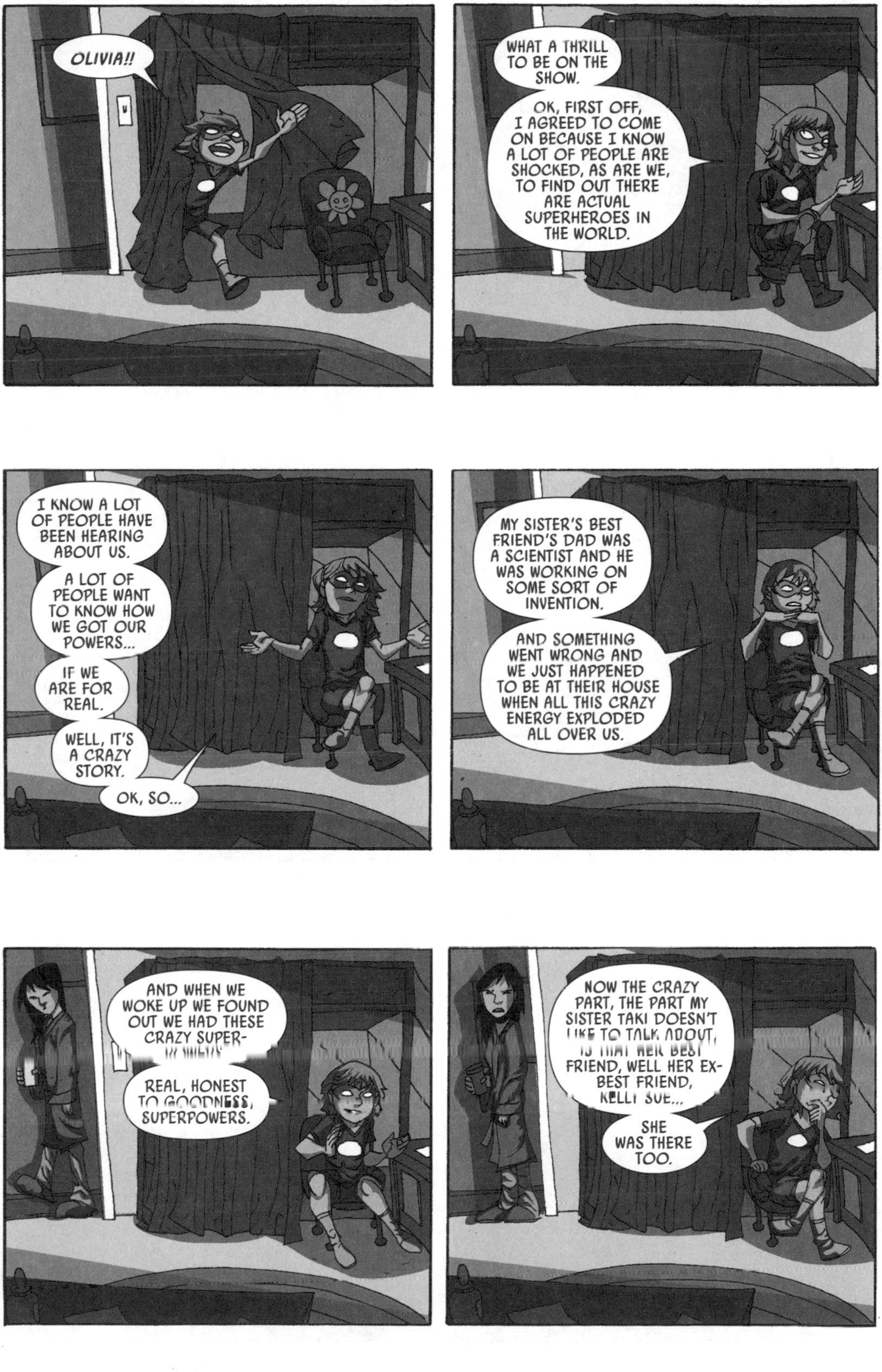
OLIVIA!!
WHAT A THRILL TO BE ON THE SHOW.
OK, FIRST OFF, I AGREED TO COME ON BECAUSE I KNOW A LOT OF PEOPLE ARE SHOCKED, AS ARE WE, TO FIND OUT THERE ARE ACTUAL SUPERHEROES IN THE WORLD.
I KNOW A LOT OF PEOPLE HAVE BEEN HEARING ABOUT US.
A LOT OF PEOPLE WANT TO KNOW HOW WE GOT OUR POWERS...
IF WE ARE FOR REAL.
WELL, IT'S A CRAZY STORY.
OK, SO...
MY SISTER'S BEST FRIEND'S DAD WAS A SCIENTIST AND HE WAS WORKING ON SOME SORT OF INVENTION.
AND SOMETHING WENT WRONG AND WE JUST HAPPENED TO BE AT THEIR HOUSE WHEN ALL THIS CRAZY ENERGY EXPLODED ALL OVER US.
AND WHEN WE WOKE UP WE FOUND OUT WE HAD THESE CRAZY SUPER-
REAL, HONEST TO GOODNESS, SUPERPOWERS.
NOW THE CRAZY PART, THE PART MY SISTER TAKI DOESN'T LIKE TO TALK ABOUT, IS THAT HER BEST FRIEND, WELL HER EX-BEST FRIEND, KELLY SUE...
SHE WAS THERE TOO.

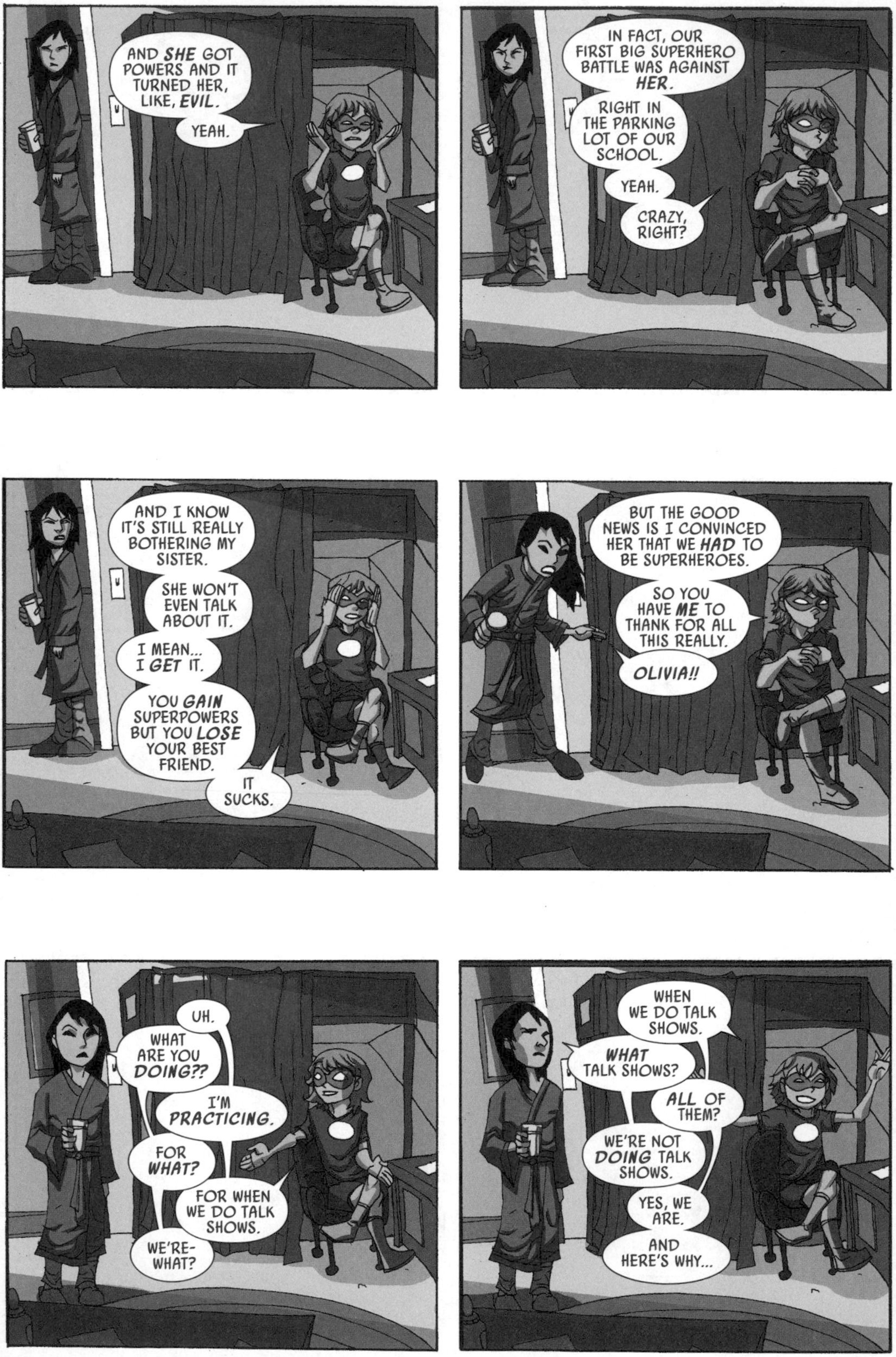
AND SHE GOT POWERS AND IT TURNED HER, LIKE, EVIL.
YEAH.
IN FACT, OUR FIRST BIG SUPERHERO BATTLE WAS AGAINST HER.
RIGHT IN THE PARKING LOT OF OUR SCHOOL.
YEAH.
CRAZY, RIGHT?
AND I KNOW IT'S STILL REALLY BOTHERING MY SISTER.
SHE WON'T EVEN TALK ABOUT IT.
I MEAN... I GET IT.
YOU GAIN SUPERPOWERS BUT YOU LOSE YOUR BEST FRIEND.
IT SUCKS.
BUT THE GOOD NEWS IS I CONVINCED HER THAT WE HAD TO BE SUPERHEROES.
SO YOU HAVE ME TO THANK FOR ALL THIS REALLY.
OLIVIA!!
UH.
WHAT ARE YOU DOING??
I'M PRACTICING.
FOR WHAT?
FOR WHEN WE DO TALK SHOWS.
WE'RE- WHAT?
WHEN WE DO TALK SHOWS.
WHAT TALK SHOWS?
ALL OF THEM?
WE'RE NOT DOING TALK SHOWS.
YES, WE ARE.
AND HERE'S WHY...

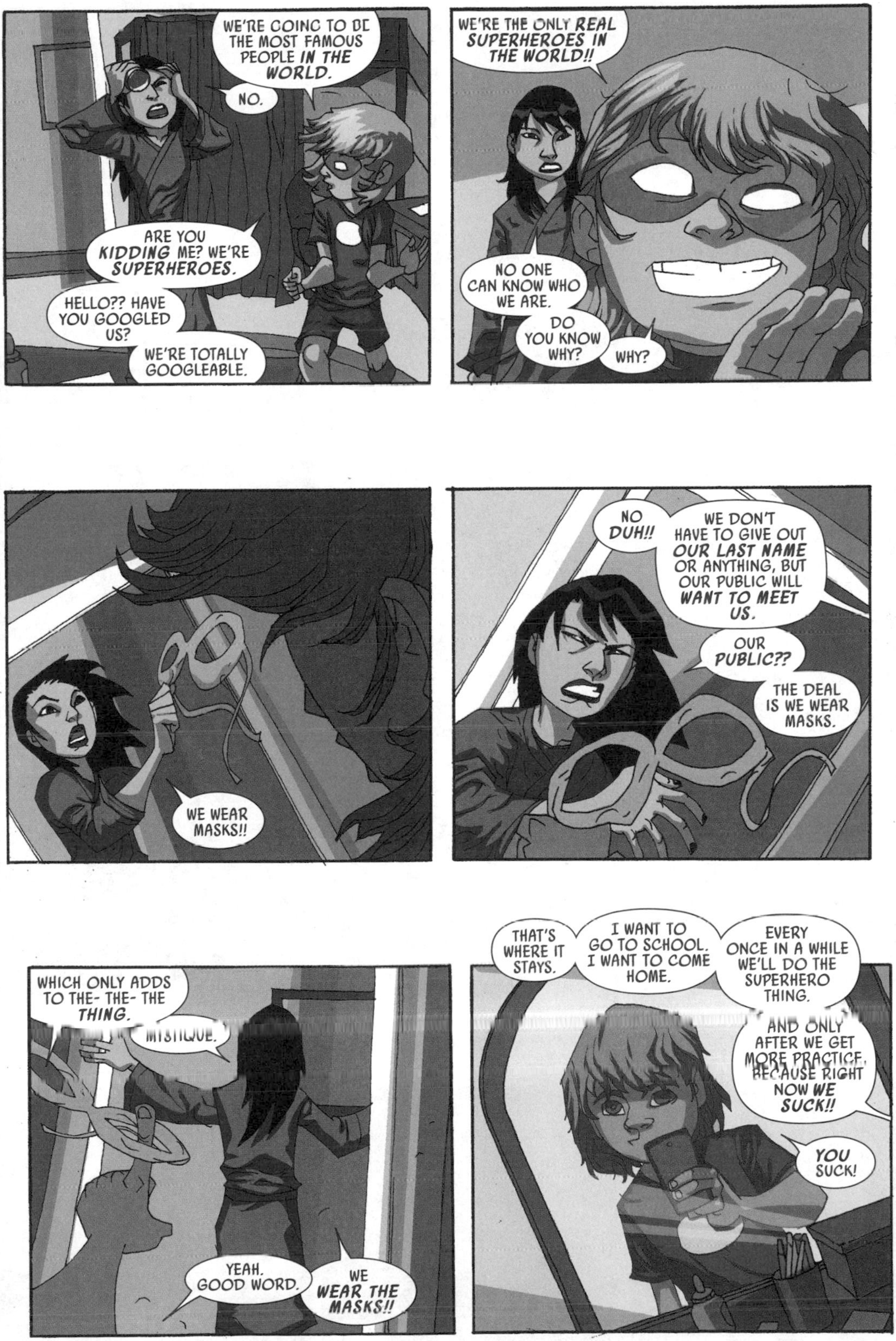

WE'RE GOING TO BE THE MOST FAMOUS PEOPLE IN THE WORLD.
NO.
ARE YOU KIDDING ME? WE'RE SUPERHEROES.
HELLO?? HAVE YOU GOOGLED US?
WE'RE TOTALLY GOOGLEABLE.
WE'RE THE ONLY REAL SUPERHEROES IN THE WORLD!!
NO ONE CAN KNOW WHO WE ARE.
DO YOU KNOW WHY?
WHY?
WE WEAR MASKS!!
NO DUH!!
WE DON'T HAVE TO GIVE OUT OUR LAST NAME OR ANYTHING, BUT OUR PUBLIC WILL WANT TO MEET US.
OUR PUBLIC??
THE DEAL IS WE WEAR MASKS.
WHICH ONLY ADDS TO THE- THE- THE THING.
MYSTIQUE.
YEAH. GOOD WORD.
WE WEAR THE MASKS!!
THAT'S WHERE IT STAYS.
I WANT TO GO TO SCHOOL. I WANT TO COME HOME.
EVERY ONCE IN A WHILE WE'LL DO THE SUPERHERO THING.
AND ONLY AFTER WE GET MORE PRACTICE, BECAUSE RIGHT NOW WE SUCK!!
YOU SUCK!

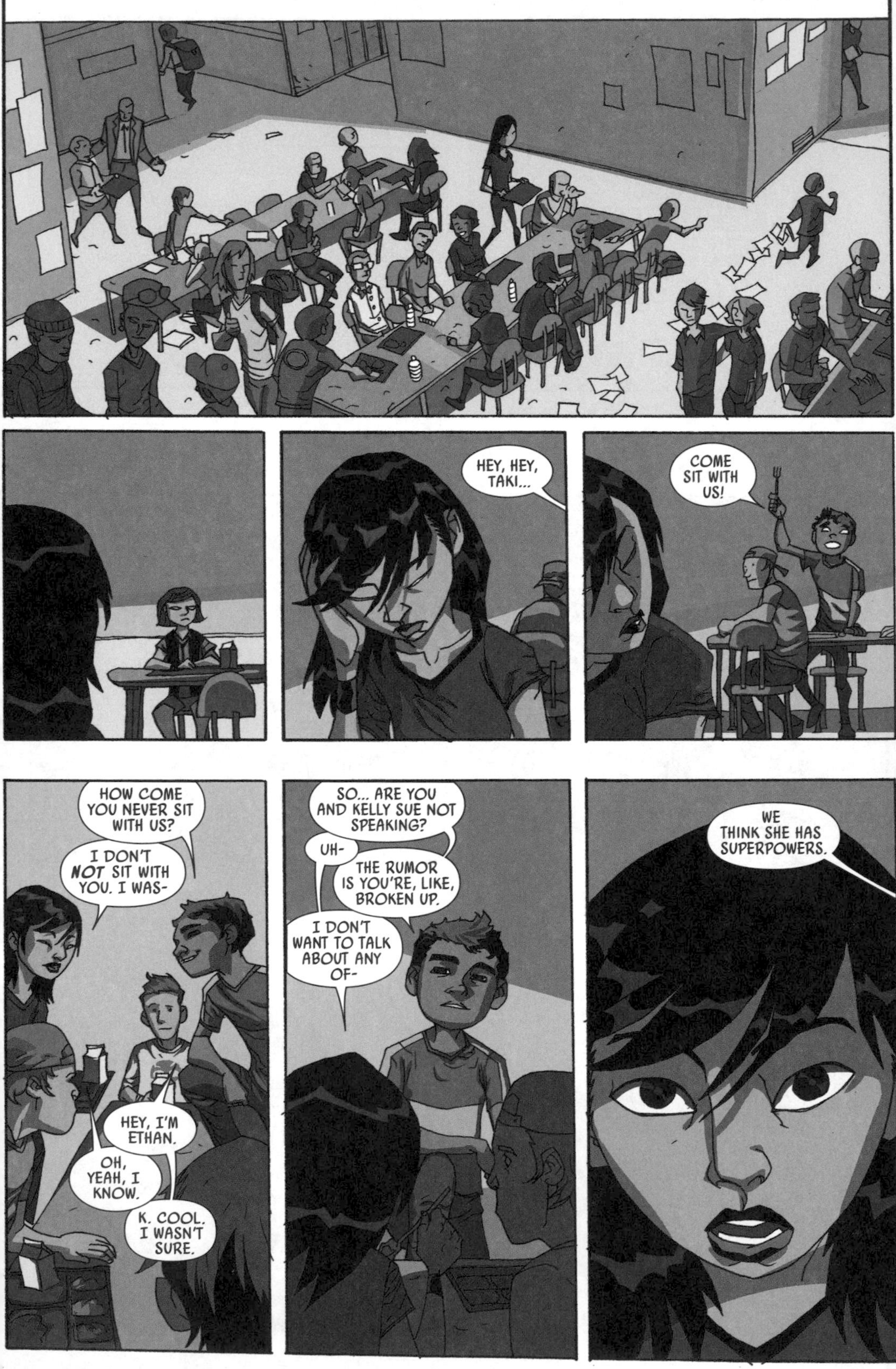
HEY, HEY, TAKI...
COME SIT WITH US!
HOW COME YOU NEVER SIT WITH US?
I DON'T *NOT* SIT WITH YOU. I WAS-
HEY, I'M ETHAN.
OH, YEAH, I KNOW.
K. COOL. I WASN'T SURE.
SO... ARE YOU AND KELLY SUE NOT SPEAKING?
UH-
THE RUMOR IS YOU'RE, LIKE, BROKEN UP.
I DON'T WANT TO TALK ABOUT ANY OF-
WE THINK SHE HAS SUPERPOWERS.

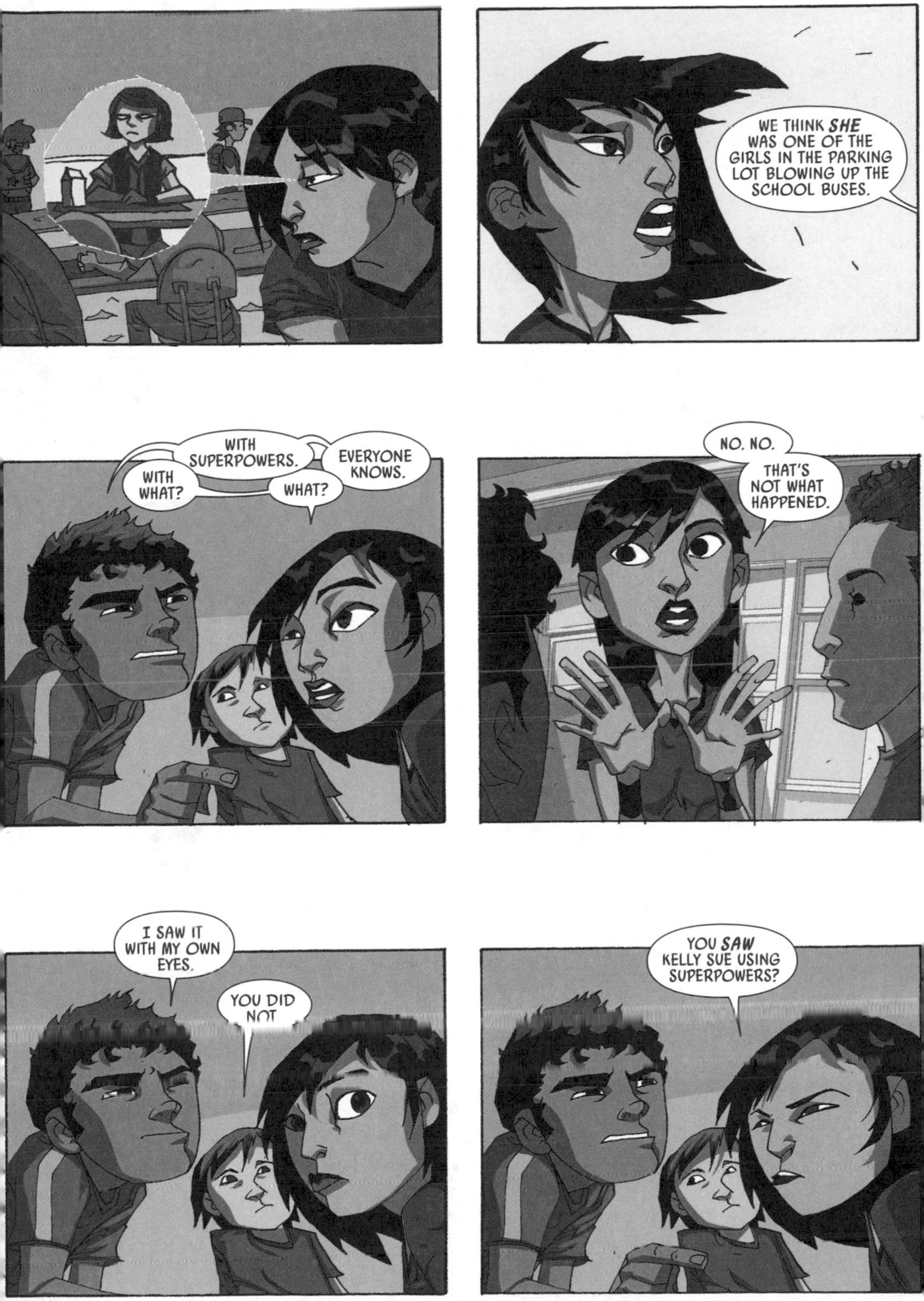
WE THINK **SHE** WAS ONE OF THE GIRLS IN THE PARKING LOT BLOWING UP THE SCHOOL BUSES.
WITH WHAT?
WITH SUPERPOWERS.
WHAT?
EVERYONE KNOWS.
NO. NO.
THAT'S NOT WHAT HAPPENED.
I SAW IT WITH MY OWN EYES.
YOU DID NOT
YOU **SAW** KELLY SUE USING SUPERPOWERS?

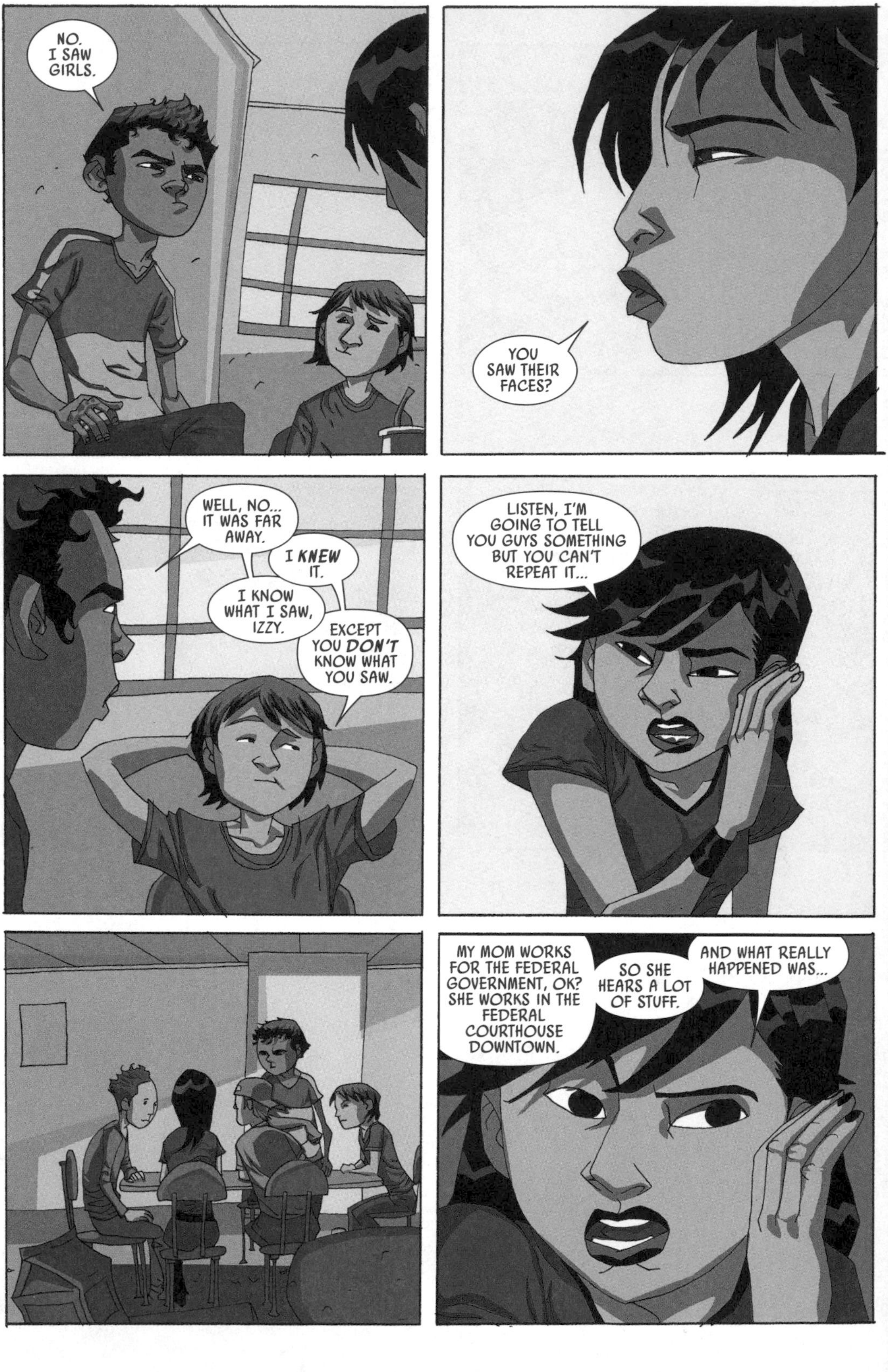
NO. I SAW GIRLS.
YOU SAW THEIR FACES?
WELL, NO... IT WAS FAR AWAY.
I KNEW IT.
I KNOW WHAT I SAW, IZZY.
EXCEPT YOU DON'T KNOW WHAT YOU SAW.
LISTEN, I'M GOING TO TELL YOU GUYS SOMETHING BUT YOU CAN'T REPEAT IT...
MY MOM WORKS FOR THE FEDERAL GOVERNMENT, OK? SHE WORKS IN THE FEDERAL COURTHOUSE DOWNTOWN.
SO SHE HEARS A LOT OF STUFF.
AND WHAT REALLY HAPPENED WAS...

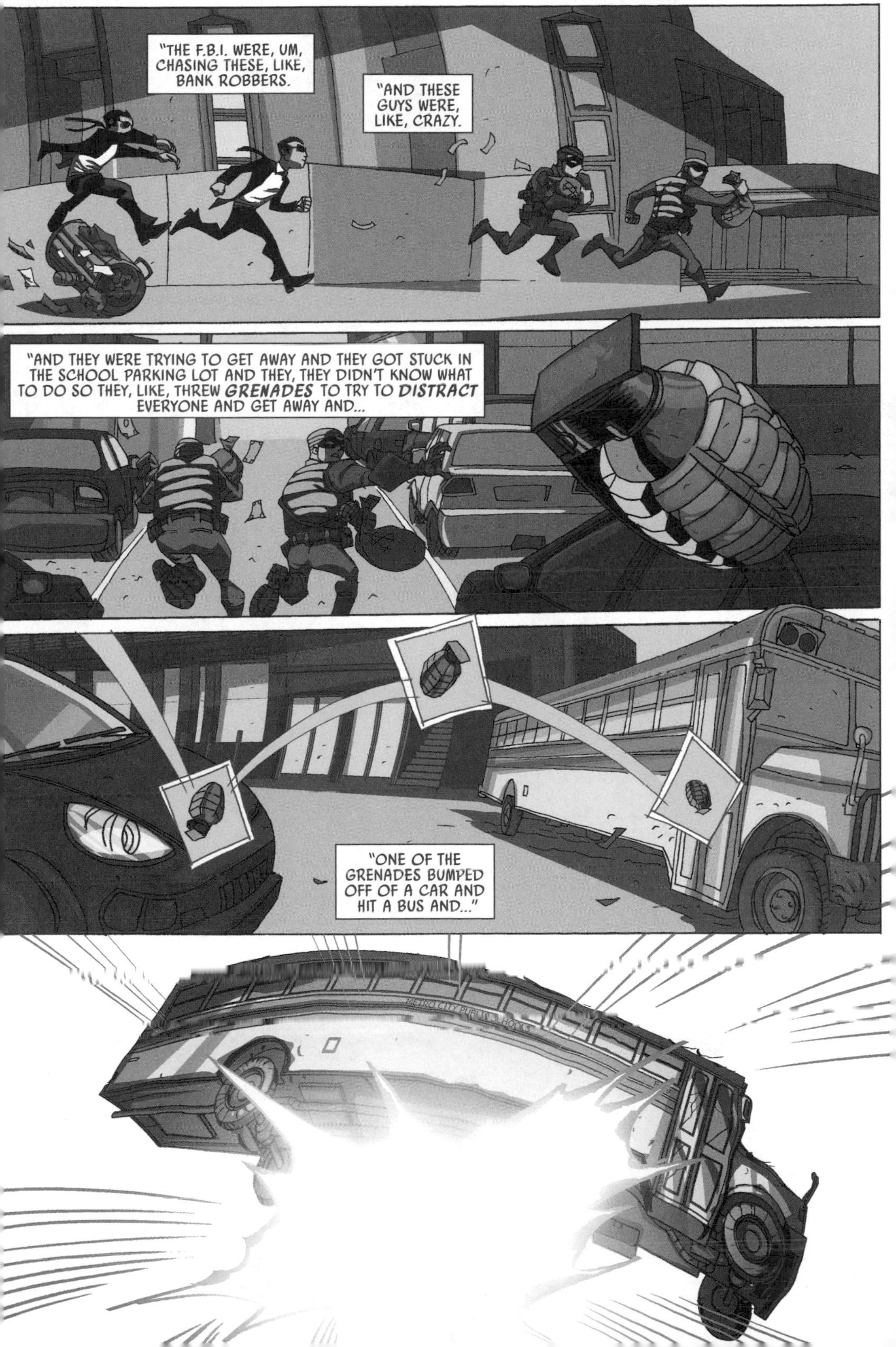
"THE F.B.I. WERE, UM, CHASING THESE, LIKE, BANK ROBBERS.
"AND THESE GUYS WERE, LIKE, CRAZY.
"AND THEY WERE TRYING TO GET AWAY AND THEY GOT STUCK IN THE SCHOOL PARKING LOT AND THEY, THEY DIDN'T KNOW WHAT TO DO SO THEY, LIKE, THREW GRENADES TO TRY TO DISTRACT EVERYONE AND GET AWAY AND...
"ONE OF THE GRENADES BUMPED OFF OF A CAR AND HIT A BUS AND..."

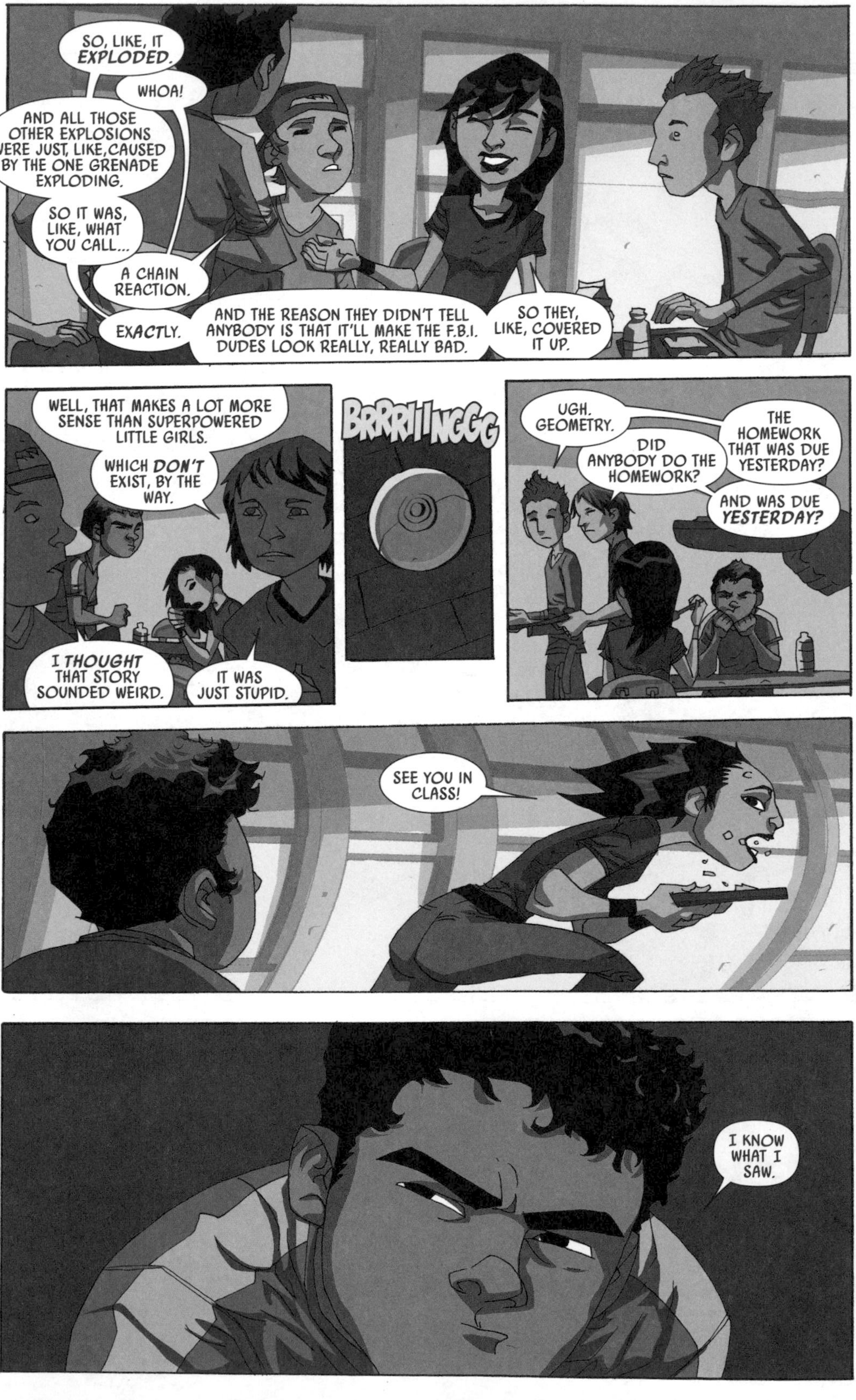
SO, LIKE, IT *EXPLODED.*
WHOA!
AND ALL THOSE OTHER EXPLOSIONS WERE JUST, LIKE,CAUSED BY THE ONE GRENADE EXPLODING.
SO IT WAS, LIKE, WHAT YOU CALL...
A CHAIN REACTION.
EXACTLY.
AND THE REASON THEY DIDN'T TELL ANYBODY IS THAT IT'LL MAKE THE F.B.I. DUDES LOOK REALLY, REALLY BAD.
SO THEY, LIKE, COVERED IT UP.
WELL, THAT MAKES A LOT MORE SENSE THAN SUPERPOWERED LITTLE GIRLS.
WHICH *DON'T* EXIST, BY THE WAY.
I *THOUGHT* THAT STORY SOUNDED WEIRD.
IT WAS JUST STUPID.
BRRRIIINGGG
UGH. GEOMETRY.
DID ANYBODY DO THE HOMEWORK?
THE HOMEWORK THAT WAS DUE YESTERDAY?
AND WAS DUE *YESTERDAY?*
SEE YOU IN CLASS!
I KNOW WHAT I SAW.

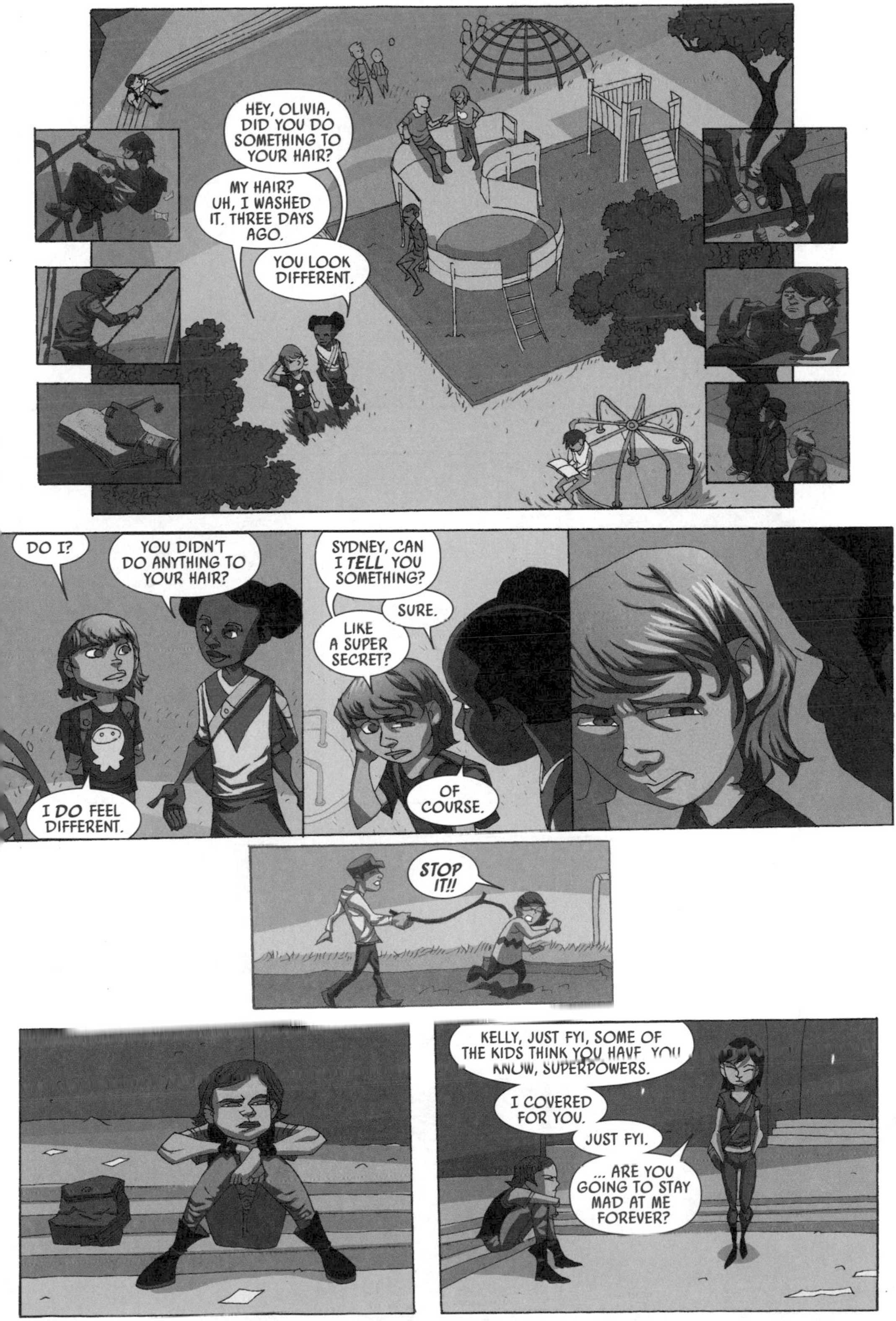
HEY, OLIVIA, DID YOU DO SOMETHING TO YOUR HAIR?
MY HAIR? UH, I WASHED IT. THREE DAYS AGO.
YOU LOOK DIFFERENT.
DO I?
YOU DIDN'T DO ANYTHING TO YOUR HAIR?
I DO FEEL DIFFERENT.
SYDNEY, CAN I TELL YOU SOMETHING?
SURE.
LIKE A SUPER SECRET?
OF COURSE.
STOP IT!!
KELLY, JUST FYI, SOME OF THE KIDS THINK YOU HAVE, YOU KNOW, SUPERPOWERS.
I COVERED FOR YOU.
JUST FYI.
... ARE YOU GOING TO STAY MAD AT ME FOREVER?

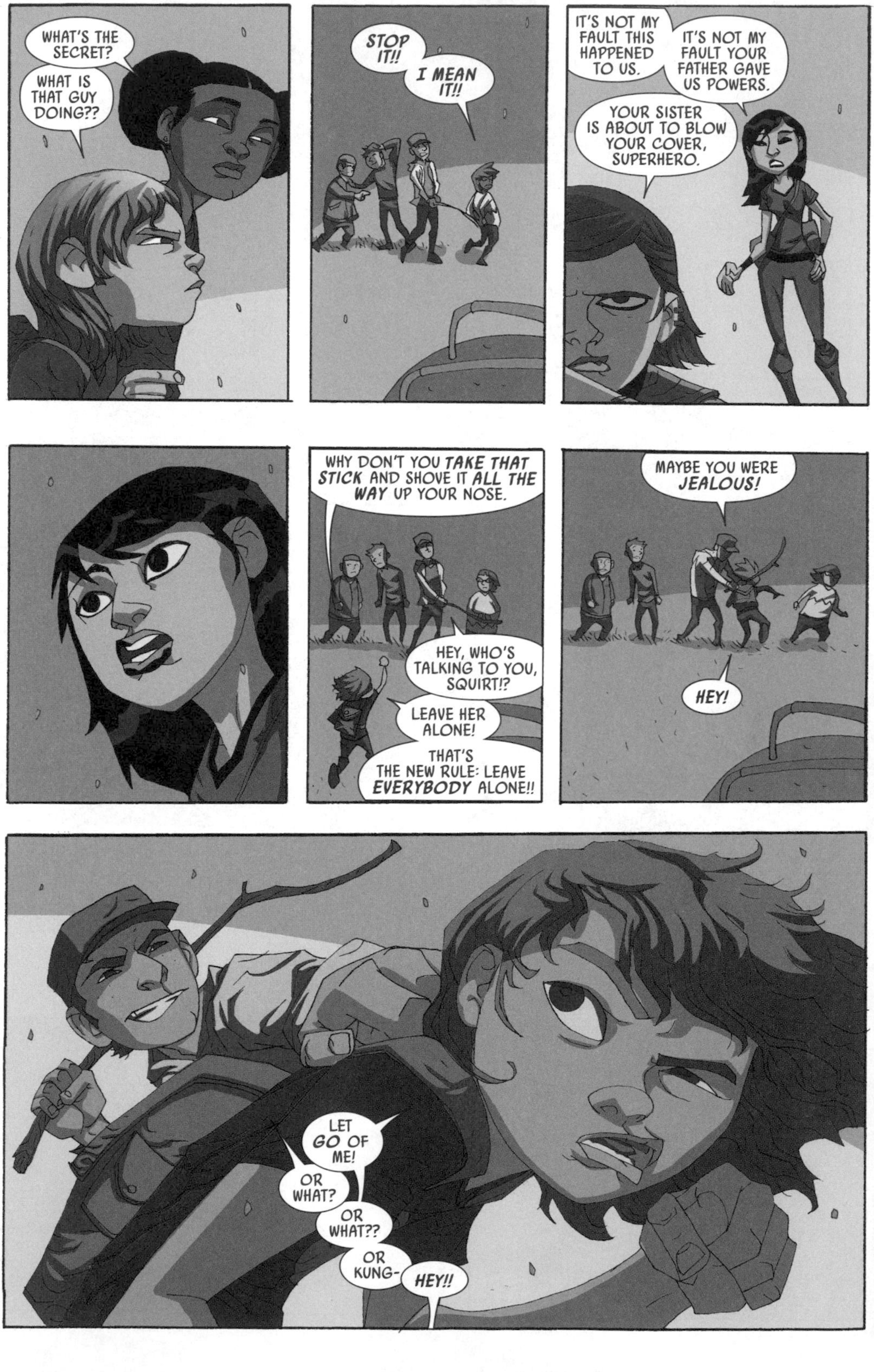
WHAT'S THE SECRET?
WHAT IS THAT GUY DOING??
STOP IT!!
I MEAN IT!!
IT'S NOT MY FAULT THIS HAPPENED TO US.
IT'S NOT MY FAULT YOUR FATHER GAVE US POWERS.
YOUR SISTER IS ABOUT TO BLOW YOUR COVER, SUPERHERO.
WHY DON'T YOU TAKE THAT STICK AND SHOVE IT ALL THE WAY UP YOUR NOSE.
HEY, WHO'S TALKING TO YOU, SQUIRT!?
LEAVE HER ALONE!
THAT'S THE NEW RULE: LEAVE EVERYBODY ALONE!!
MAYBE YOU WERE JEALOUS!
HEY!
LET GO OF ME!
OR WHAT?
OR WHAT??
OR KUNG-
HEY!!

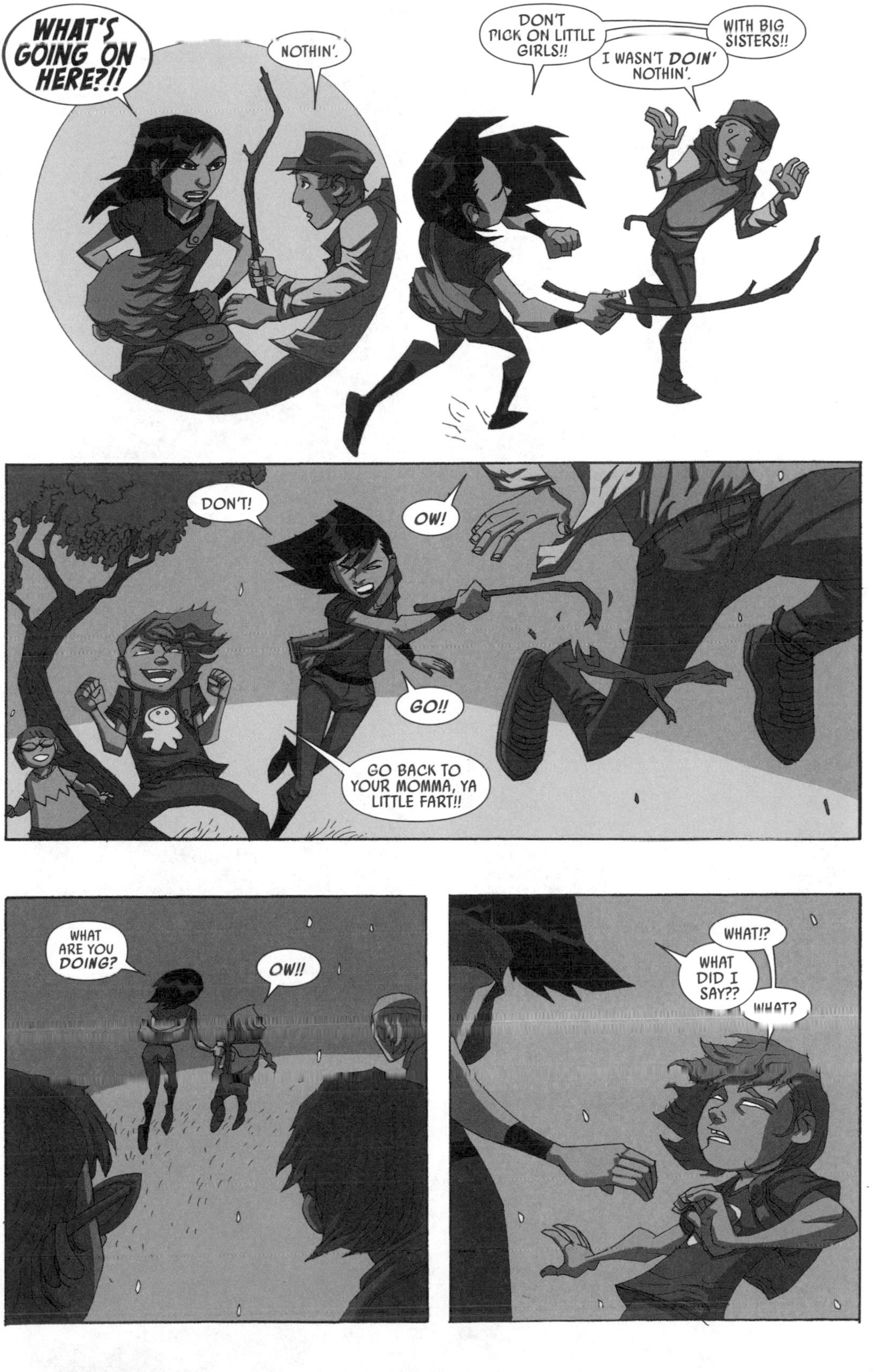
WHAT'S GOING ON HERE?!!
NOTHIN'.
DON'T PICK ON LITTLE GIRLS!!
WITH BIG SISTERS!!
I WASN'T DOIN' NOTHIN'.
DON'T!
OW!
GO!!
GO BACK TO YOUR MOMMA, YA LITTLE FART!!
WHAT ARE YOU DOING?
OW!!
WHAT!?
WHAT DID I SAY??
WHAT?

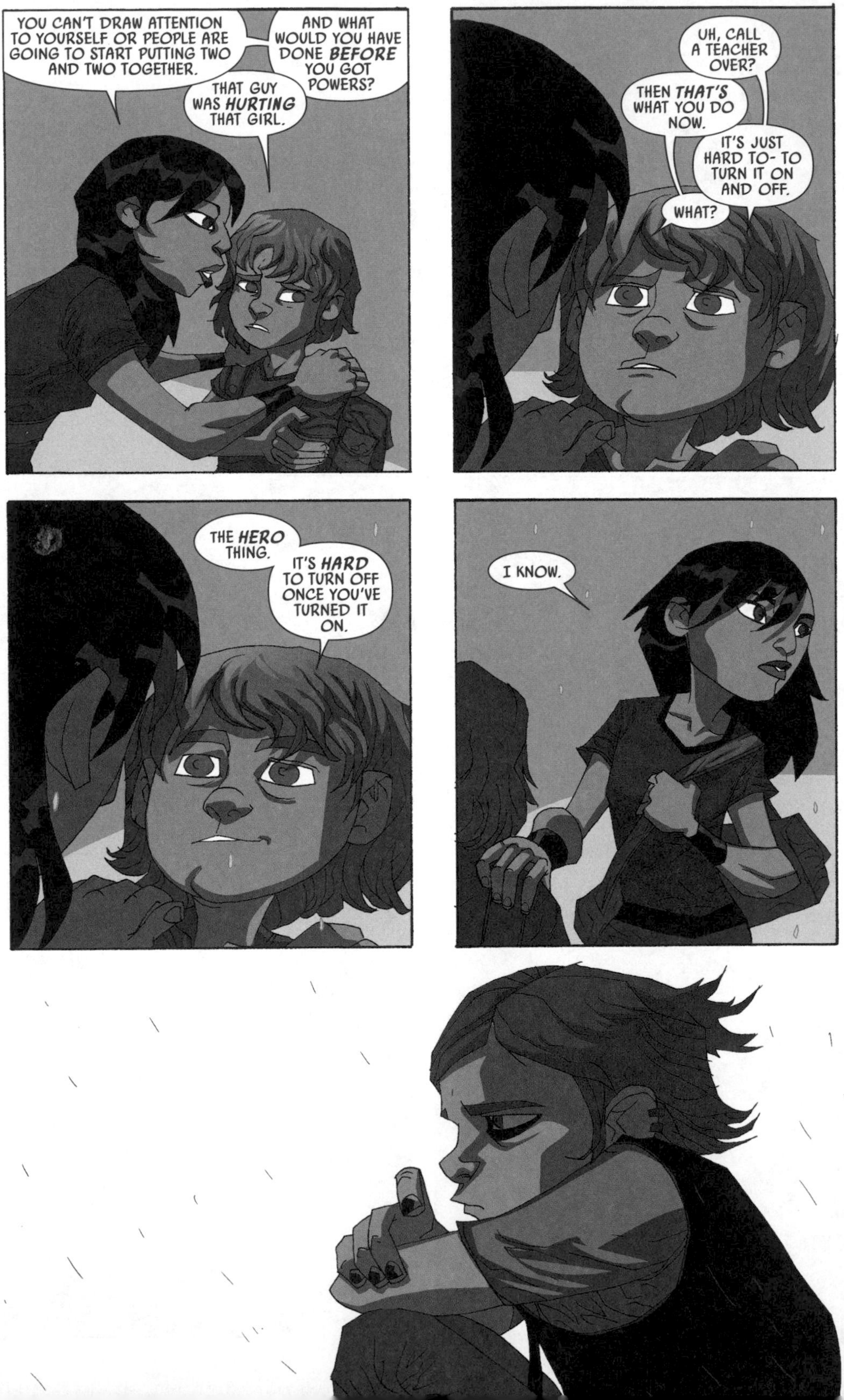
YOU CAN'T DRAW ATTENTION TO YOURSELF OR PEOPLE ARE GOING TO START PUTTING TWO AND TWO TOGETHER.
THAT GUY WAS HURTING THAT GIRL.
AND WHAT WOULD YOU HAVE DONE BEFORE YOU GOT POWERS?
UH, CALL A TEACHER OVER?
THEN THAT'S WHAT YOU DO NOW.
IT'S JUST HARD TO- TO TURN IT ON AND OFF.
WHAT?
THE HERO THING.
IT'S HARD TO TURN OFF ONCE YOU'VE TURNED IT ON.
I KNOW.

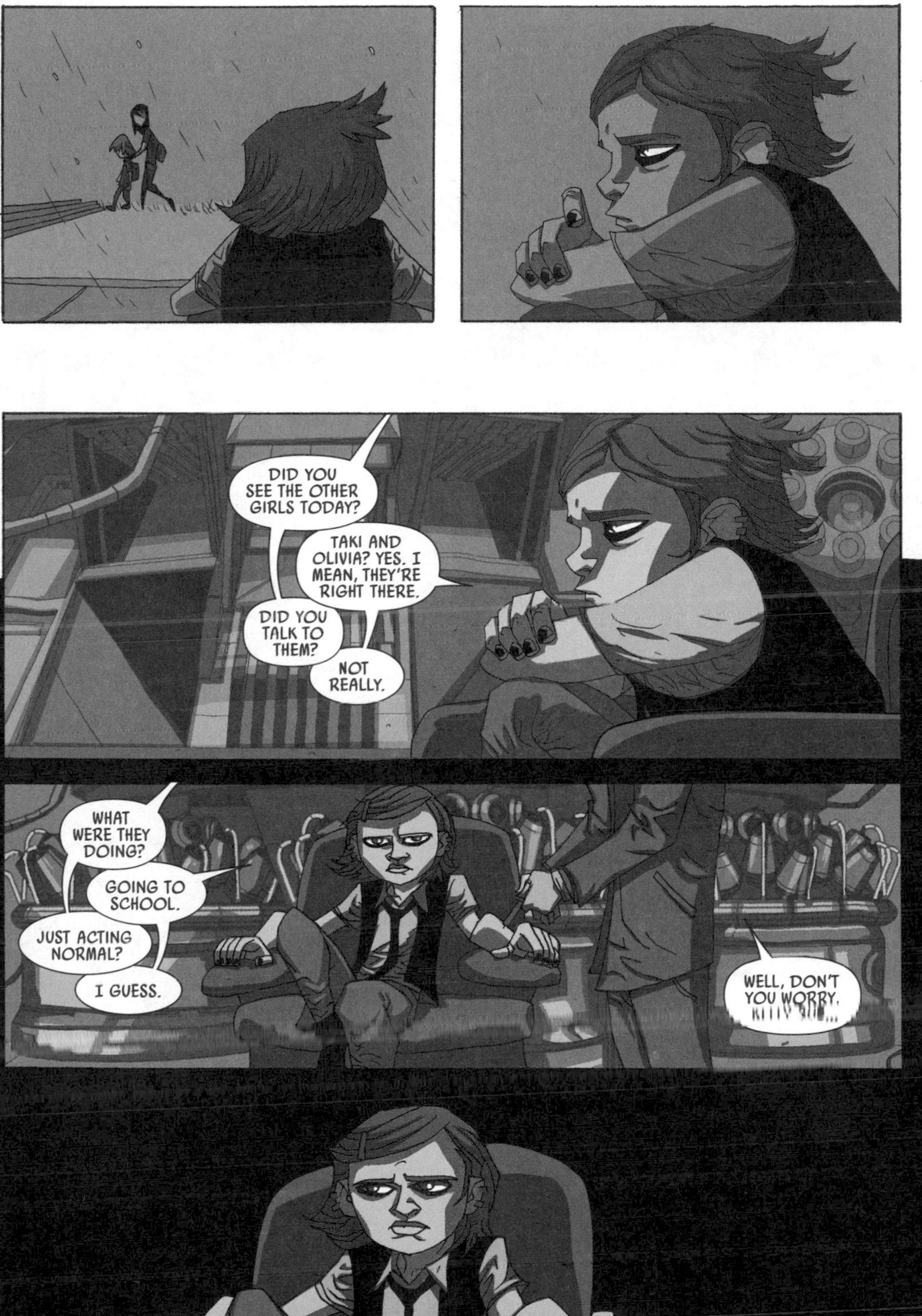
DID YOU SEE THE OTHER GIRLS TODAY?
TAKI AND OLIVIA? YES. I MEAN, THEY'RE RIGHT THERE.
DID YOU TALK TO THEM?
NOT REALLY.
WHAT WERE THEY DOING?
GOING TO SCHOOL.
JUST ACTING NORMAL?
I GUESS.
WELL, DON'T YOU WORRY.

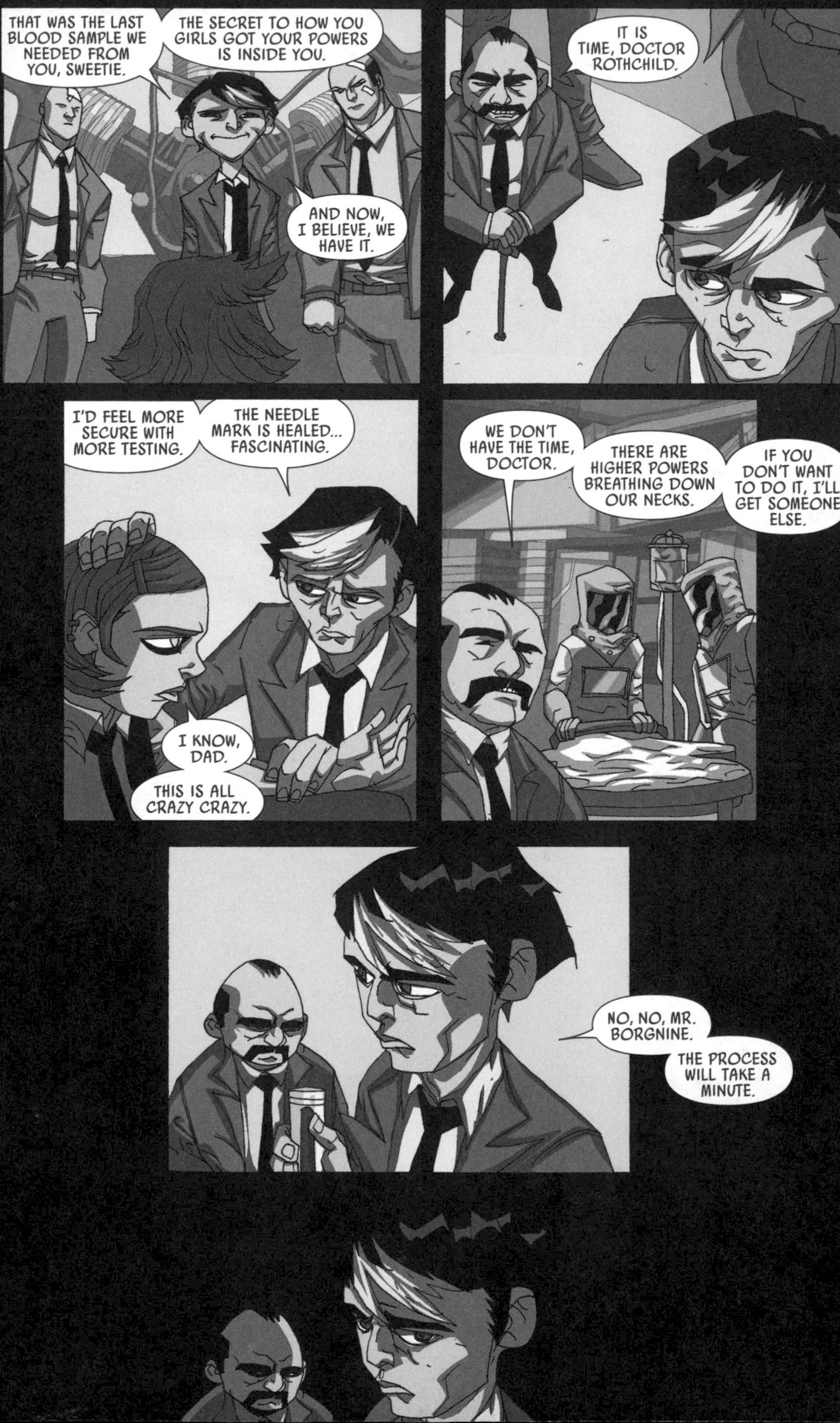
THAT WAS THE LAST BLOOD SAMPLE WE NEEDED FROM YOU, SWEETIE.
THE SECRET TO HOW YOU GIRLS GOT YOUR POWERS IS INSIDE YOU.
AND NOW, I BELIEVE, WE HAVE IT.
IT IS TIME, DOCTOR ROTHCHILD.
I'D FEEL MORE SECURE WITH MORE TESTING.
THE NEEDLE MARK IS HEALED... FASCINATING.
I KNOW, DAD.
THIS IS ALL CRAZY CRAZY.
WE DON'T HAVE THE TIME, DOCTOR.
THERE ARE HIGHER POWERS BREATHING DOWN OUR NECKS.
IF YOU DON'T WANT TO DO IT, I'LL GET SOMEONE ELSE.
NO, NO, MR. BORGNINE.
THE PROCESS WILL TAKE A MINUTE.

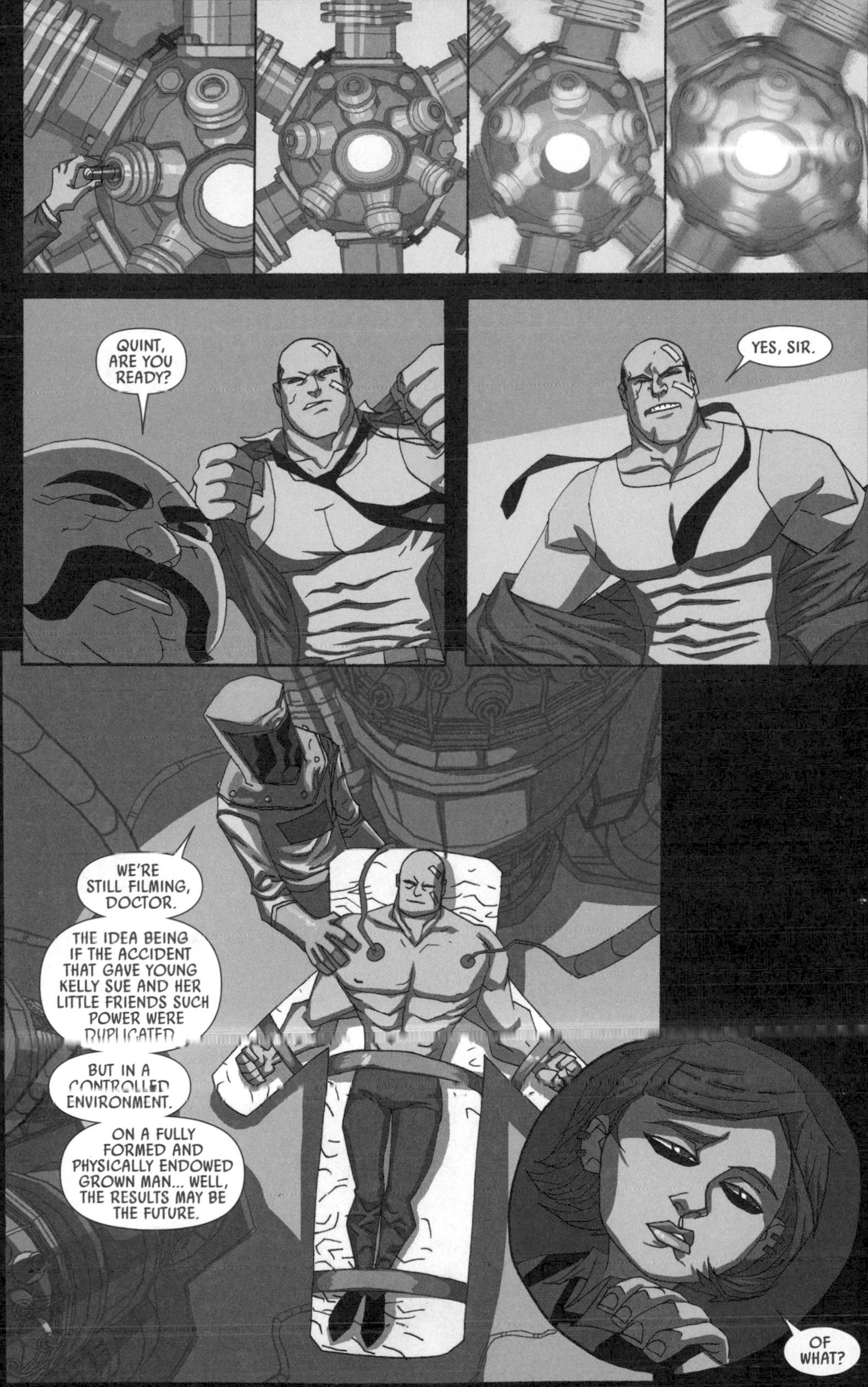
QUINT, ARE YOU READY?
YES, SIR.
WE'RE STILL FILMING, DOCTOR.
THE IDEA BEING IF THE ACCIDENT THAT GAVE YOUNG KELLY SUE AND HER LITTLE FRIENDS SUCH POWER WERE DUPLICATED
BUT IN A CONTROLLED ENVIRONMENT.
ON A FULLY FORMED AND PHYSICALLY ENDOWED GROWN MAN... WELL, THE RESULTS MAY BE THE FUTURE.
OF WHAT?

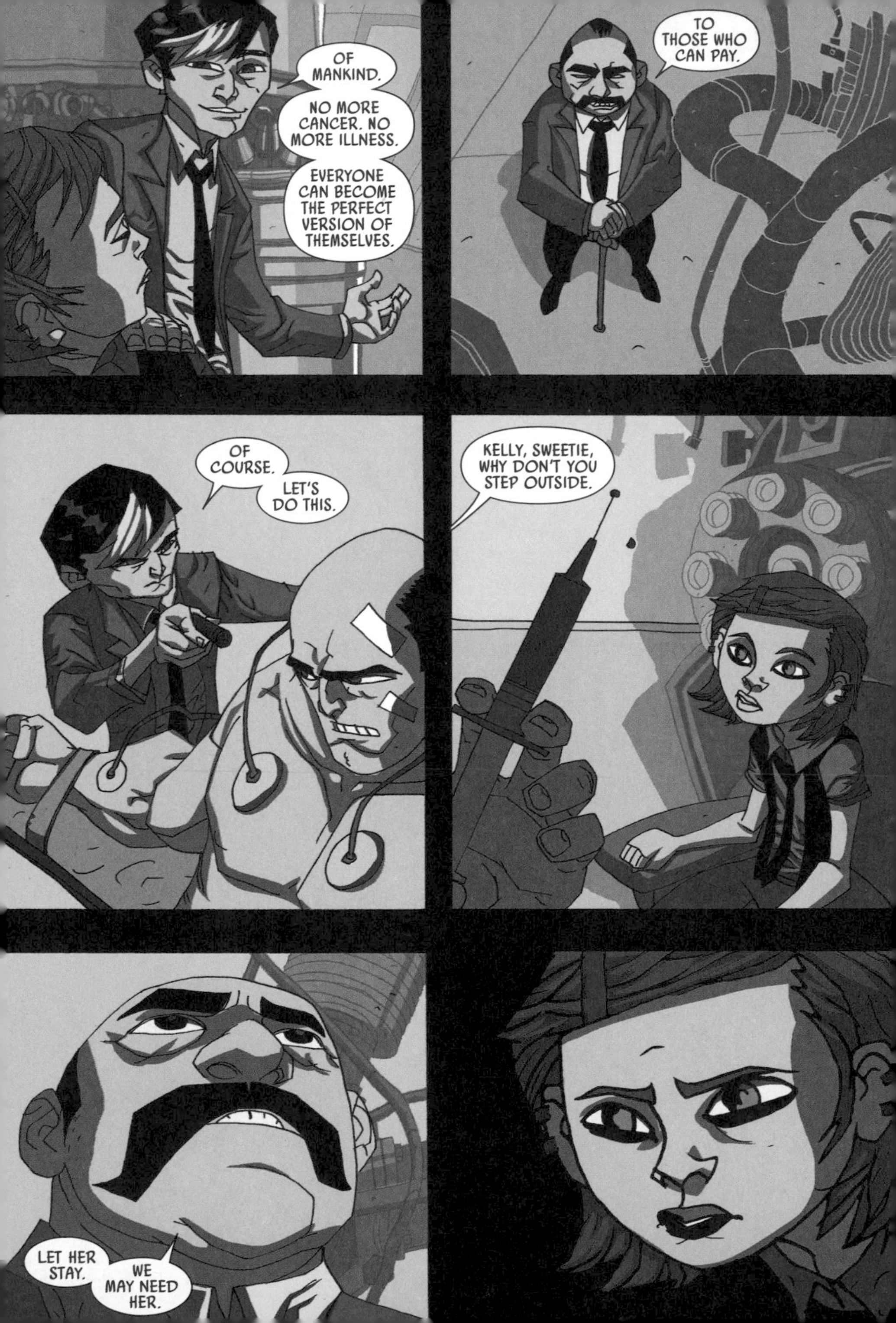
OF MANKIND.
NO MORE CANCER. NO MORE ILLNESS.
EVERYONE CAN BECOME THE PERFECT VERSION OF THEMSELVES.
TO THOSE WHO CAN PAY.
OF COURSE.
LET'S DO THIS.
KELLY, SWEETIE, WHY DON'T YOU STEP OUTSIDE.
LET HER STAY.
WE MAY NEED HER.

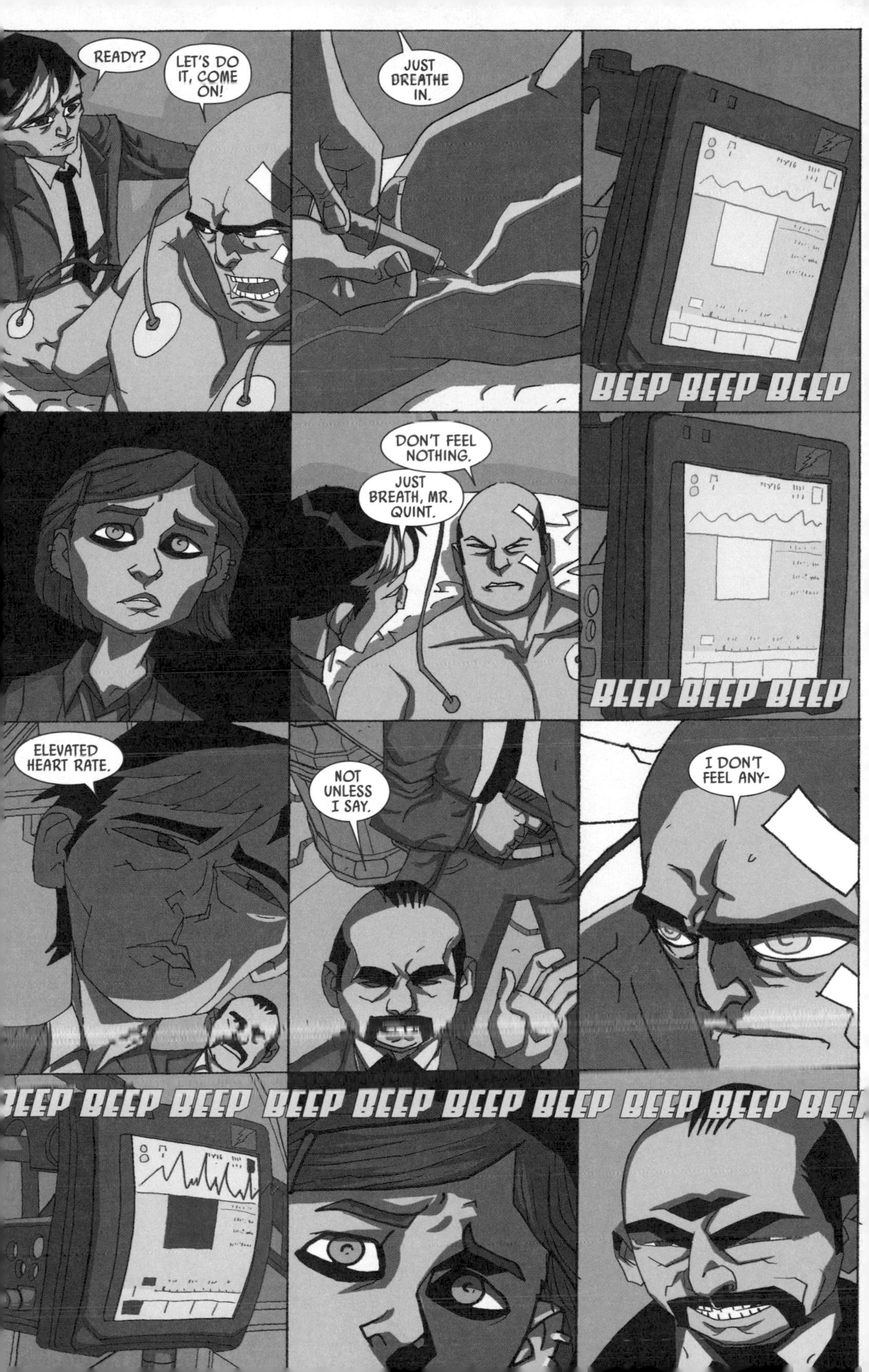
READY?
LET'S DO IT, COME ON!
JUST BREATHE IN.
BEEP BEEP BEEP
DON'T FEEL NOTHING.
JUST BREATH, MR. QUINT.
BEEP BEEP BEEP
ELEVATED HEART RATE.
NOT UNLESS I SAY.
I DON'T FEEL ANY-
BEEP BEEP BEEP BEEP BEEP BEEP BEEP BEEP BEEP

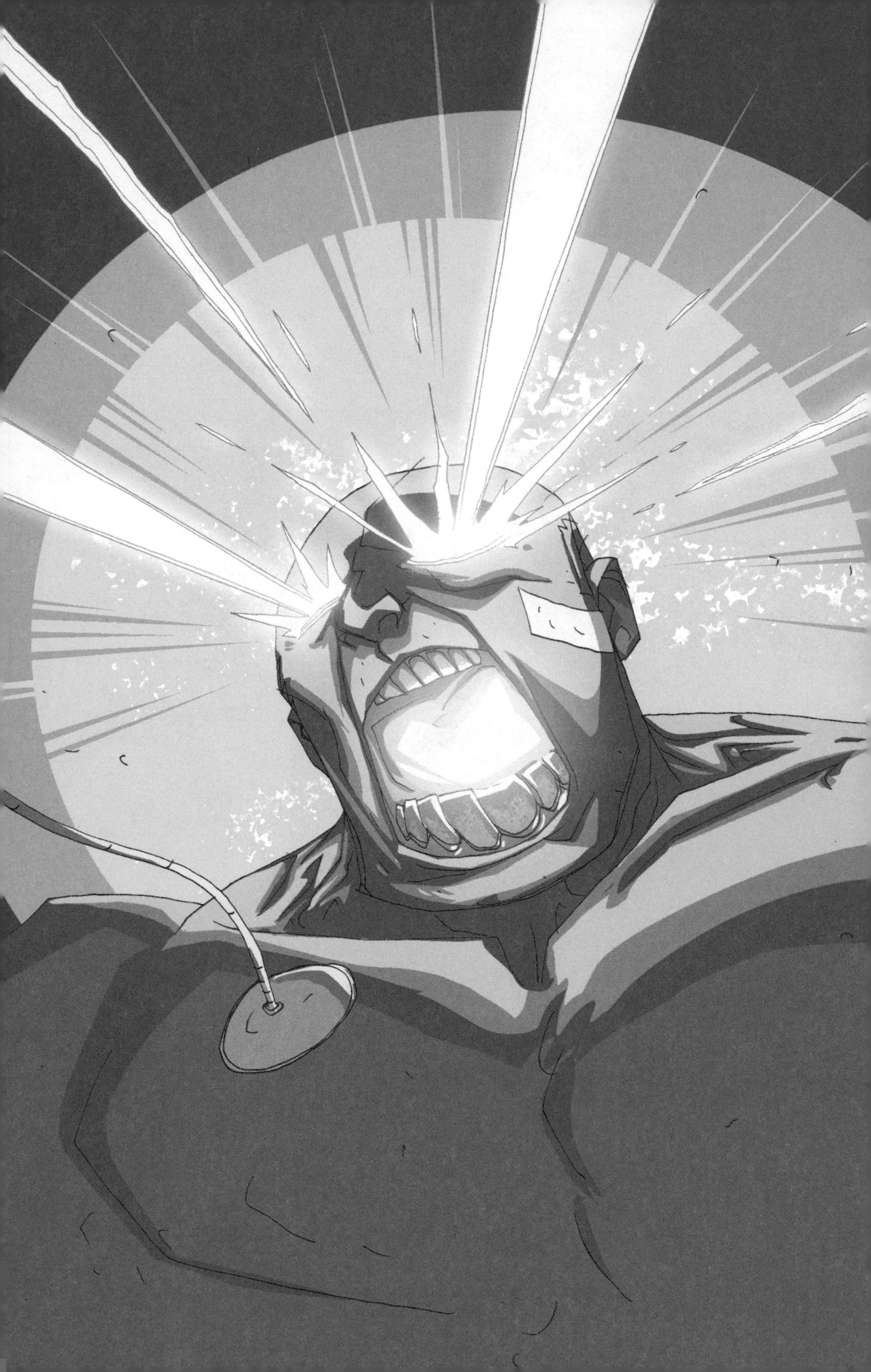

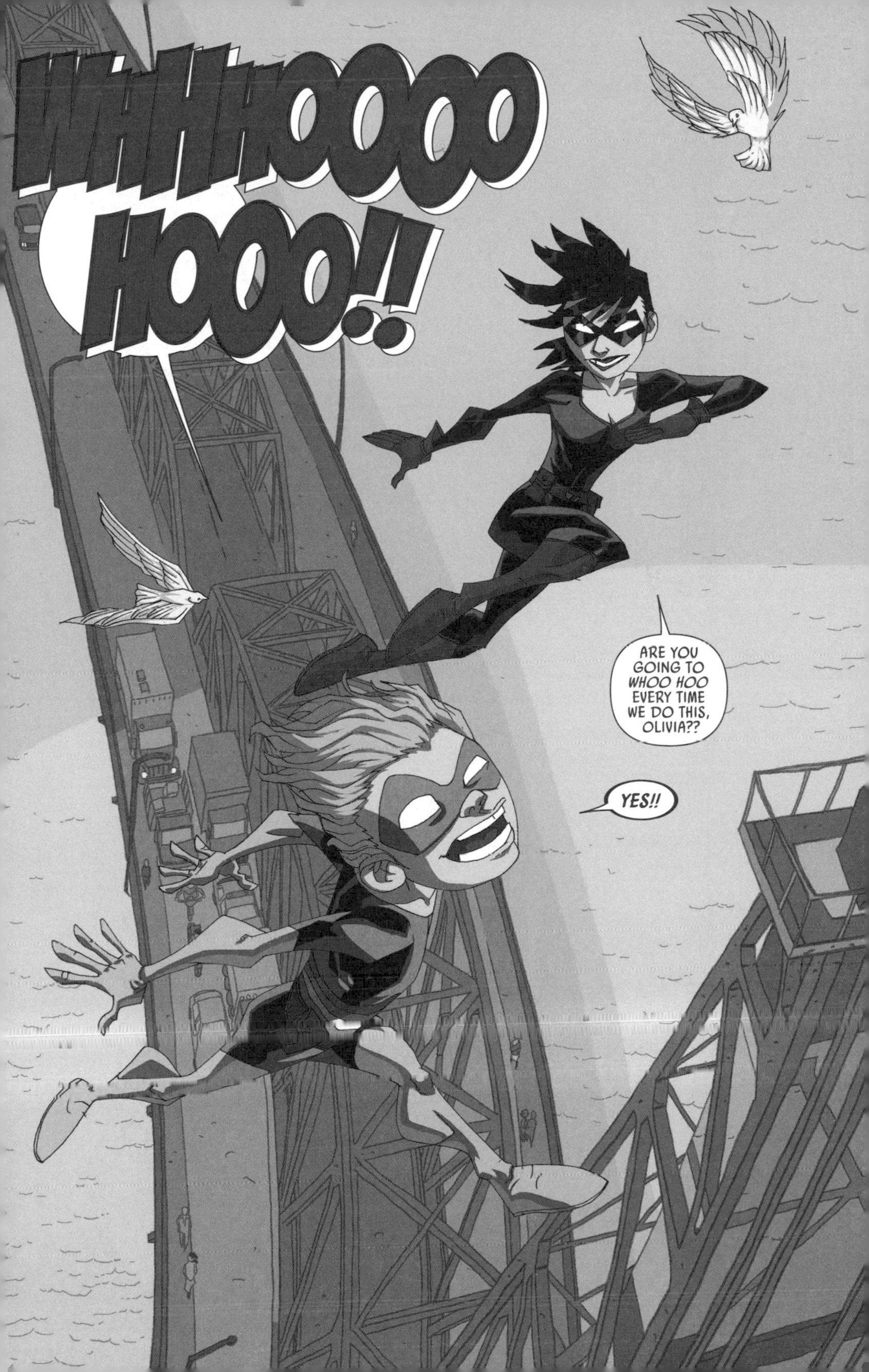
WHHHOOOOO HOOO!!
ARE YOU GOING TO WHOO HOO EVERY TIME WE DO THIS, OLIVIA??
YES!!

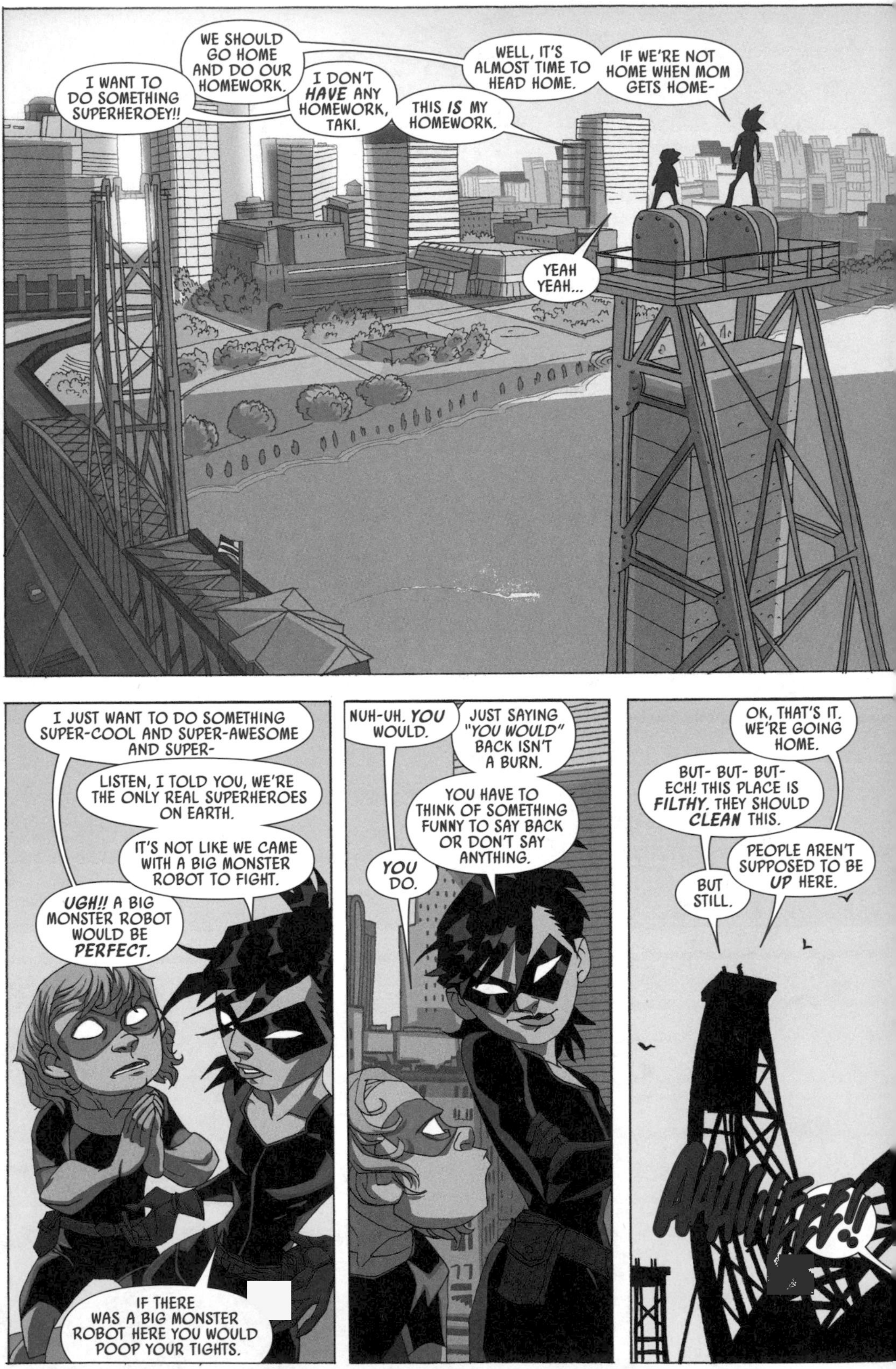
I WANT TO DO SOMETHING SUPERHEROEY!!
WE SHOULD GO HOME AND DO OUR HOMEWORK.
I DON'T HAVE ANY HOMEWORK, TAKI.
THIS IS MY HOMEWORK.
WELL, IT'S ALMOST TIME TO HEAD HOME.
IF WE'RE NOT HOME WHEN MOM GETS HOME-
YEAH YEAH...
I JUST WANT TO DO SOMETHING SUPER-COOL AND SUPER-AWESOME AND SUPER-
LISTEN, I TOLD YOU, WE'RE THE ONLY REAL SUPERHEROES ON EARTH.
IT'S NOT LIKE WE CAME WITH A BIG MONSTER ROBOT TO FIGHT.
UGH!! A BIG MONSTER ROBOT WOULD BE PERFECT.
IF THERE WAS A BIG MONSTER ROBOT HERE YOU WOULD POOP YOUR TIGHTS.
NUH-UH. YOU WOULD.
JUST SAYING "YOU WOULD" BACK ISN'T A BURN.
YOU HAVE TO THINK OF SOMETHING FUNNY TO SAY BACK OR DON'T SAY ANYTHING.
YOU DO.
OK, THAT'S IT. WE'RE GOING HOME.
BUT- BUT- BUT- ECH! THIS PLACE IS FILTHY. THEY SHOULD CLEAN THIS.
PEOPLE AREN'T SUPPOSED TO BE UP HERE.
BUT STILL.

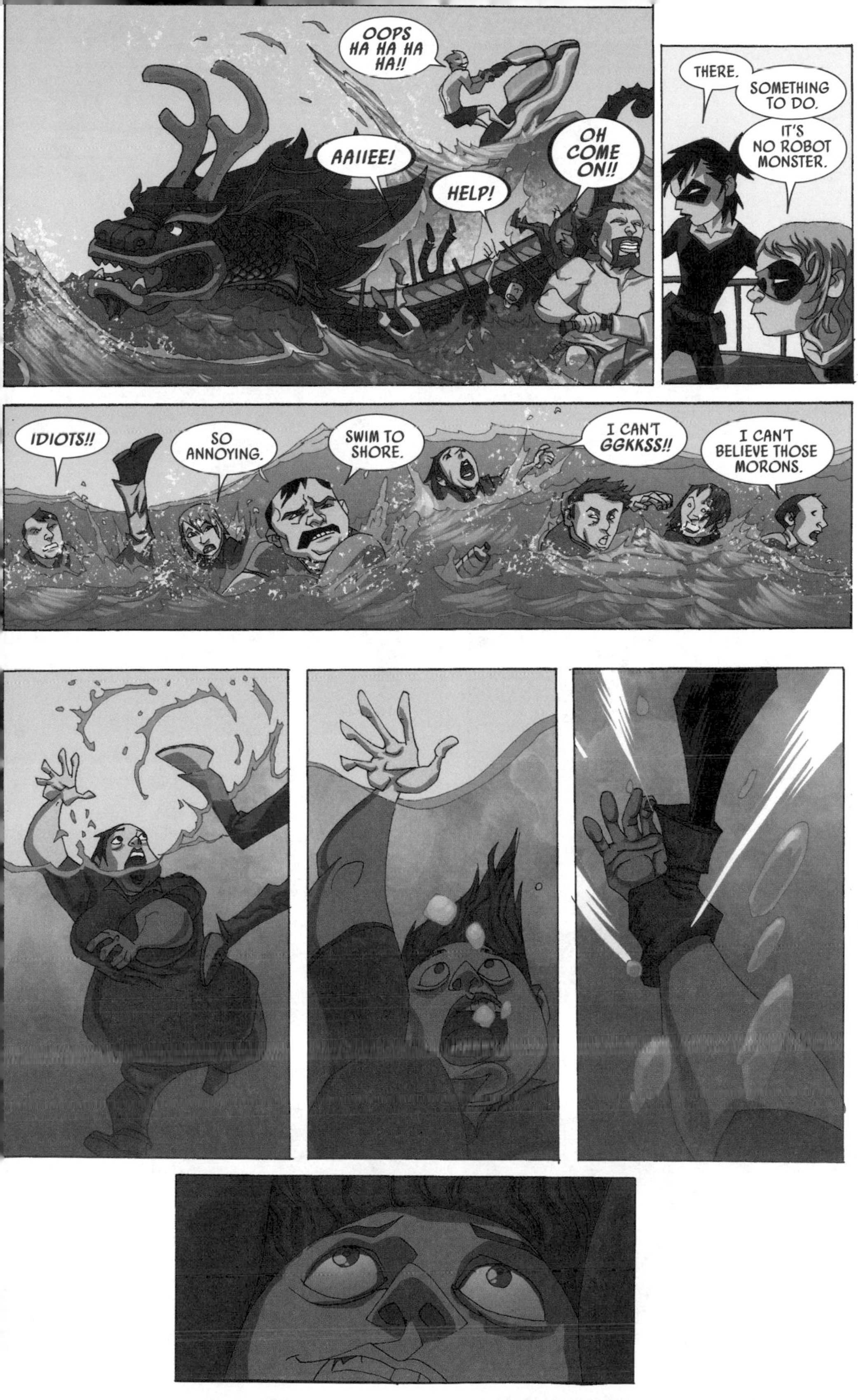
OOPS HA HA HA HA!!
AAIIEE!
HELP!
OH COME ON!!
THERE.
SOMETHING TO DO.
IT'S NO ROBOT MONSTER.
IDIOTS!!
SO ANNOYING.
SWIM TO SHORE.
I CAN'T GGKKSS!!
I CAN'T BELIEVE THOSE MORONS.

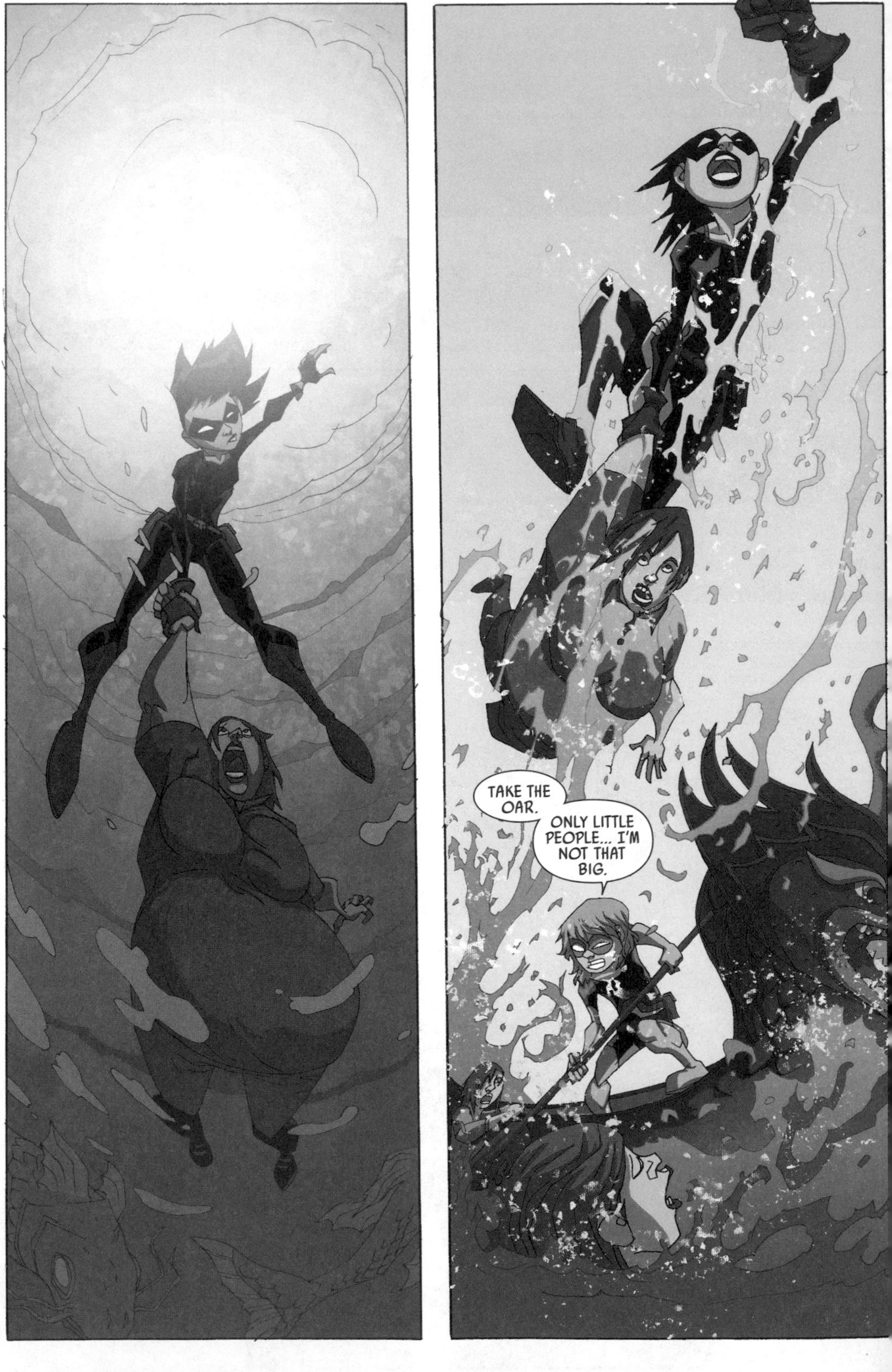
TAKE THE OAR.
ONLY LITTLE PEOPLE... I'M NOT THAT BIG.

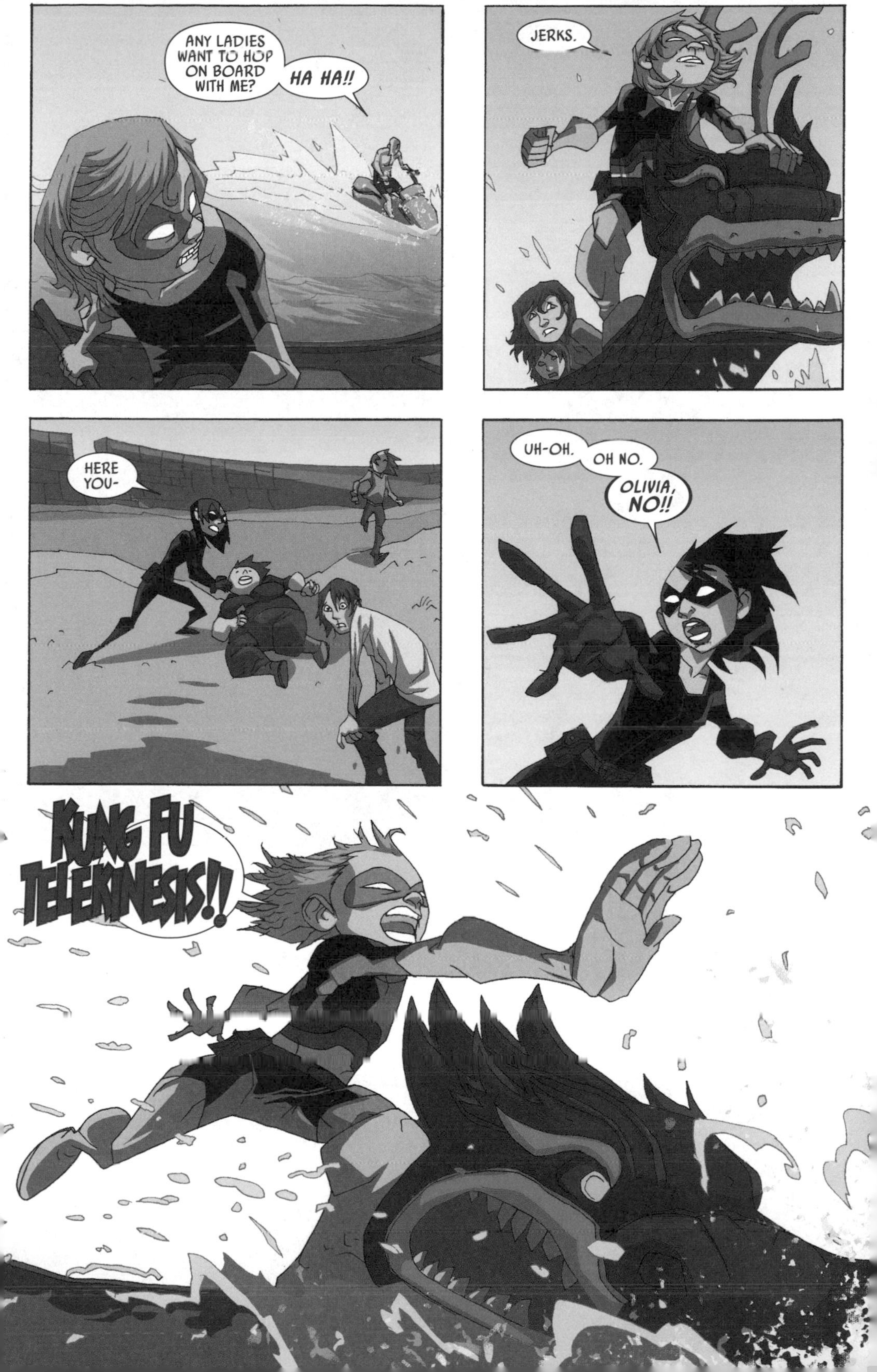
ANY LADIES WANT TO HOP ON BOARD WITH ME?
HA HA!!
JERKS.
HERE YOU-
UH-OH.
OH NO.
OLIVIA, NO!!
KUNG FU TELEKINESIS!!

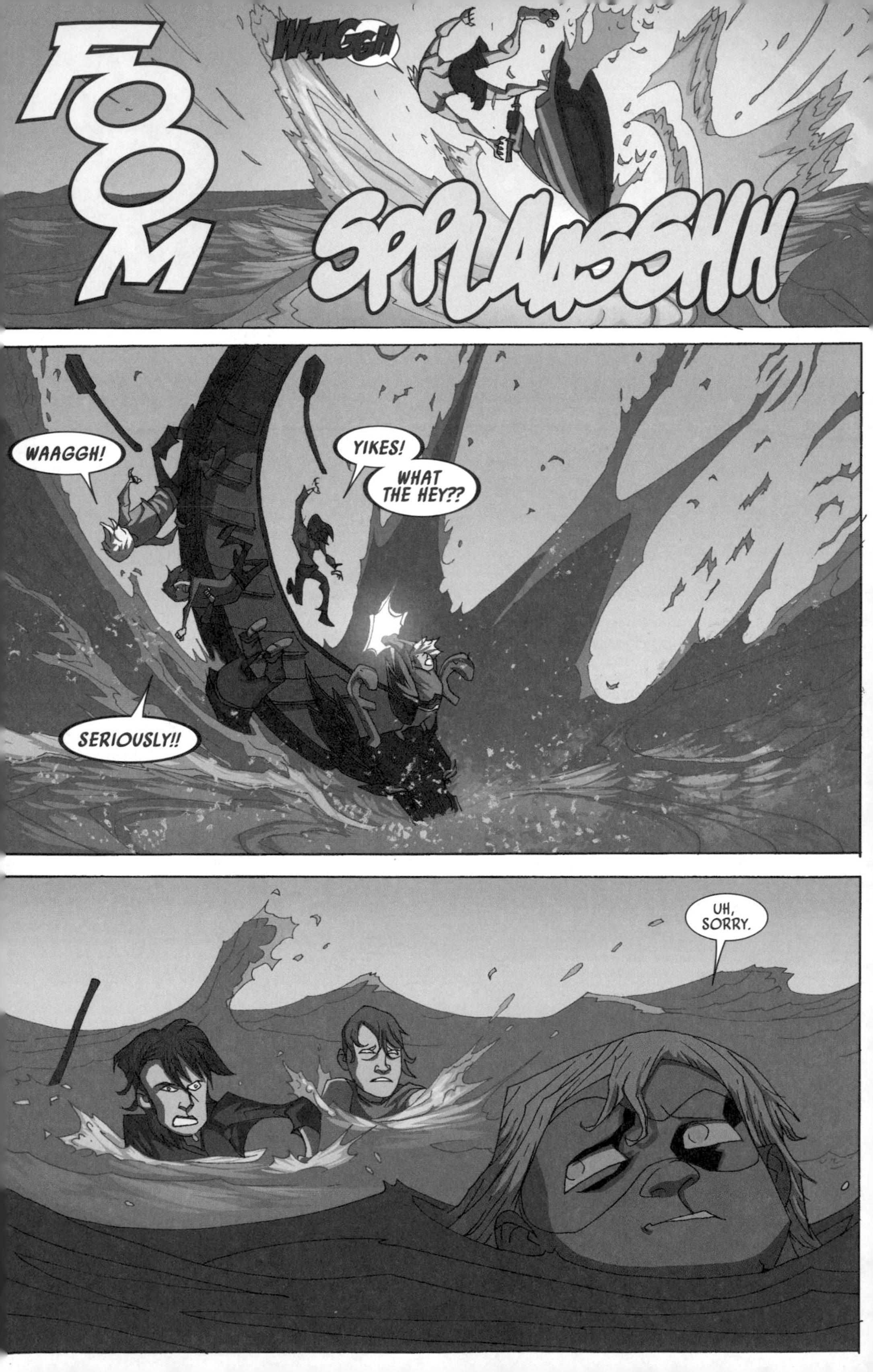
FOOM
WAAGGH
SPPLAASSHH
WAAGGH!
YIKES!
WHAT THE HEY??
SERIOUSLY!!
UH, SORRY.

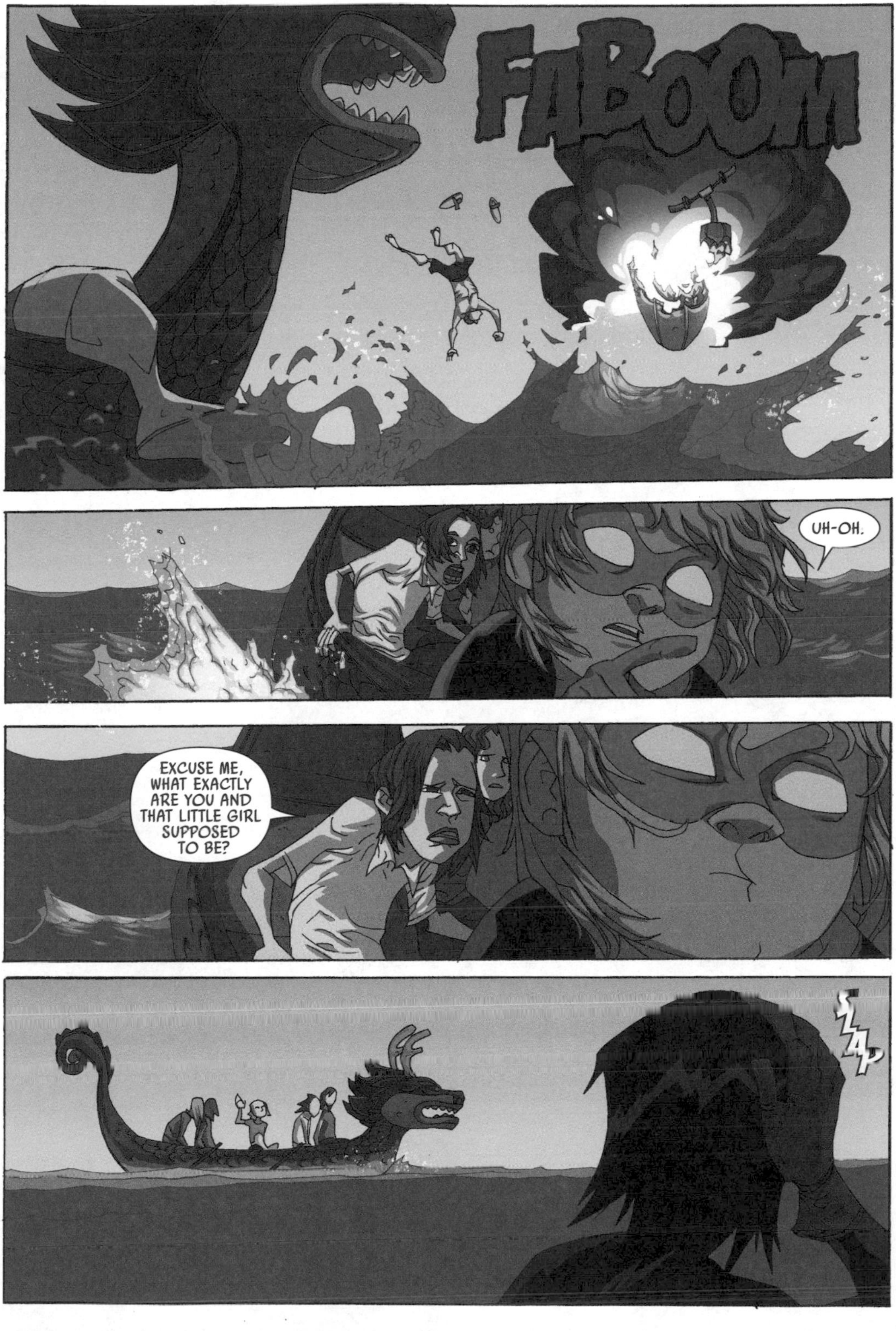
FABOOM
UH-OH.
EXCUSE ME, WHAT EXACTLY ARE YOU AND THAT LITTLE GIRL SUPPOSED TO BE?
SLAP

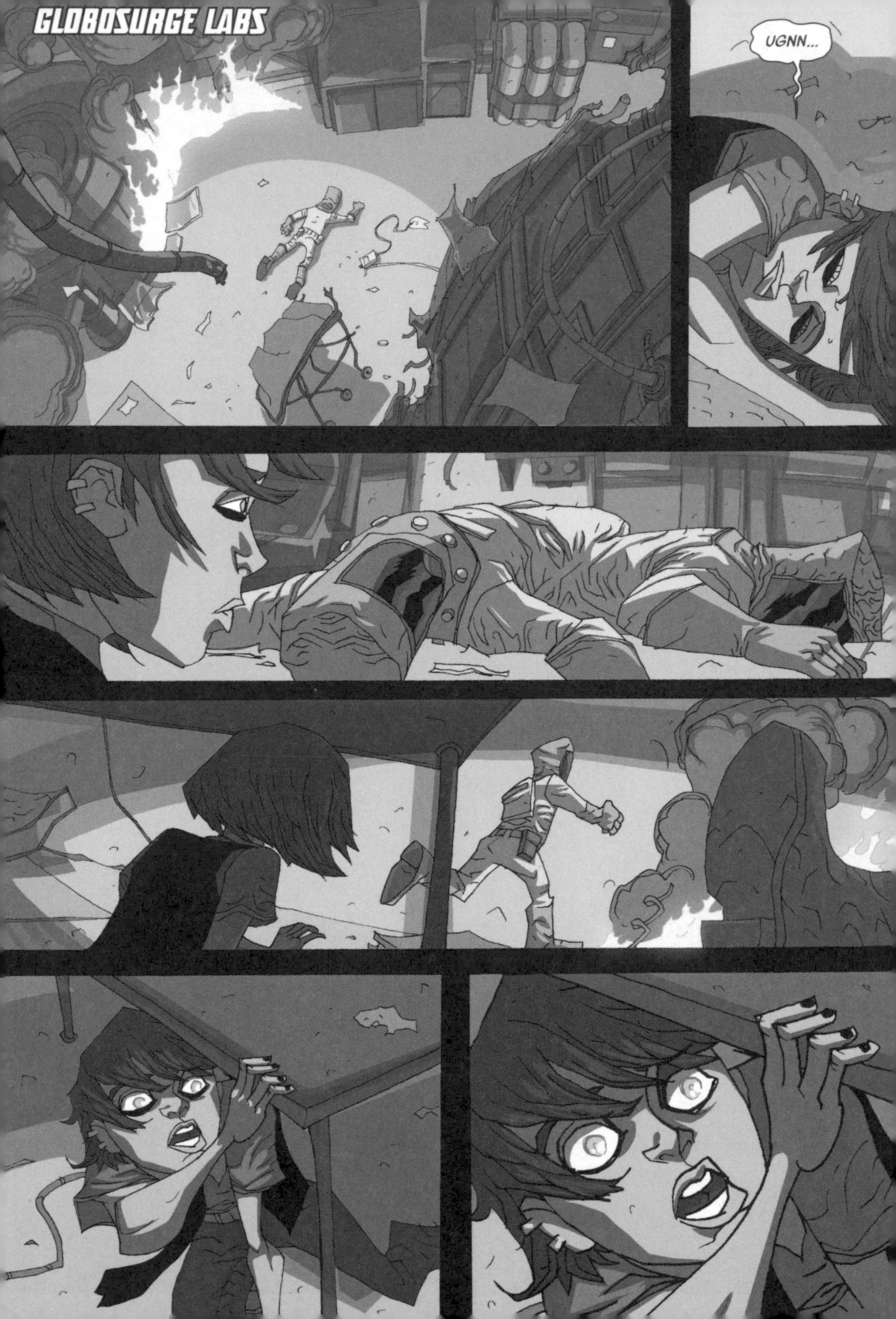
GLOBOSURGE LABS
UGNN...

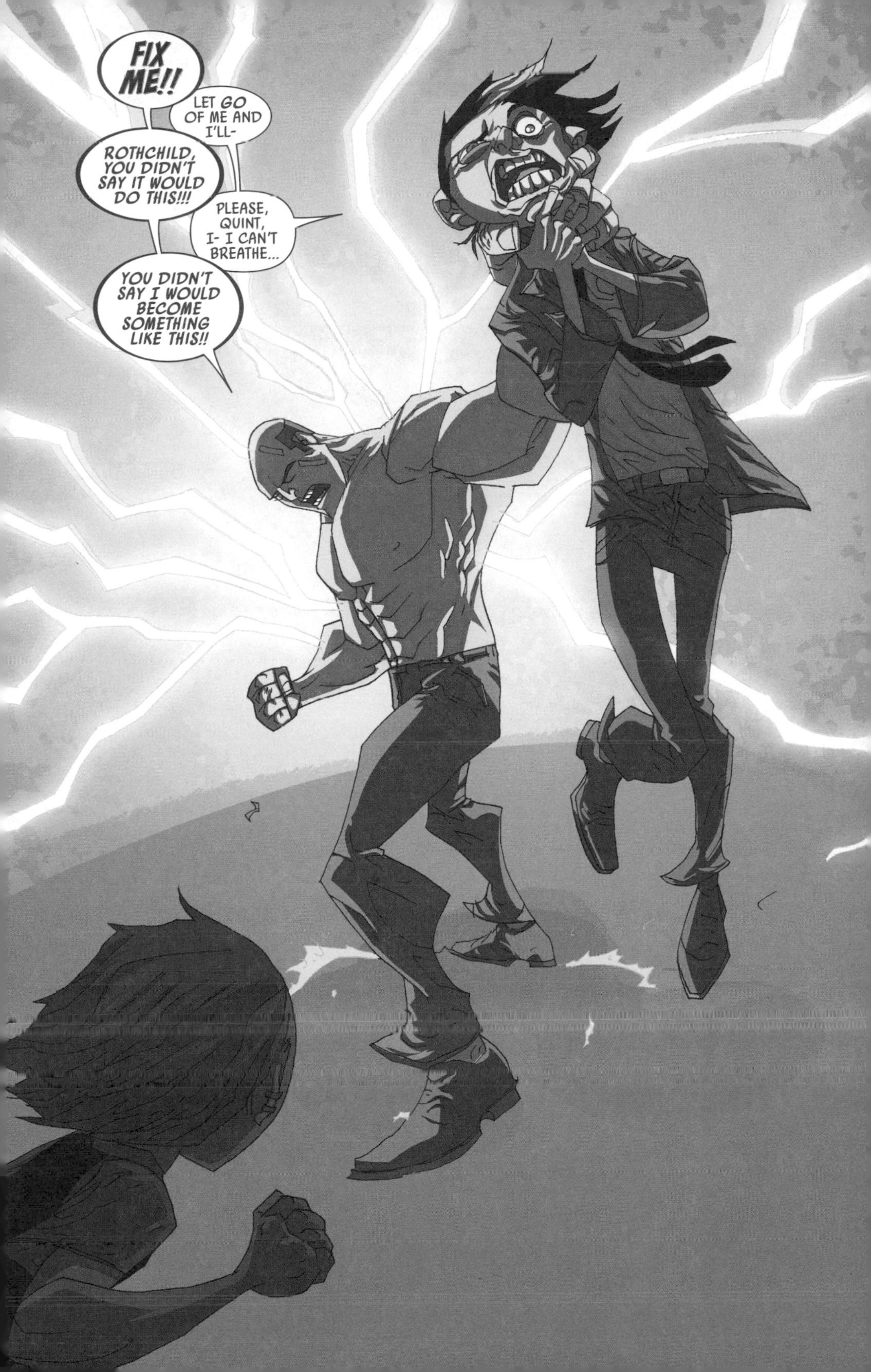
FIX ME!!
LET GO OF ME AND I'LL-
ROTHCHILD, YOU DIDN'T SAY IT WOULD DO THIS!!!
PLEASE, QUINT, I- I CAN'T BREATHE...
YOU DIDN'T SAY I WOULD BECOME SOMETHING LIKE THIS!!

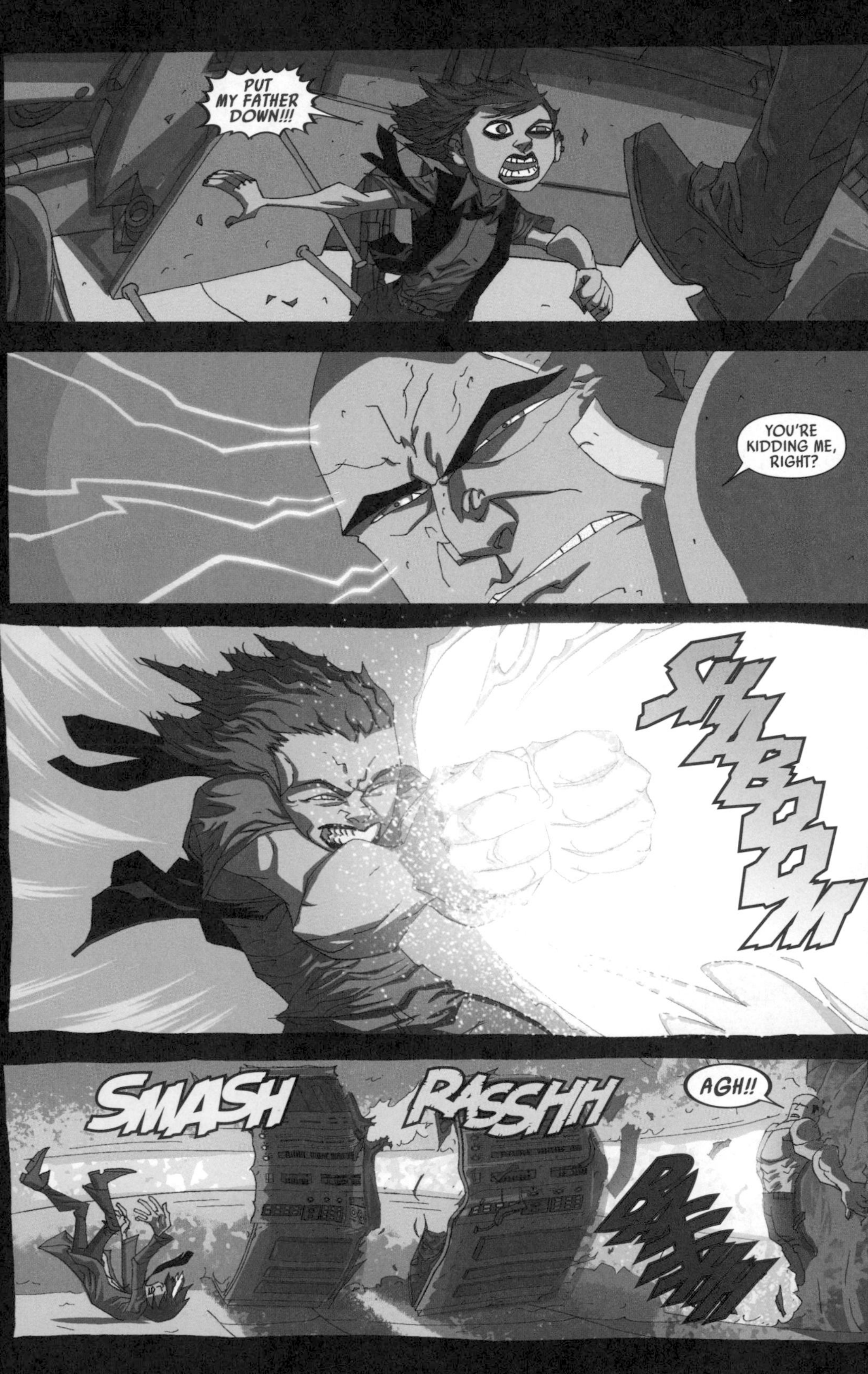
PUT MY FATHER DOWN!!!
YOU'RE KIDDING ME, RIGHT?
SHABOOM
SMASH
RASSHH
AGH!!

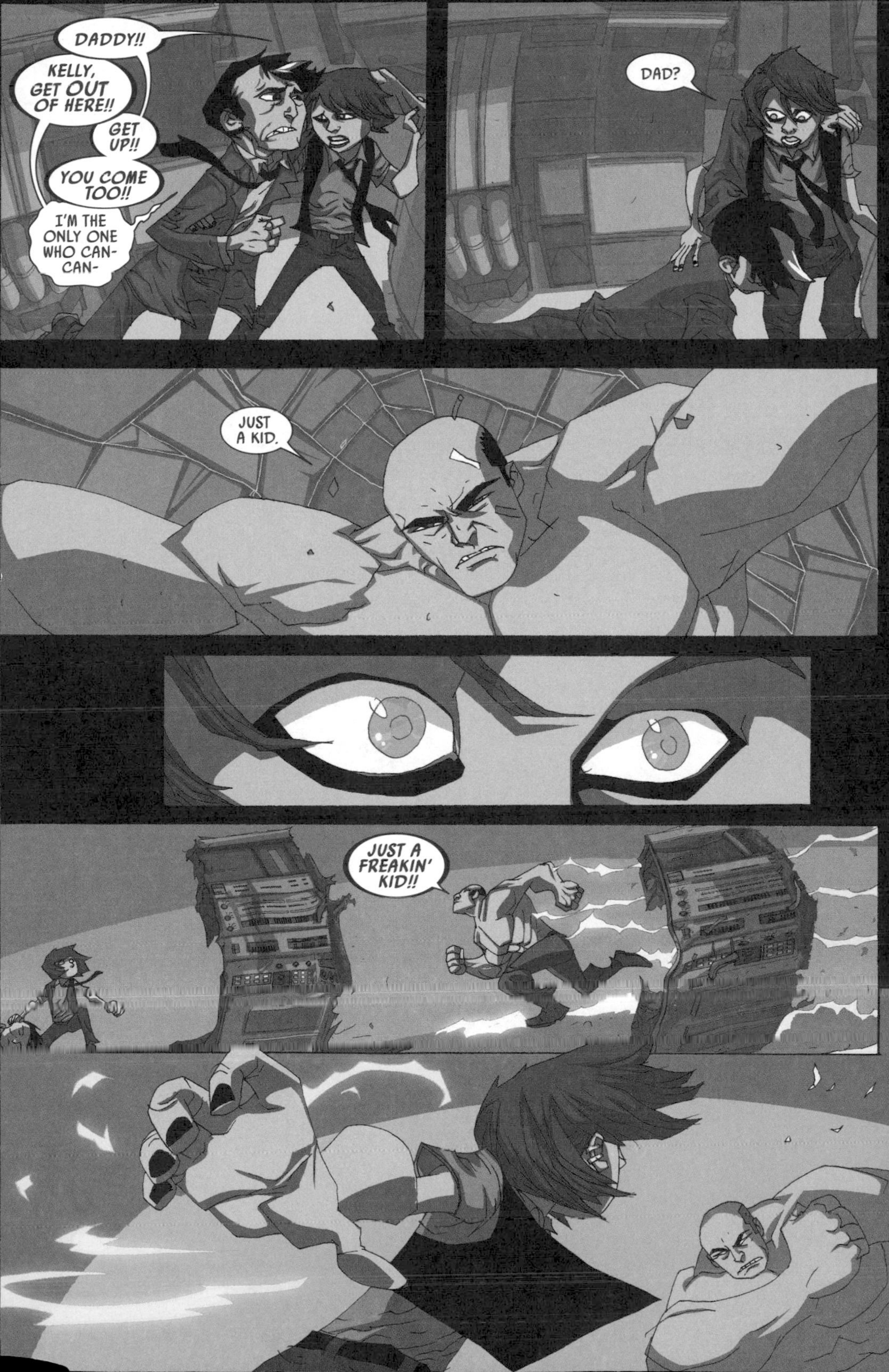
DADDY!!
KELLY, GET OUT OF HERE!!
GET UP!!
YOU COME TOO!!
I'M THE ONLY ONE WHO CAN-CAN-
DAD?
JUST A KID.
JUST A FREAKIN' KID!!

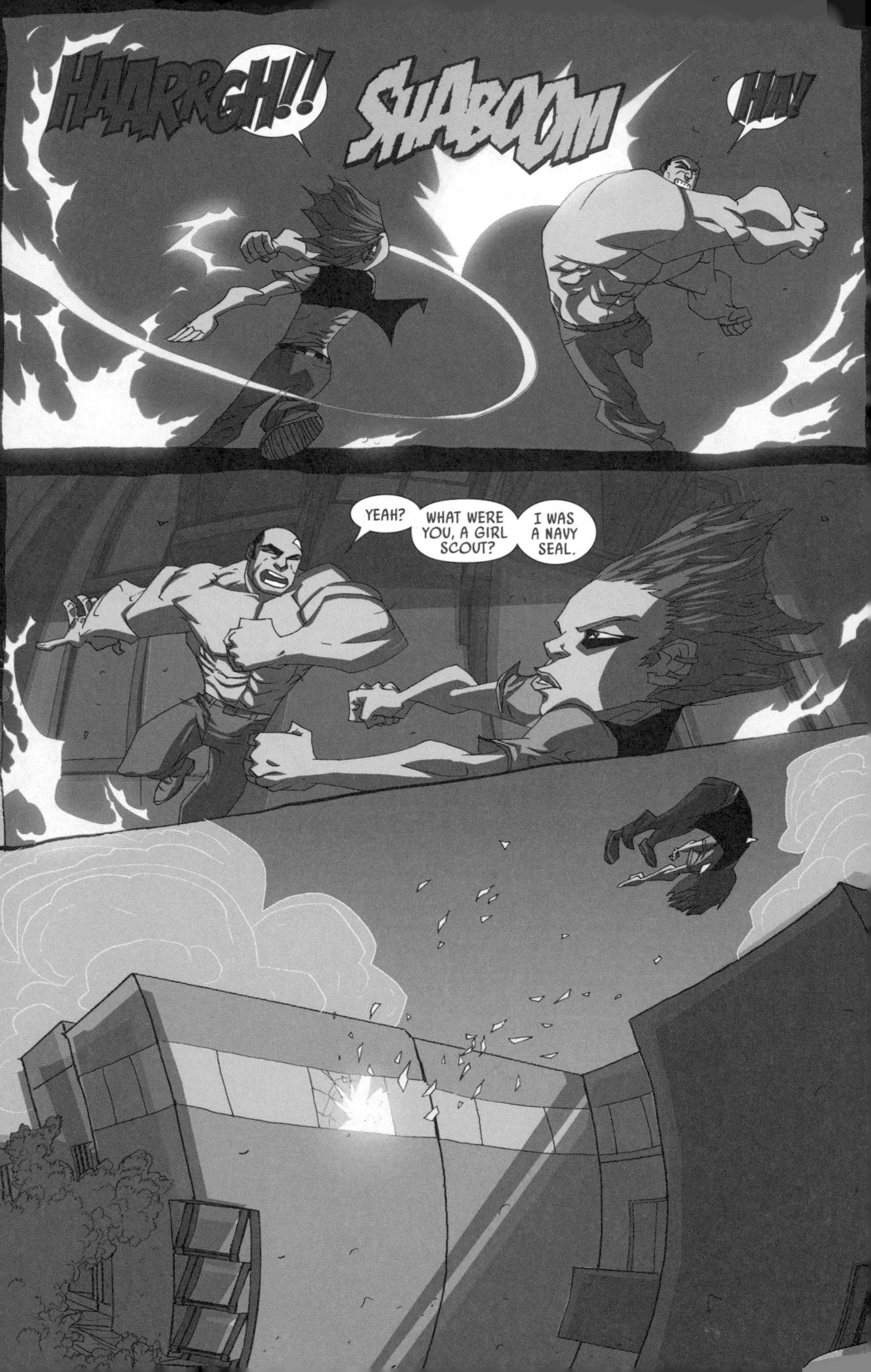
HAARRGH!!
SHABOOM
HA!
YEAH?
WHAT WERE YOU, A GIRL SCOUT?
I WAS A NAVY SEAL.

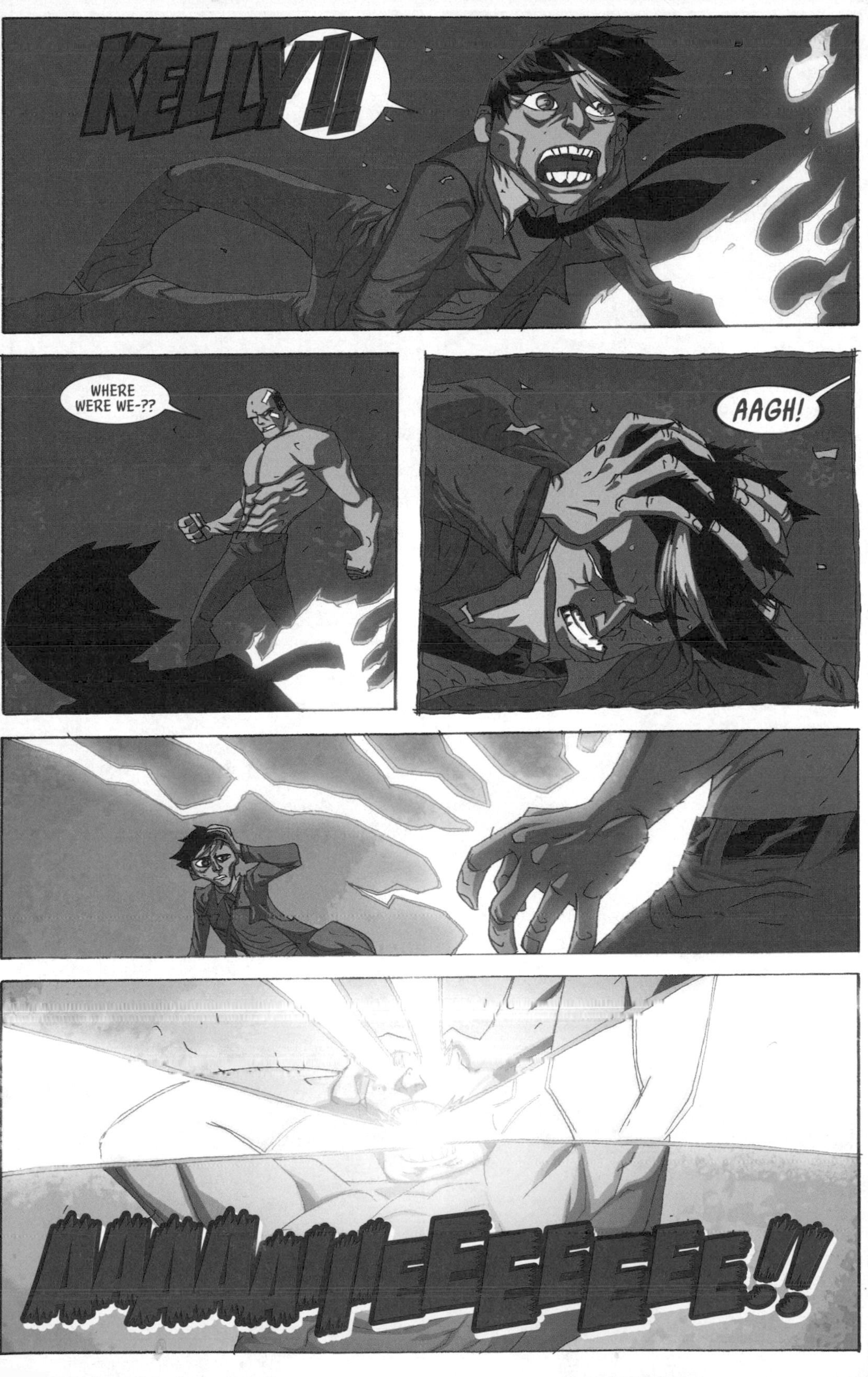
KELLY!!
WHERE WERE WE-??
AAGH!
AAAAAIIEEEEEEEEE!!

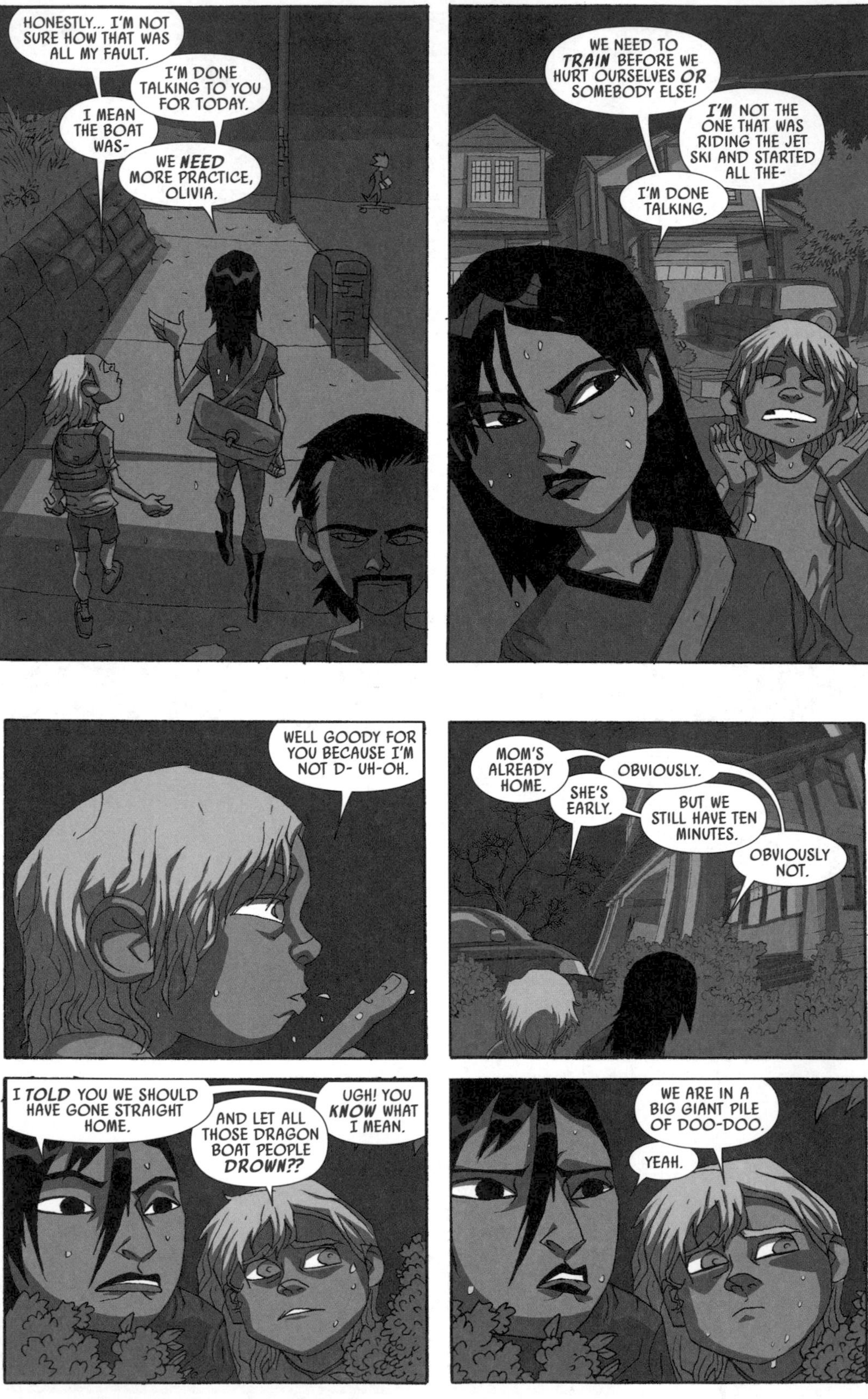
HONESTLY... I'M NOT SURE HOW THAT WAS ALL MY FAULT.
I'M DONE TALKING TO YOU FOR TODAY.
I MEAN THE BOAT WAS-
WE NEED MORE PRACTICE, OLIVIA.
WE NEED TO TRAIN BEFORE WE HURT OURSELVES OR SOMEBODY ELSE!
I'M NOT THE ONE THAT WAS RIDING THE JET SKI AND STARTED ALL THE-
I'M DONE TALKING.
WELL GOODY FOR YOU BECAUSE I'M NOT D- UH-OH.
MOM'S ALREADY HOME.
OBVIOUSLY.
SHE'S EARLY.
BUT WE STILL HAVE TEN MINUTES.
OBVIOUSLY NOT.
I TOLD YOU WE SHOULD HAVE GONE STRAIGHT HOME.
AND LET ALL THOSE DRAGON BOAT PEOPLE DROWN??
UGH! YOU KNOW WHAT I MEAN.
WE ARE IN A BIG GIANT PILE OF DOO-DOO.
YEAH.

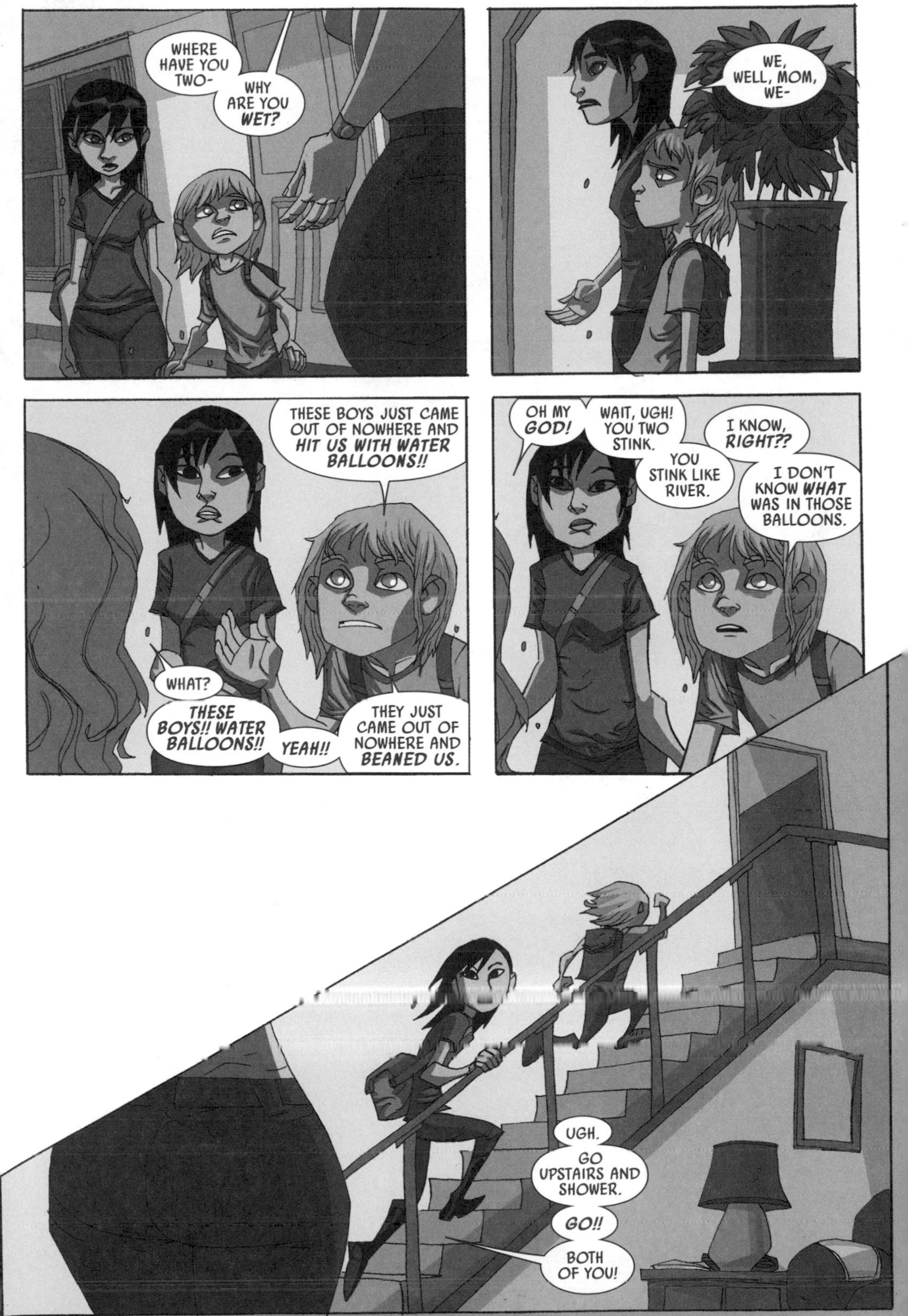
WHERE HAVE YOU TWO-
WHY ARE YOU WET?
WE, WELL, MOM, WE-
THESE BOYS JUST CAME OUT OF NOWHERE AND HIT US WITH WATER BALLOONS!!
WHAT?
THESE BOYS!! WATER BALLOONS!!
YEAH!!
THEY JUST CAME OUT OF NOWHERE AND BEANED US.
OH MY GOD!
WAIT, UGH! YOU TWO STINK.
YOU STINK LIKE RIVER.
I KNOW, RIGHT??
I DON'T KNOW WHAT WAS IN THOSE BALLOONS.
UGH.
GO UPSTAIRS AND SHOWER.
GO!!
BOTH OF YOU!

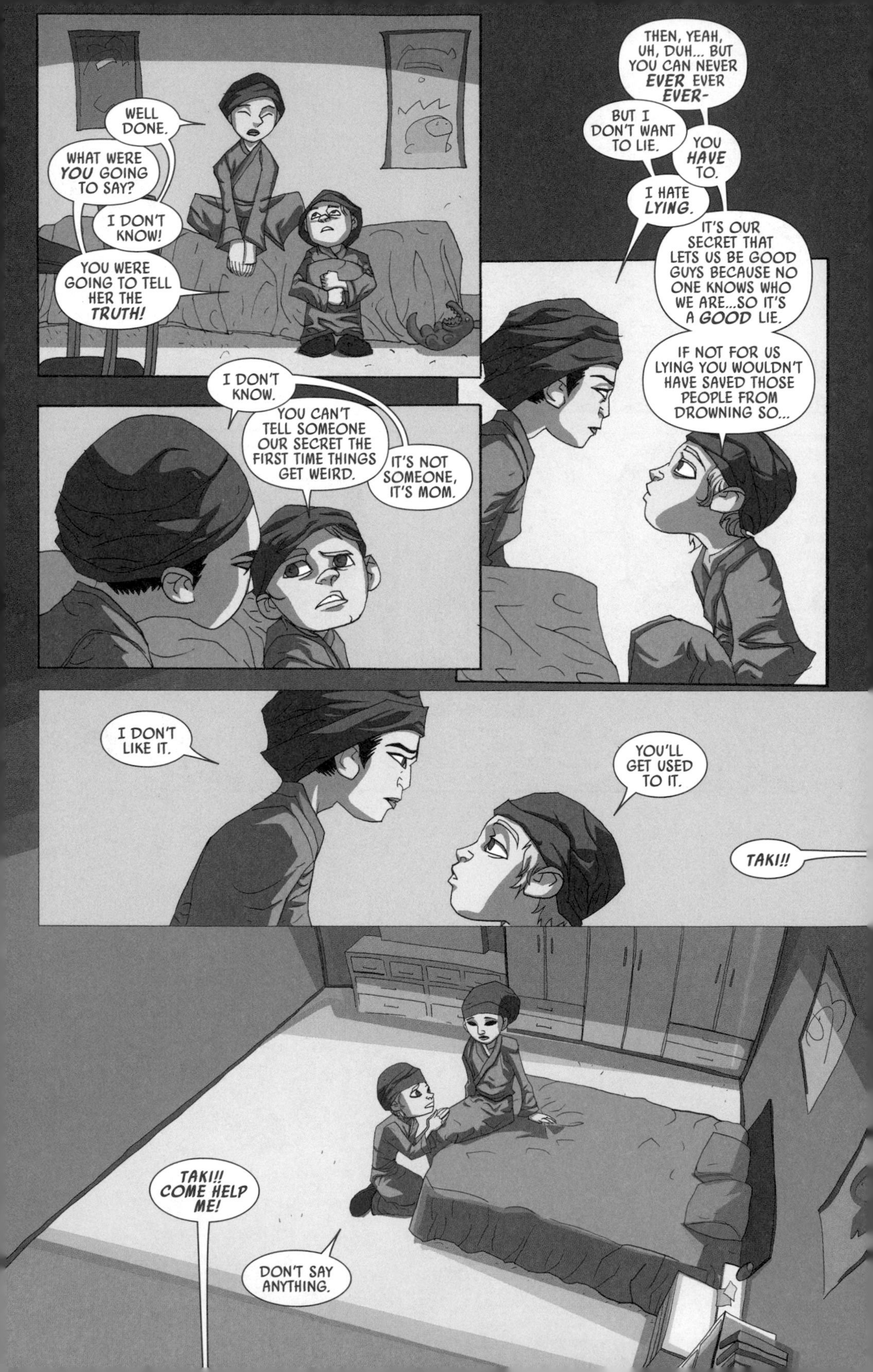
WELL DONE.
WHAT WERE YOU GOING TO SAY?
I DON'T KNOW!
YOU WERE GOING TO TELL HER THE TRUTH!
THEN, YEAH, UH, DUH... BUT YOU CAN NEVER EVER EVER EVER-
BUT I DON'T WANT TO LIE.
YOU HAVE TO.
I HATE LYING.
IT'S OUR SECRET THAT LETS US BE GOOD GUYS BECAUSE NO ONE KNOWS WHO WE ARE...SO IT'S A GOOD LIE.
IF NOT FOR US LYING YOU WOULDN'T HAVE SAVED THOSE PEOPLE FROM DROWNING SO...
I DON'T KNOW.
YOU CAN'T TELL SOMEONE OUR SECRET THE FIRST TIME THINGS GET WEIRD.
IT'S NOT SOMEONE, IT'S MOM.
I DON'T LIKE IT.
YOU'LL GET USED TO IT.
TAKI!!
TAKI!! COME HELP ME!
DON'T SAY ANYTHING.

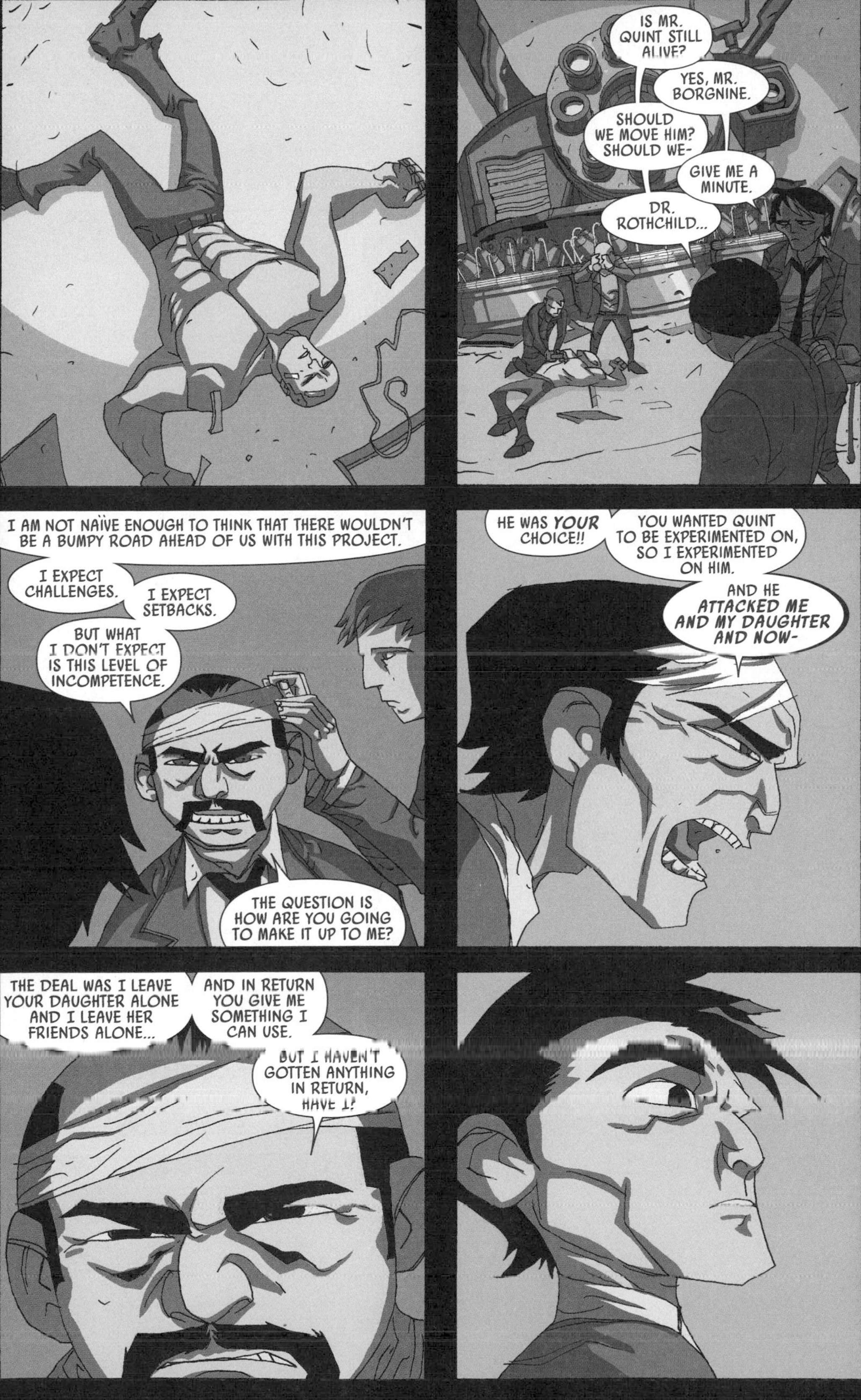
IS MR. QUINT STILL ALIVE?
YES, MR. BORGNINE.
SHOULD WE MOVE HIM? SHOULD WE-
GIVE ME A MINUTE.
DR. ROTHCHILD...
I AM NOT NAÏVE ENOUGH TO THINK THAT THERE WOULDN'T BE A BUMPY ROAD AHEAD OF US WITH THIS PROJECT.
I EXPECT CHALLENGES.
I EXPECT SETBACKS.
BUT WHAT I DON'T EXPECT IS THIS LEVEL OF INCOMPETENCE.
THE QUESTION IS HOW ARE YOU GOING TO MAKE IT UP TO ME?
HE WAS *YOUR* CHOICE!!
YOU WANTED QUINT TO BE EXPERIMENTED ON, SO I EXPERIMENTED ON HIM.
AND HE *ATTACKED ME AND MY DAUGHTER AND NOW-*
THE DEAL WAS I LEAVE YOUR DAUGHTER ALONE AND I LEAVE HER FRIENDS ALONE...
AND IN RETURN YOU GIVE ME SOMETHING I CAN USE.
BUT I HAVEN'T GOTTEN ANYTHING IN RETURN, HAVE I?

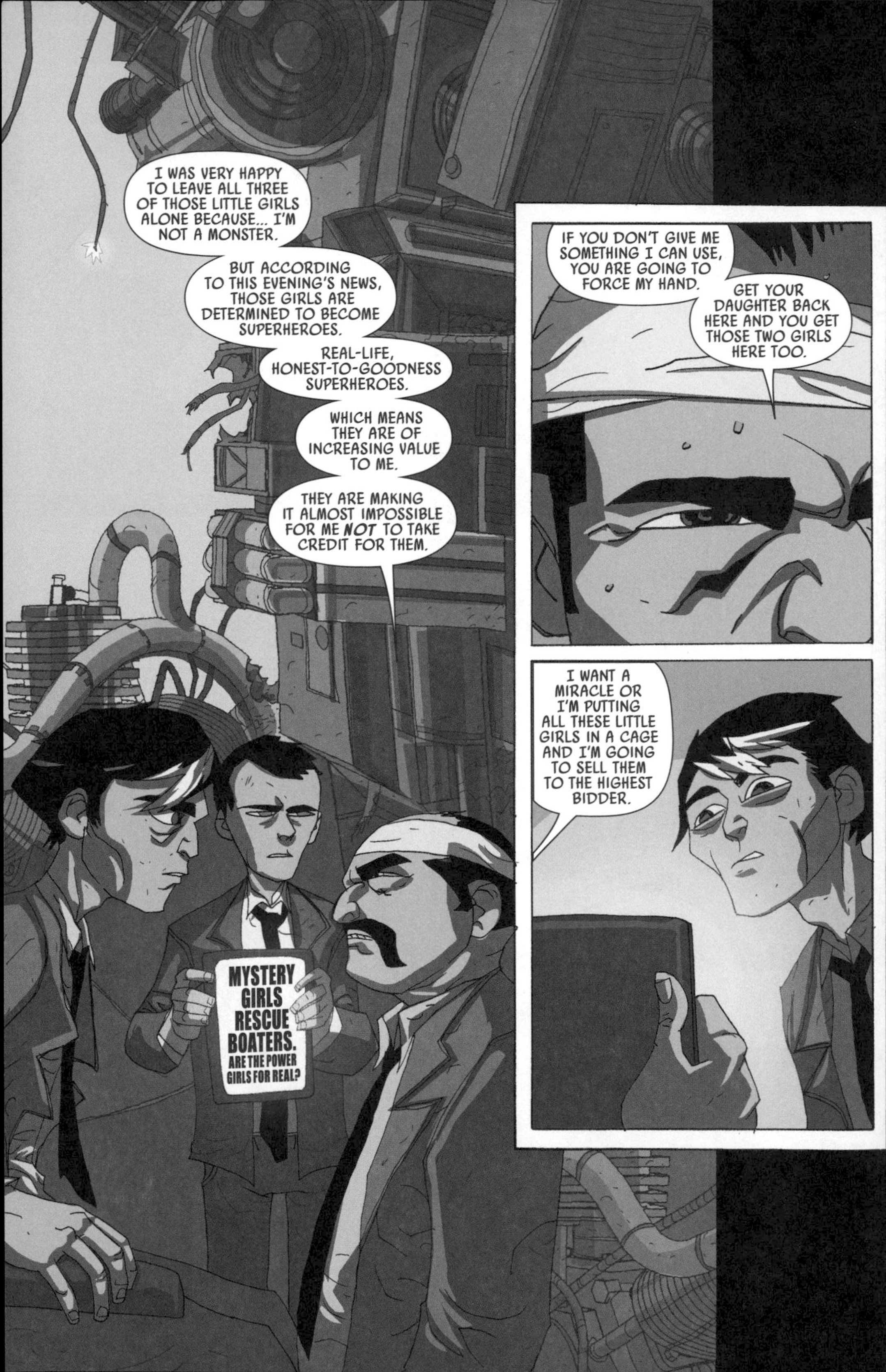
I WAS VERY HAPPY TO LEAVE ALL THREE OF THOSE LITTLE GIRLS ALONE BECAUSE... I'M NOT A MONSTER.
BUT ACCORDING TO THIS EVENING'S NEWS, THOSE GIRLS ARE DETERMINED TO BECOME SUPERHEROES.
REAL-LIFE, HONEST-TO-GOODNESS SUPERHEROES.
WHICH MEANS THEY ARE OF INCREASING VALUE TO ME.
THEY ARE MAKING IT ALMOST IMPOSSIBLE FOR ME *NOT* TO TAKE CREDIT FOR THEM.
MYSTERY GIRLS RESCUE BOATERS.
ARE THE POWER GIRLS FOR REAL?
IF YOU DON'T GIVE ME SOMETHING I CAN USE, YOU ARE GOING TO FORCE MY HAND.
GET YOUR DAUGHTER BACK HERE AND YOU GET THOSE TWO GIRLS HERE TOO.
I WANT A MIRACLE OR I'M PUTTING ALL THESE LITTLE GIRLS IN A CAGE AND I'M GOING TO SELL THEM TO THE HIGHEST BIDDER.

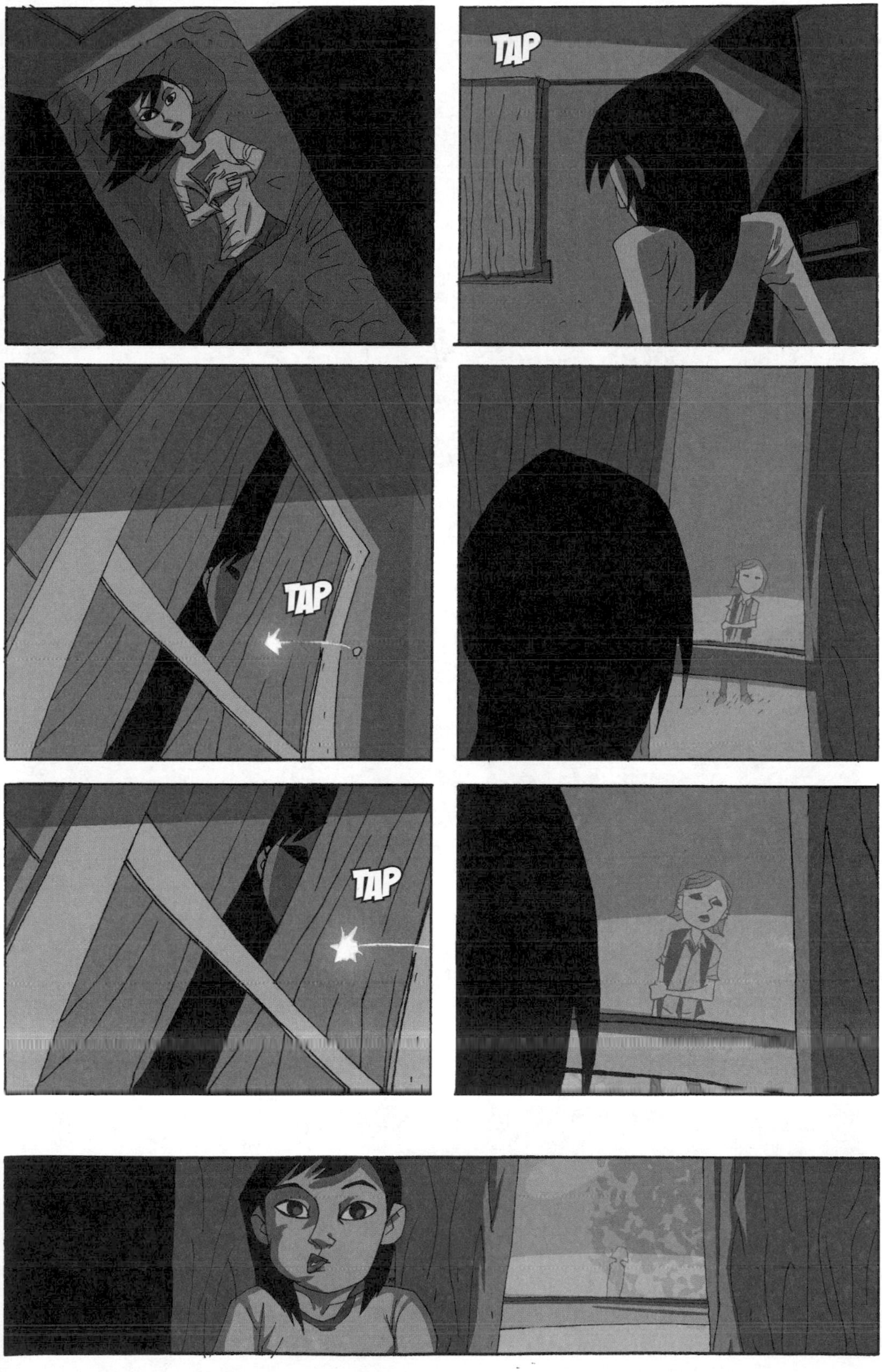
TAP
TAP
TAP

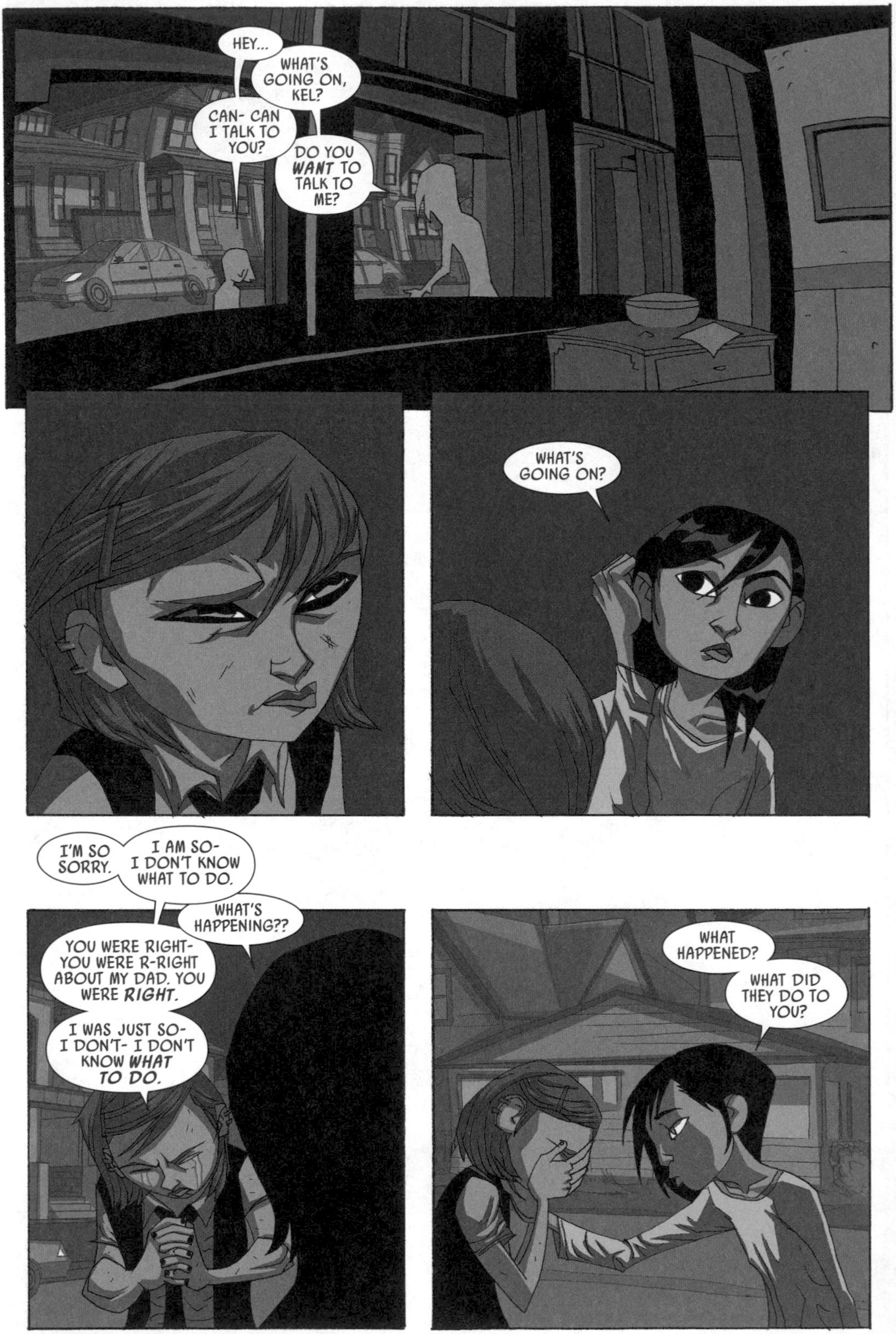
HEY...
WHAT'S GOING ON, KEL?
CAN- CAN I TALK TO YOU?
DO YOU *WANT* TO TALK TO ME?
WHAT'S GOING ON?
I'M SO SORRY.
I AM SO- I DON'T KNOW WHAT TO DO.
WHAT'S HAPPENING??
YOU WERE RIGHT- YOU WERE R-RIGHT ABOUT MY DAD. YOU WERE *RIGHT*.
I WAS JUST SO- I DON'T- I DON'T KNOW *WHAT TO DO*.
WHAT HAPPENED?
WHAT DID THEY DO TO YOU?

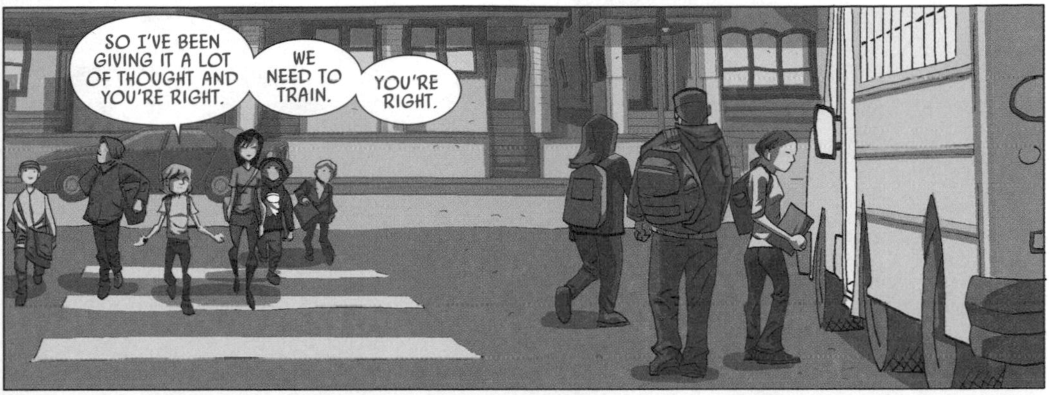
SO I'VE BEEN GIVING IT A LOT OF THOUGHT AND YOU'RE RIGHT.
WE NEED TO TRAIN.
YOU'RE RIGHT.

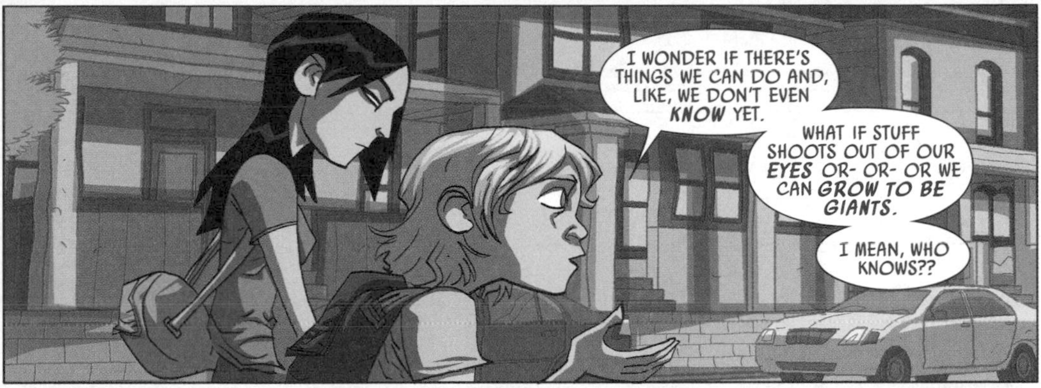
I WONDER IF THERE'S THINGS WE CAN DO AND, LIKE, WE DON'T EVEN KNOW YET.
WHAT IF STUFF SHOOTS OUT OF OUR EYES OR- OR- OR WE CAN GROW TO BE GIANTS.
I MEAN, WHO KNOWS??

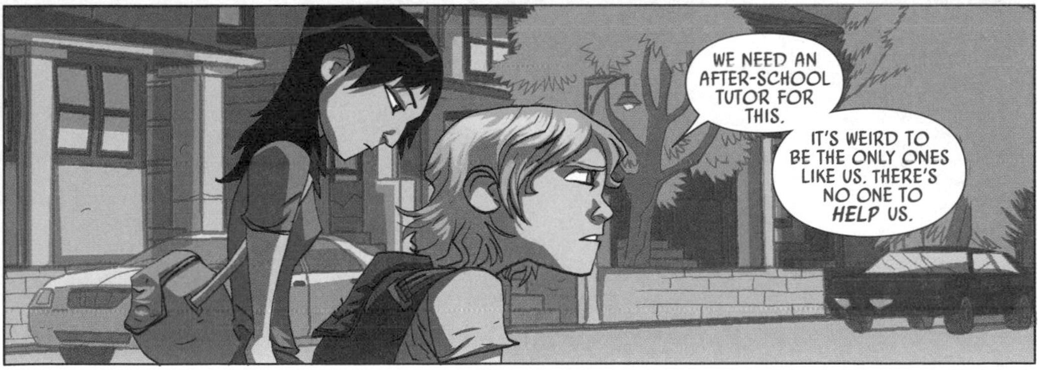
WE NEED AN AFTER-SCHOOL TUTOR FOR THIS.
IT'S WEIRD TO BE THE ONLY ONES LIKE US. THERE'S NO ONE TO HELP US.

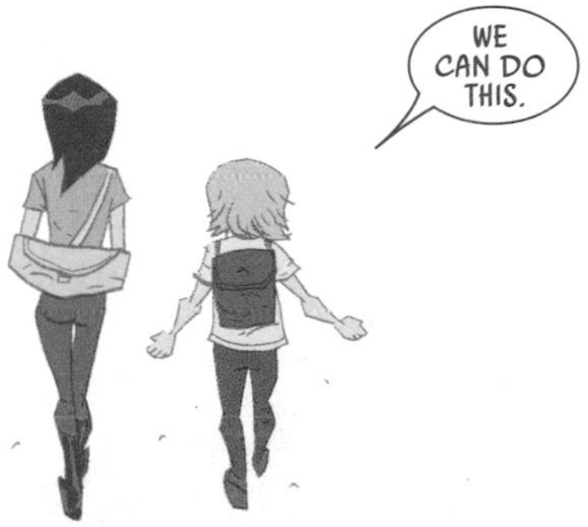
WE CAN DO THIS.

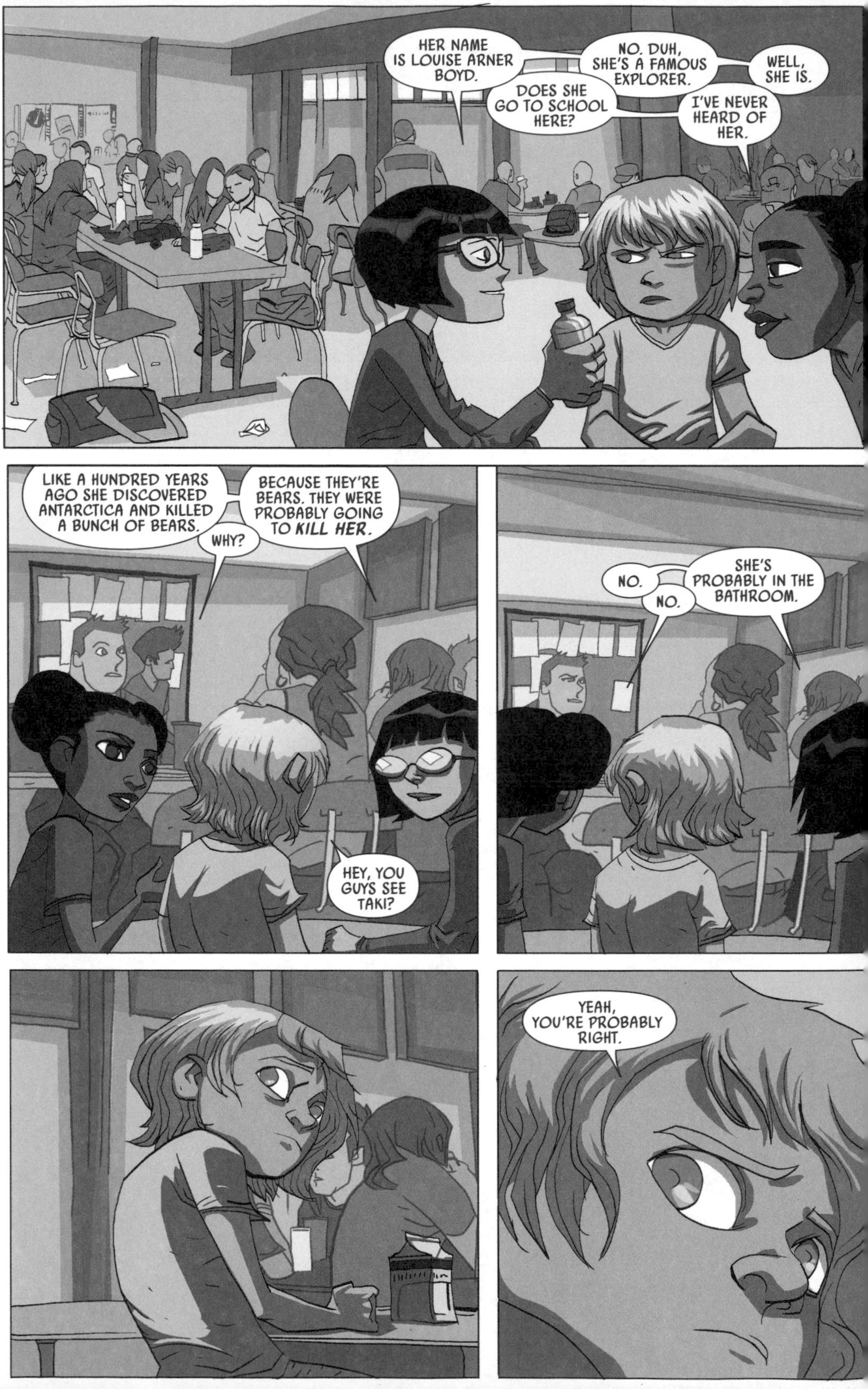
HER NAME IS LOUISE ARNER BOYD.
DOES SHE GO TO SCHOOL HERE?
NO. DUH, SHE'S A FAMOUS EXPLORER.
I'VE NEVER HEARD OF HER.
WELL, SHE IS.
LIKE A HUNDRED YEARS AGO SHE DISCOVERED ANTARCTICA AND KILLED A BUNCH OF BEARS.
WHY?
BECAUSE THEY'RE BEARS. THEY WERE PROBABLY GOING TO KILL HER.
HEY, YOU GUYS SEE TAKI?
NO.
NO.
SHE'S PROBABLY IN THE BATHROOM.
YEAH, YOU'RE PROBABLY RIGHT.

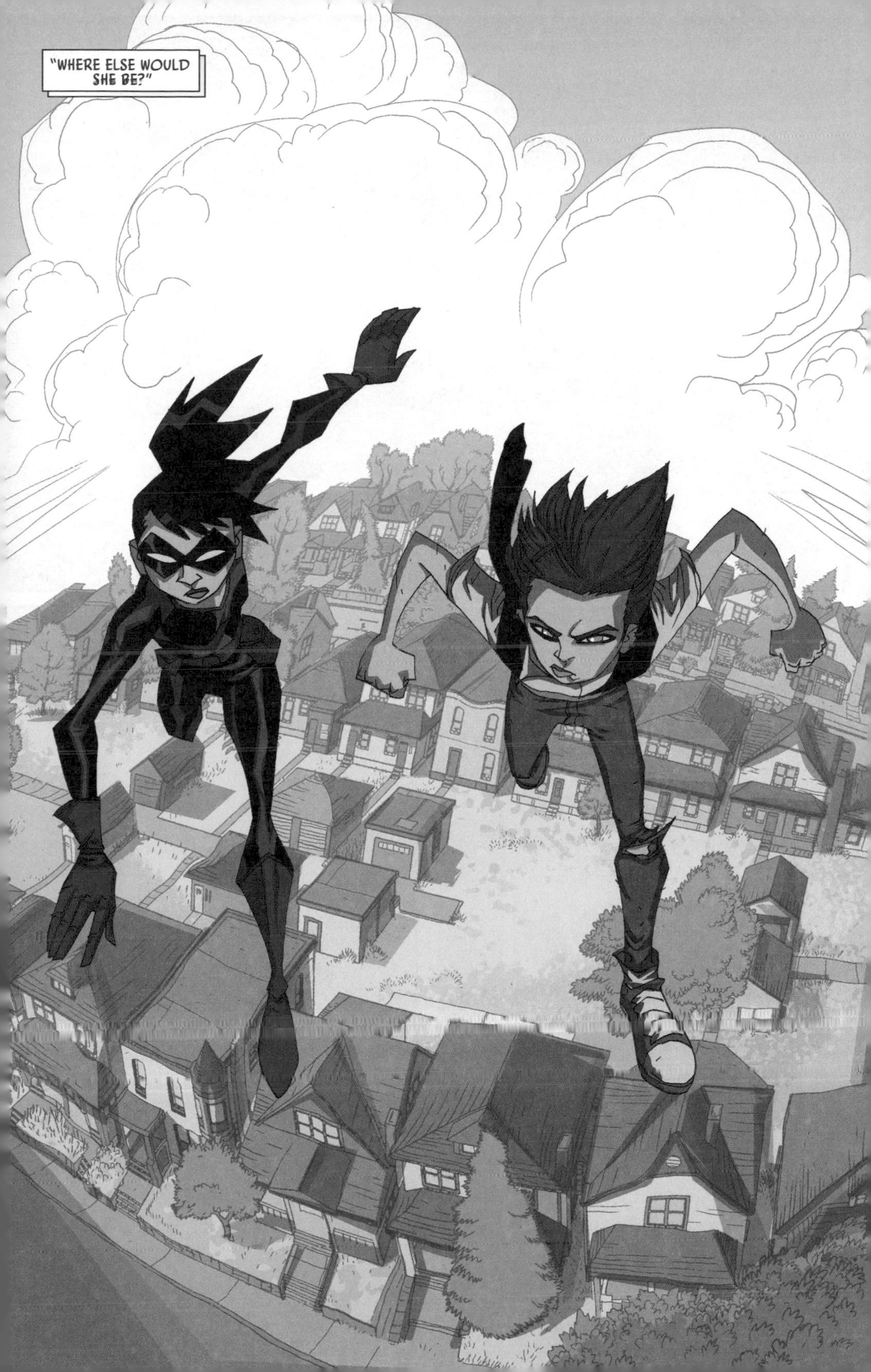
"WHERE ELSE WOULD SHE BE?"

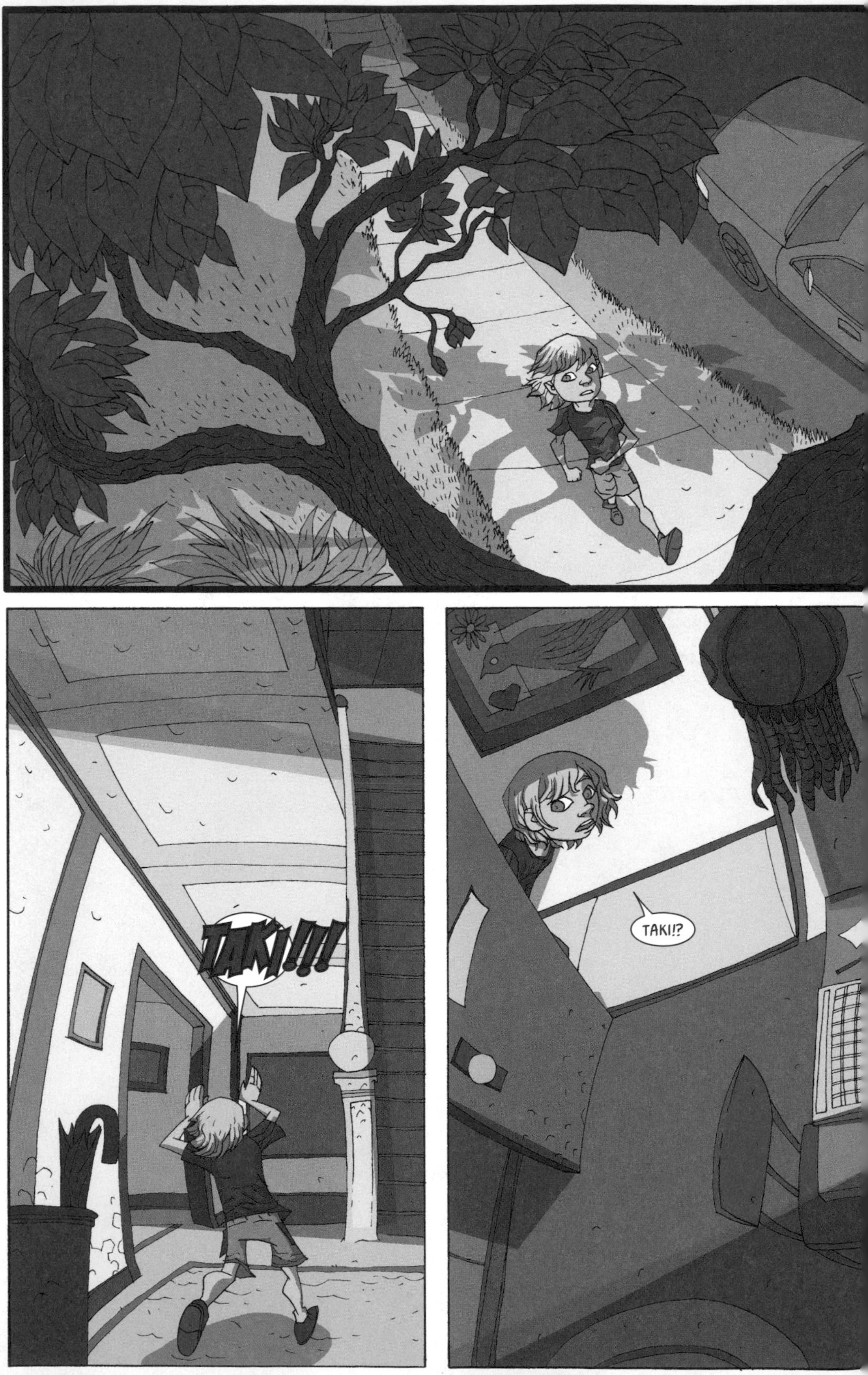
TAKI!!!
TAKI!?

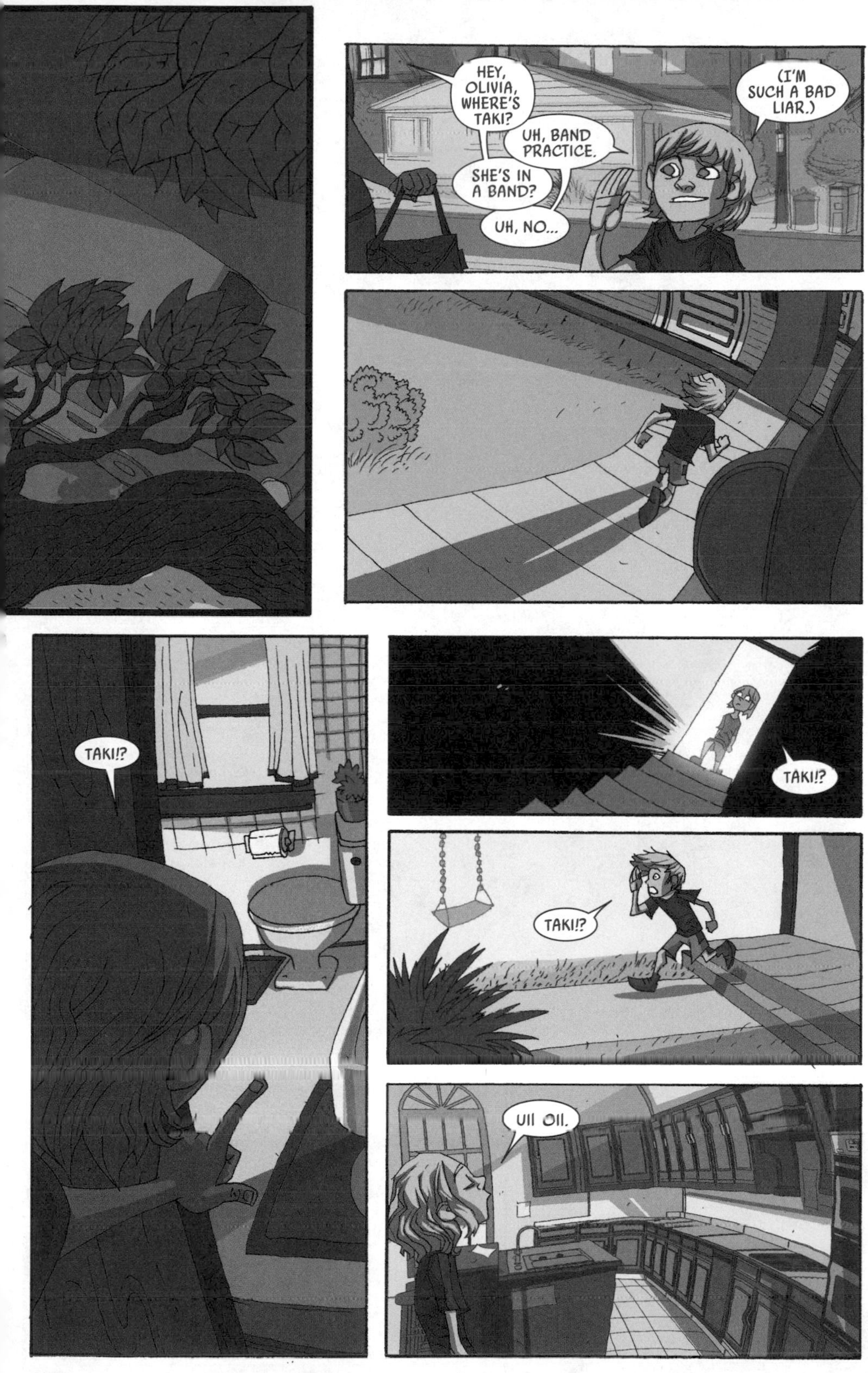
HEY, OLIVIA, WHERE'S TAKI?
UH, BAND PRACTICE.
SHE'S IN A BAND?
UH, NO...
(I'M SUCH A BAD LIAR.)
TAKI!?
TAKI!?
TAKI!?
UH OH.

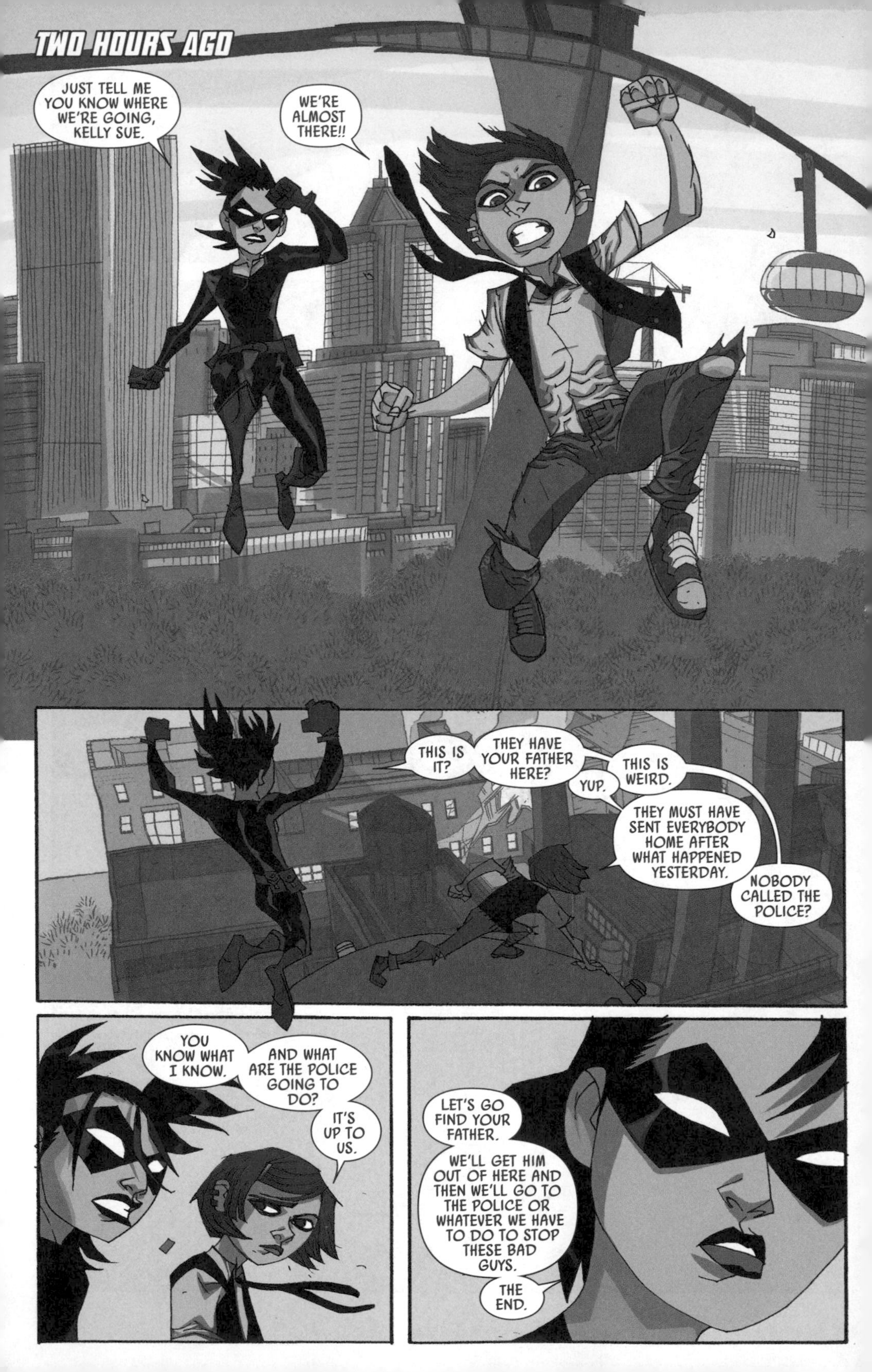
TWO HOURS AGO
JUST TELL ME YOU KNOW WHERE WE'RE GOING, KELLY SUE.
WE'RE ALMOST THERE!!
THIS IS IT?
THEY HAVE YOUR FATHER HERE?
YUP.
THIS IS WEIRD.
THEY MUST HAVE SENT EVERYBODY HOME AFTER WHAT HAPPENED YESTERDAY.
NOBODY CALLED THE POLICE?
YOU KNOW WHAT I KNOW.
AND WHAT ARE THE POLICE GOING TO DO?
IT'S UP TO US.
LET'S GO FIND YOUR FATHER.
WE'LL GET HIM OUT OF HERE AND THEN WE'LL GO TO THE POLICE OR WHATEVER WE HAVE TO DO TO STOP THESE BAD GUYS.
THE END.

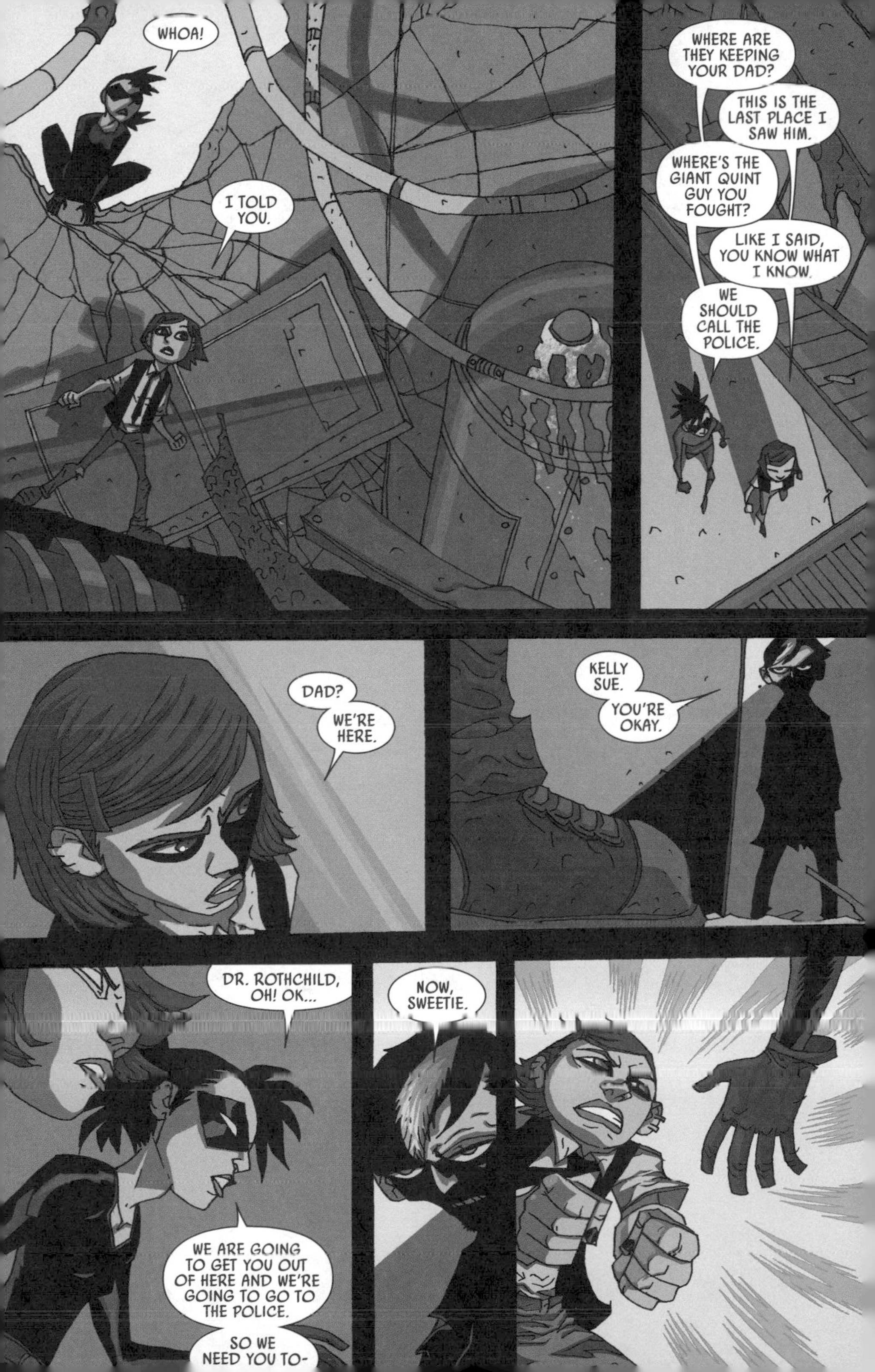
WHOA!
I TOLD YOU.
WHERE ARE THEY KEEPING YOUR DAD?
THIS IS THE LAST PLACE I SAW HIM.
WHERE'S THE GIANT QUINT GUY YOU FOUGHT?
LIKE I SAID, YOU KNOW WHAT I KNOW.
WE SHOULD CALL THE POLICE.
DAD?
WE'RE HERE.
KELLY SUE.
YOU'RE OKAY.
DR. ROTHCHILD, OH! OK...
WE ARE GOING TO GET YOU OUT OF HERE AND WE'RE GOING TO GO TO THE POLICE.
SO WE NEED YOU TO-
NOW, SWEETIE.

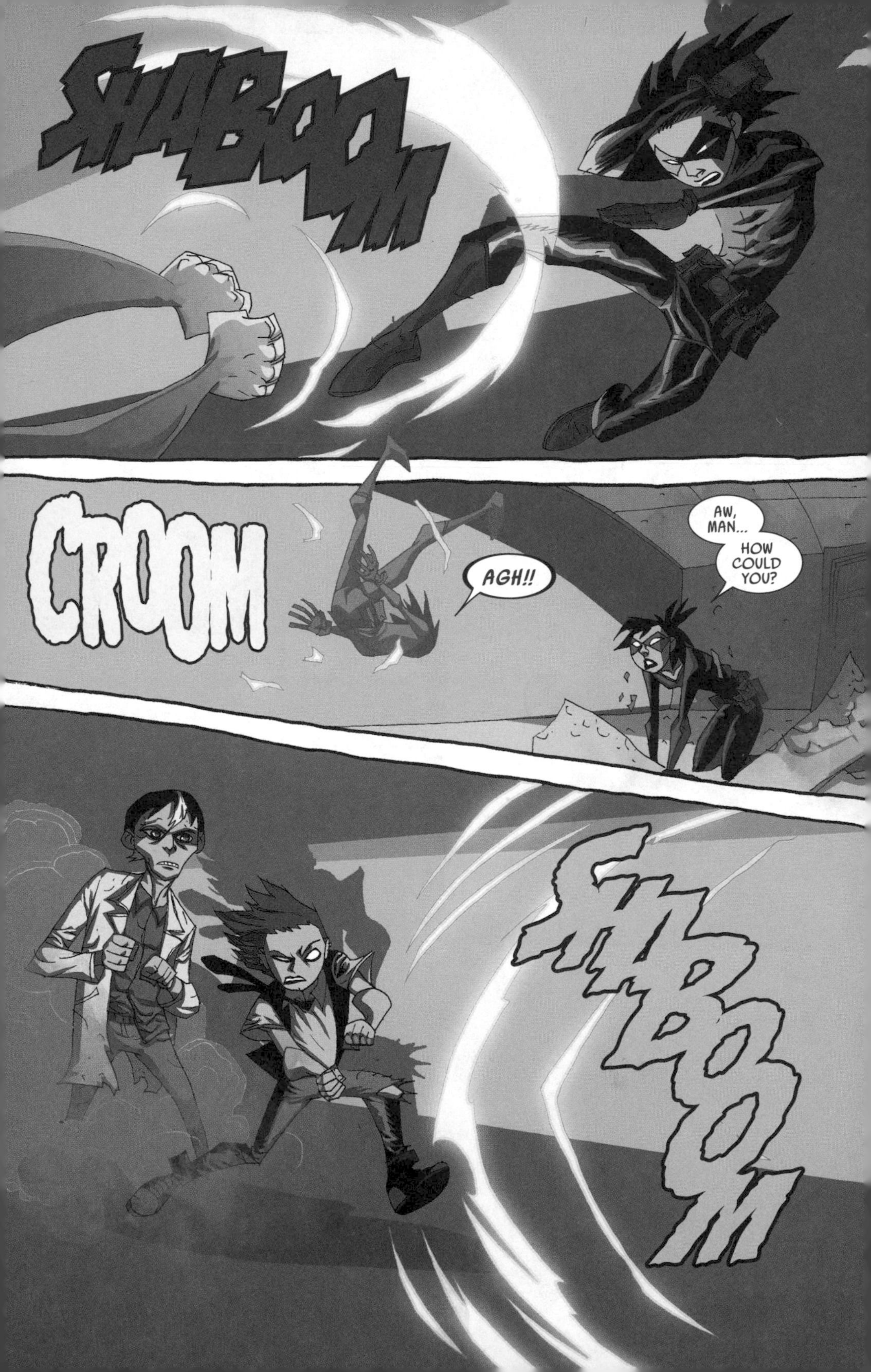
SHABOOM
CROOM
AGH!!
AW, MAN...
HOW COULD YOU?
SHABOOM

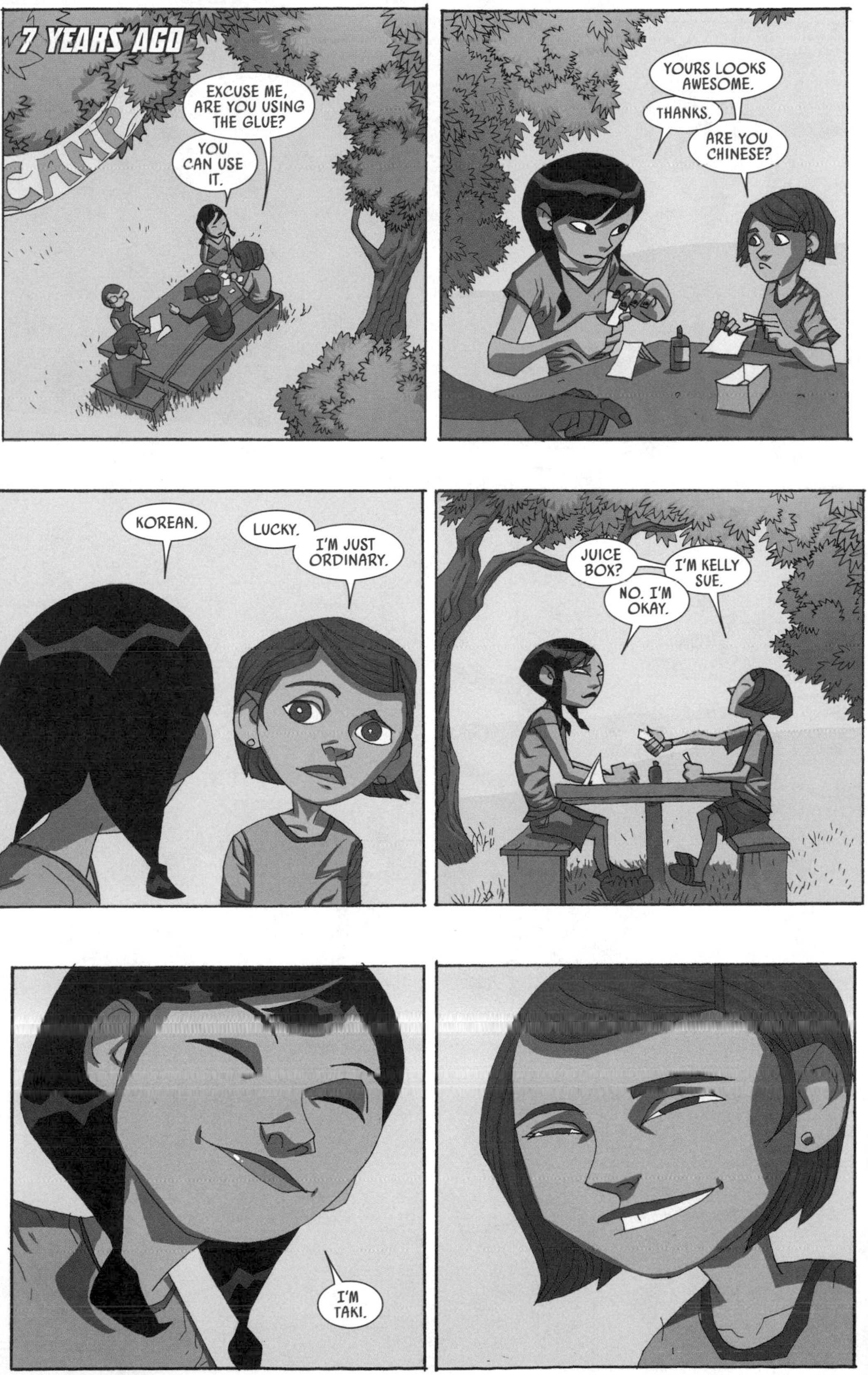
7 YEARS AGO
CAMP
EXCUSE ME, ARE YOU USING THE GLUE?
YOU CAN USE IT.
YOURS LOOKS AWESOME.
THANKS.
ARE YOU CHINESE?
KOREAN.
LUCKY.
I'M JUST ORDINARY.
JUICE BOX?
NO. I'M OKAY.
I'M KELLY SUE.
I'M TAKI.

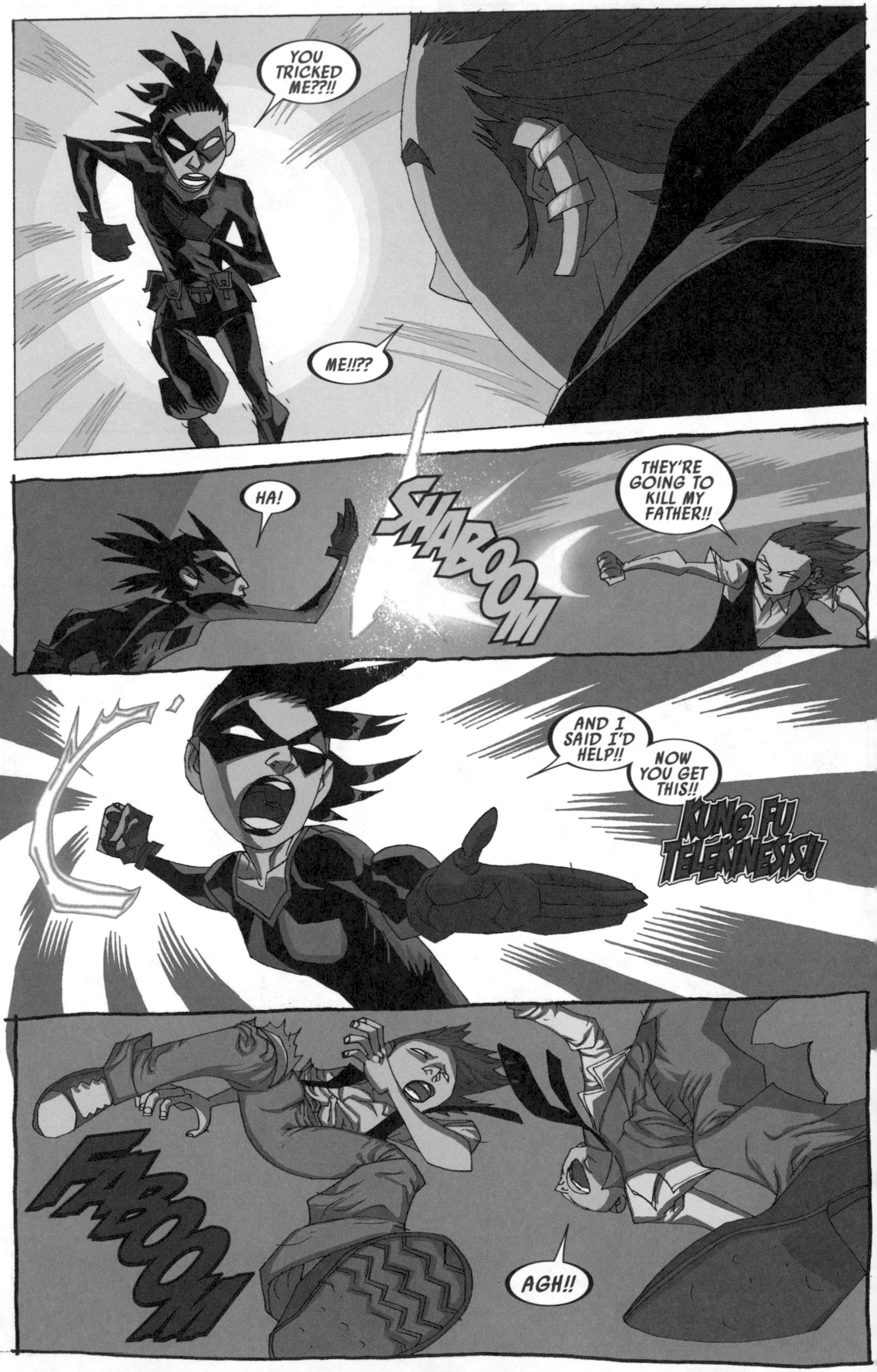
YOU TRICKED ME??!!
ME!!??
HA!
SHABOOM
THEY'RE GOING TO KILL MY FATHER!!
AND I SAID I'D HELP!!
NOW YOU GET THIS!!
KUNG FU TELEKINESIS!
FABOOM
AGH!!

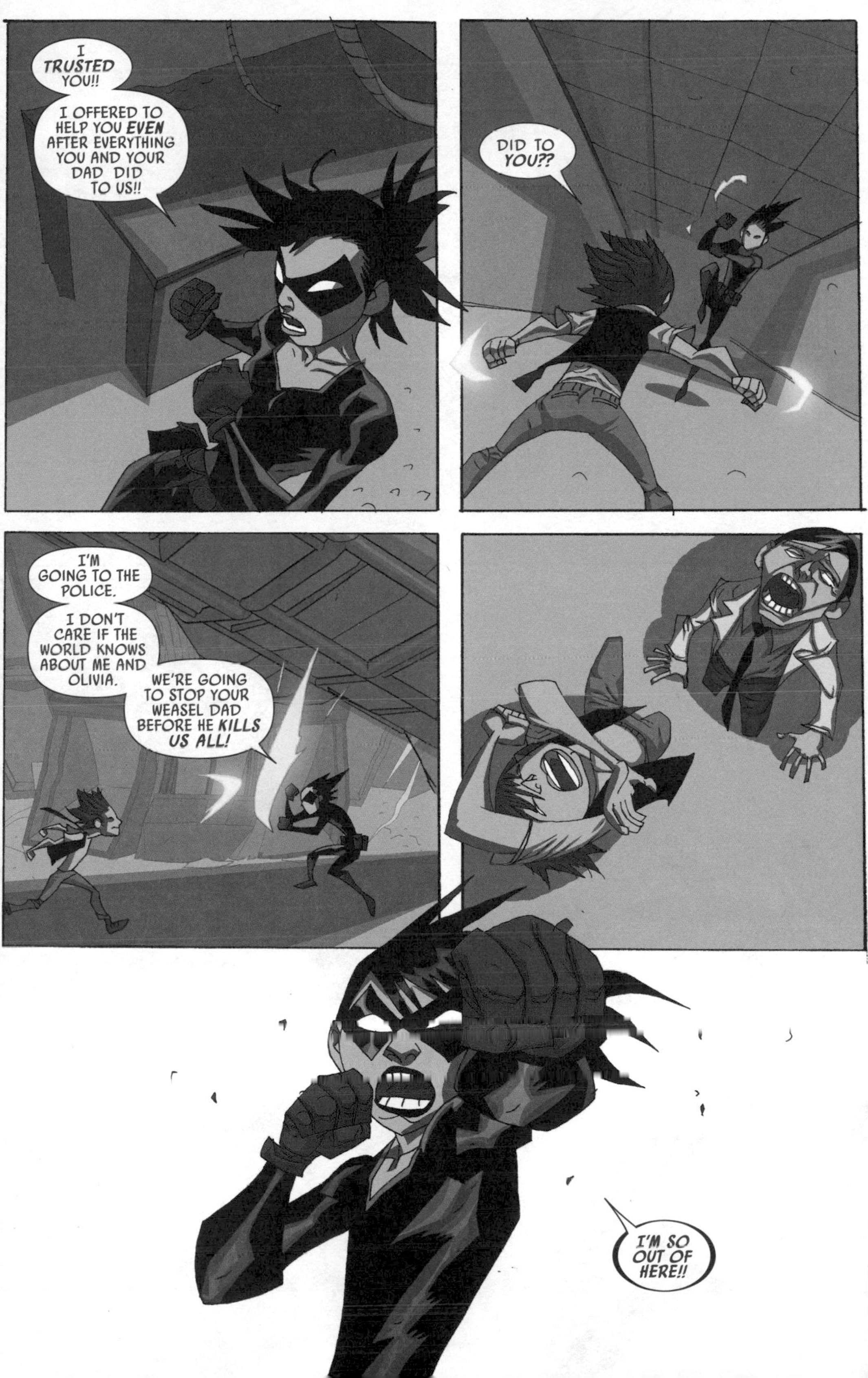
I TRUSTED YOU!!
I OFFERED TO HELP YOU EVEN AFTER EVERYTHING YOU AND YOUR DAD DID TO US!!
DID TO YOU??
I'M GOING TO THE POLICE.
I DON'T CARE IF THE WORLD KNOWS ABOUT ME AND OLIVIA.
WE'RE GOING TO STOP YOUR WEASEL DAD BEFORE HE KILLS US ALL!
I'M SO OUT OF HERE!!

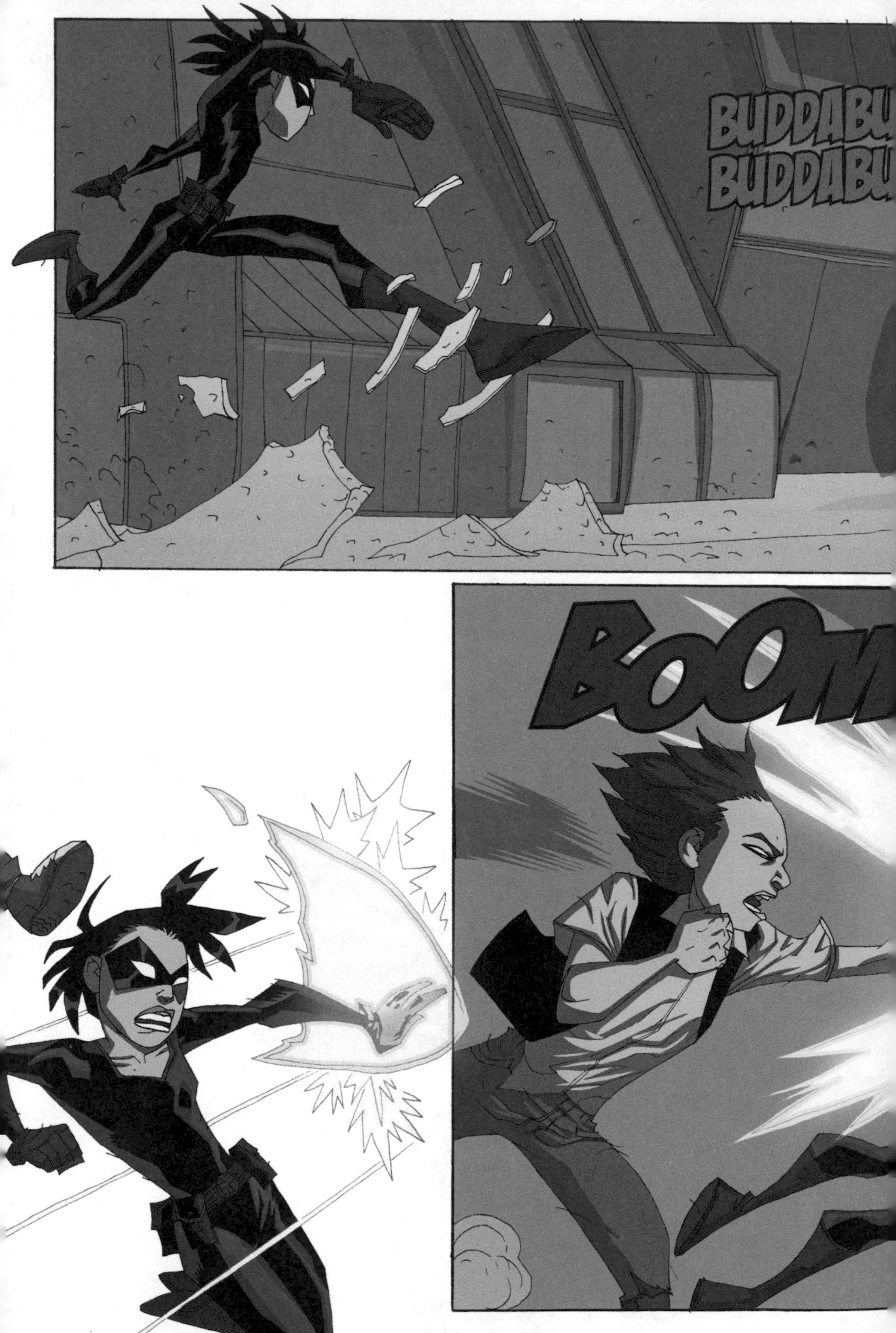
BUDDABU
BUDDABU
BOO

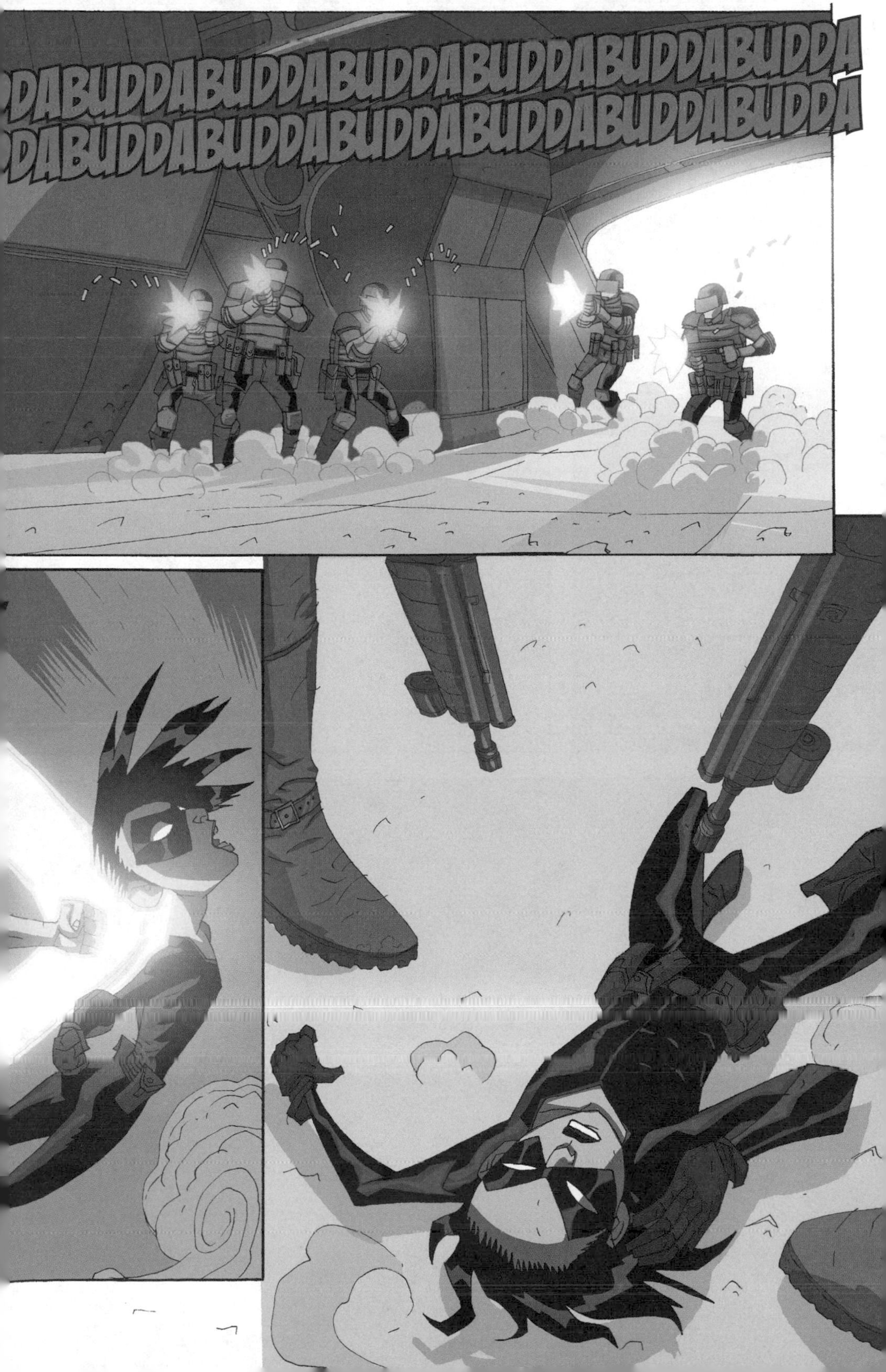
DABUDDABUDDABUDDABUDDABUDDABUDDA
DABUDDABUDDABUDDABUDDABUDDABUDDA

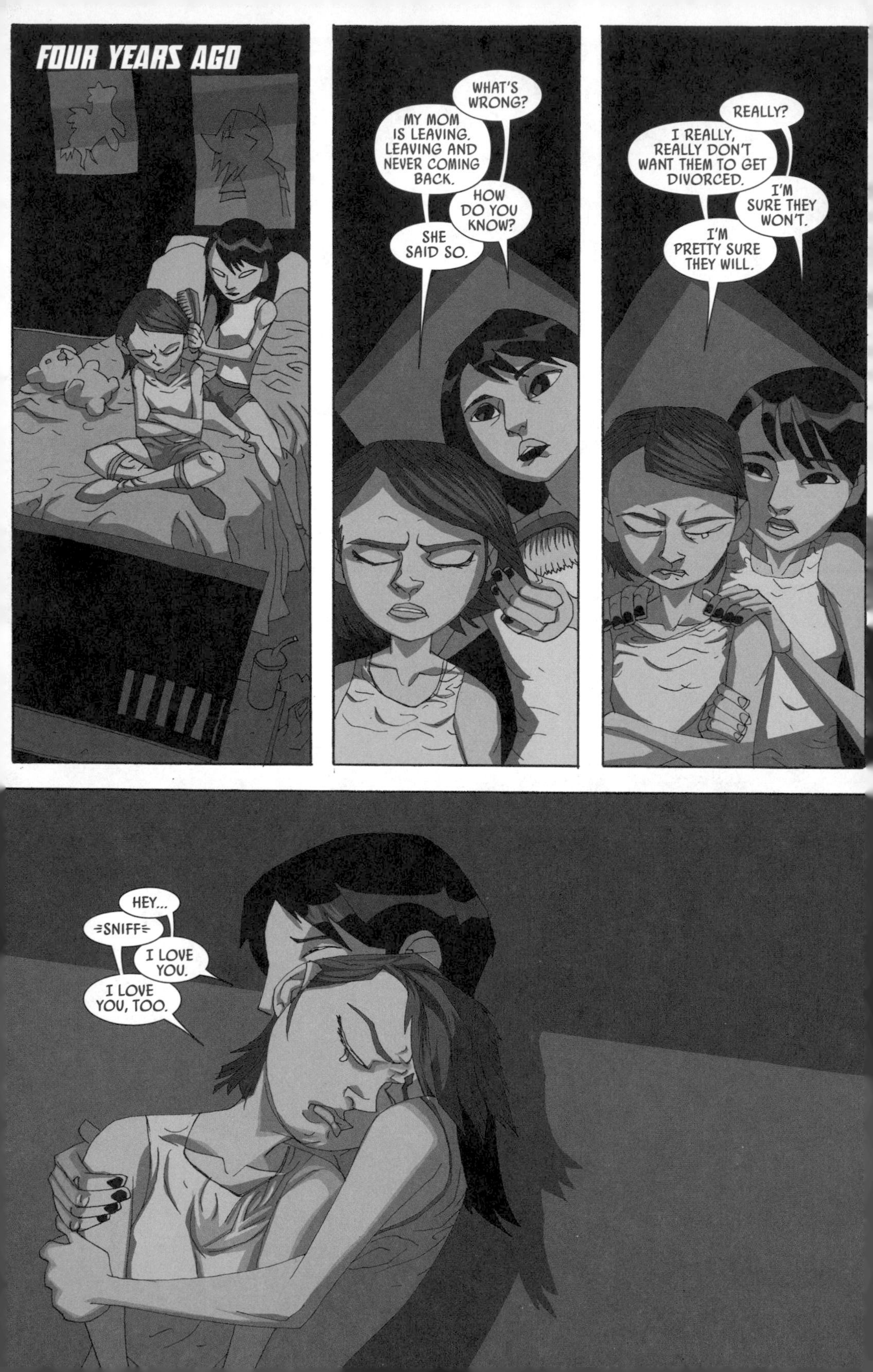
FOUR YEARS AGO
WHAT'S WRONG?
MY MOM IS LEAVING. LEAVING AND NEVER COMING BACK.
HOW DO YOU KNOW?
SHE SAID SO.
REALLY?
I REALLY, REALLY DON'T WANT THEM TO GET DIVORCED.
I'M SURE THEY WON'T.
I'M PRETTY SURE THEY WILL.
HEY...
=SNIFF=
I LOVE YOU.
I LOVE YOU, TOO.

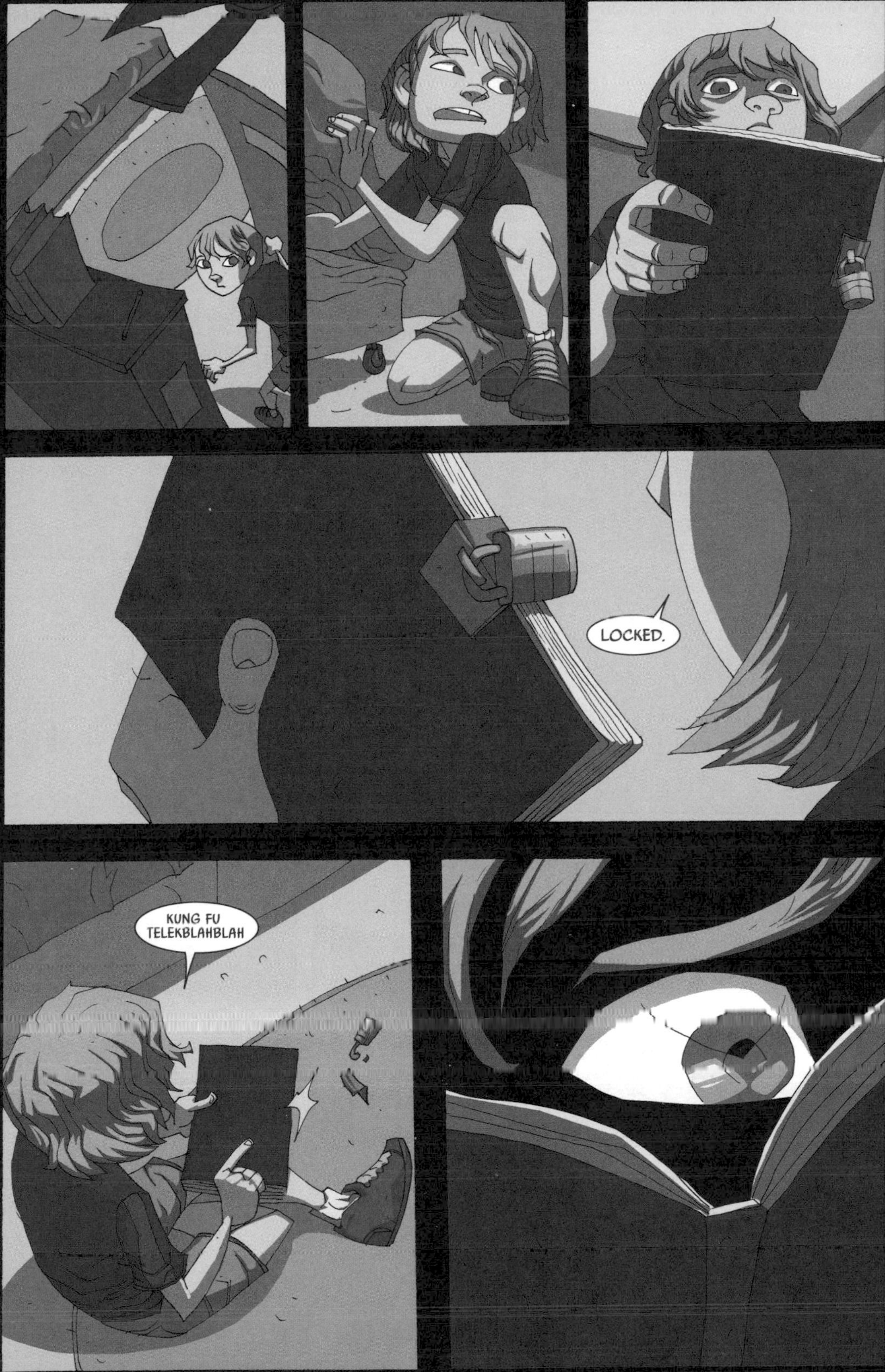
LOCKED.
KUNG FU TELEKBLAHBLAH

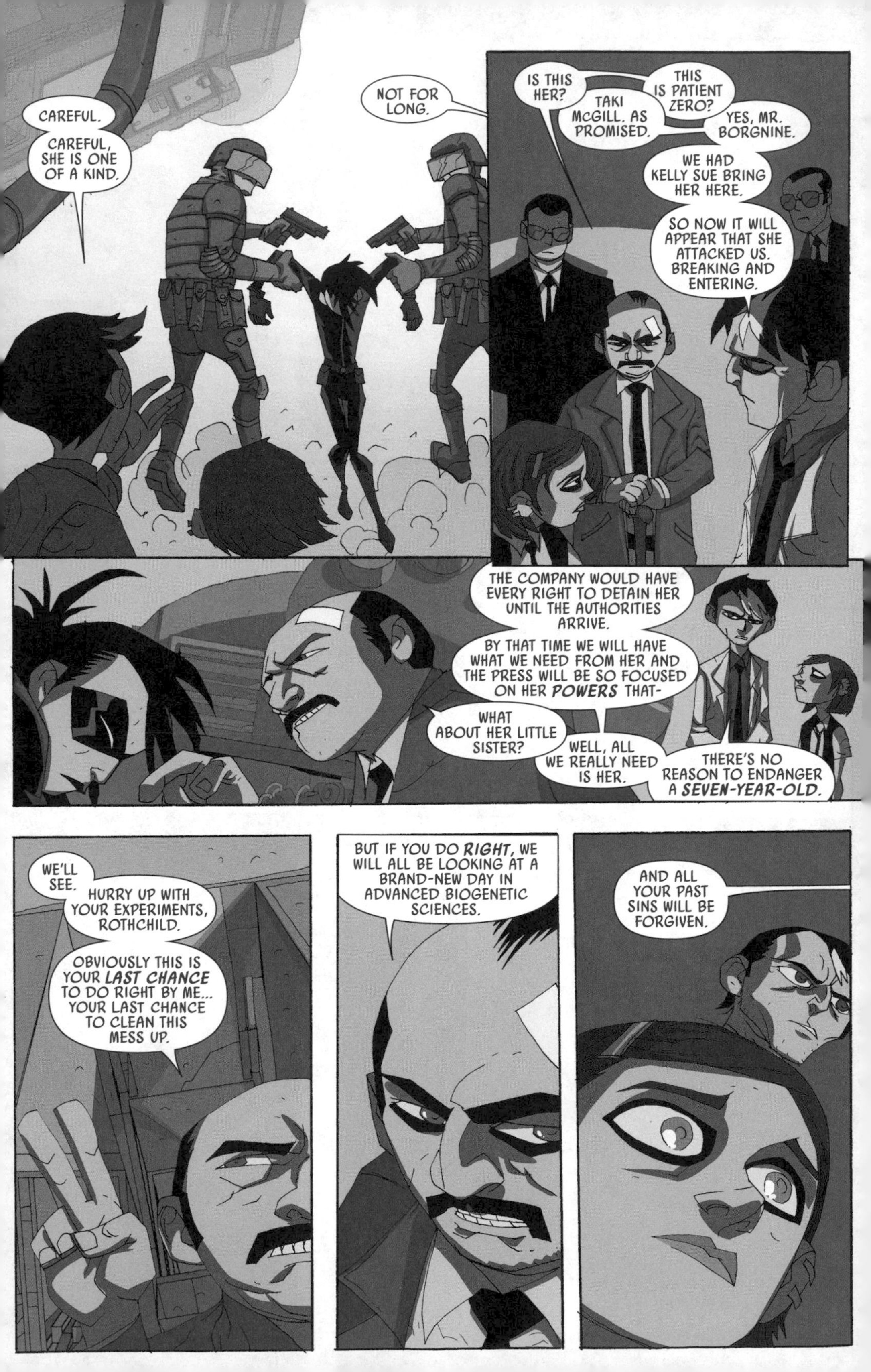
CAREFUL.
CAREFUL, SHE IS ONE OF A KIND.
NOT FOR LONG.
IS THIS HER?
THIS IS PATIENT ZERO?
TAKI McGILL, AS PROMISED.
YES, MR. BORGNINE.
WE HAD KELLY SUE BRING HER HERE.
SO NOW IT WILL APPEAR THAT SHE ATTACKED US. BREAKING AND ENTERING.
THE COMPANY WOULD HAVE EVERY RIGHT TO DETAIN HER UNTIL THE AUTHORITIES ARRIVE.
BY THAT TIME WE WILL HAVE WHAT WE NEED FROM HER AND THE PRESS WILL BE SO FOCUSED ON HER POWERS THAT-
WHAT ABOUT HER LITTLE SISTER?
WELL, ALL WE REALLY NEED IS HER.
THERE'S NO REASON TO ENDANGER A SEVEN-YEAR-OLD.
WE'LL SEE.
HURRY UP WITH YOUR EXPERIMENTS, ROTHCHILD.
OBVIOUSLY THIS IS YOUR LAST CHANCE TO DO RIGHT BY ME... YOUR LAST CHANCE TO CLEAN THIS MESS UP.
BUT IF YOU DO RIGHT, WE WILL ALL BE LOOKING AT A BRAND-NEW DAY IN ADVANCED BIOGENETIC SCIENCES.
AND ALL YOUR PAST SINS WILL BE FORGIVEN.

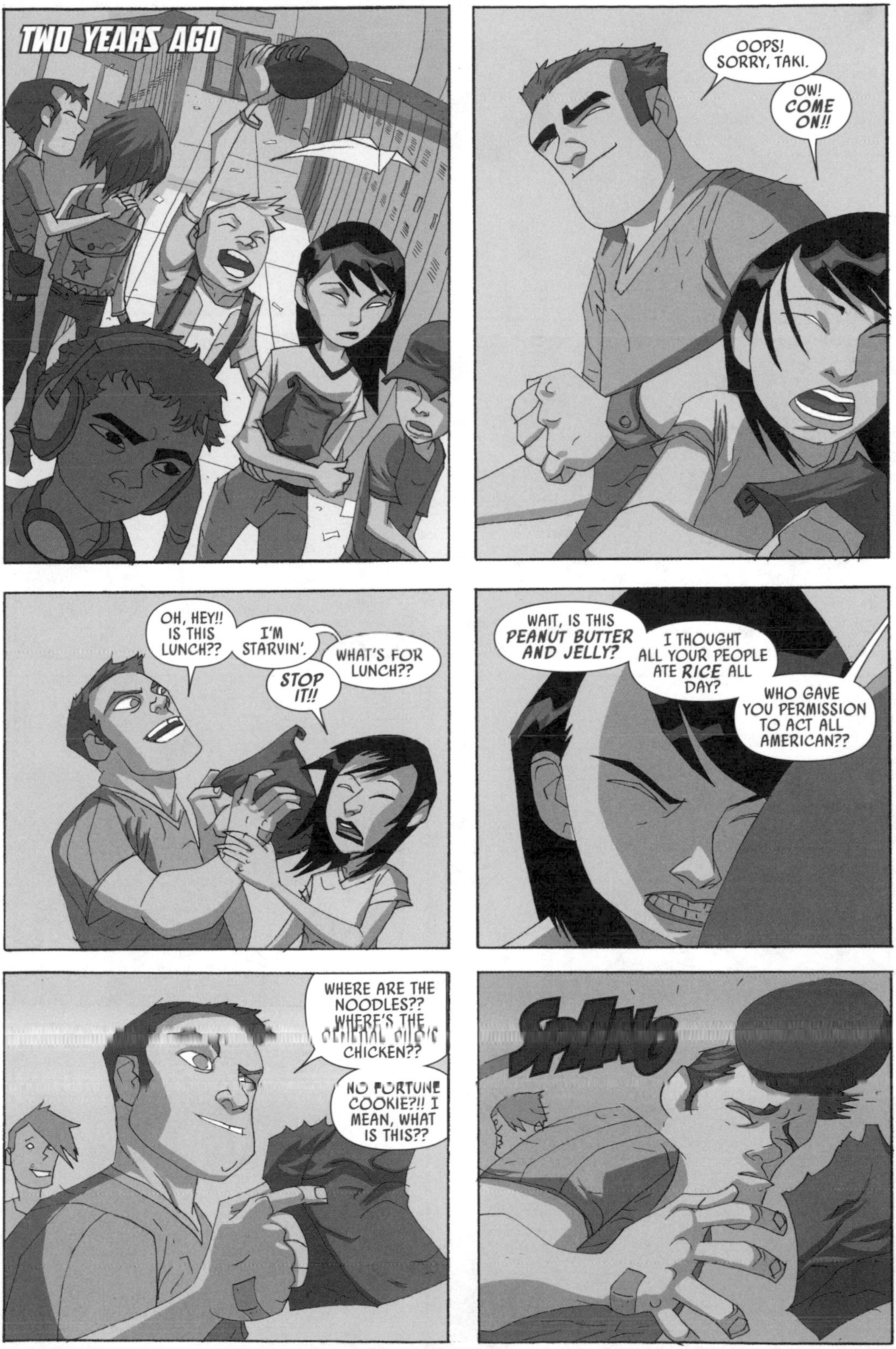
TWO YEARS AGO
OOPS! SORRY, TAKI.
OW! COME ON!!
OH, HEY!! IS THIS LUNCH??
I'M STARVIN'.
WHAT'S FOR LUNCH??
STOP IT!!
WAIT, IS THIS PEANUT BUTTER AND JELLY?
I THOUGHT ALL YOUR PEOPLE ATE RICE ALL DAY?
WHO GAVE YOU PERMISSION TO ACT ALL AMERICAN??
WHERE ARE THE NOODLES?? WHERE'S THE
CHICKEN??
NO FORTUNE COOKIE?!! I MEAN, WHAT IS THIS??
SPANG

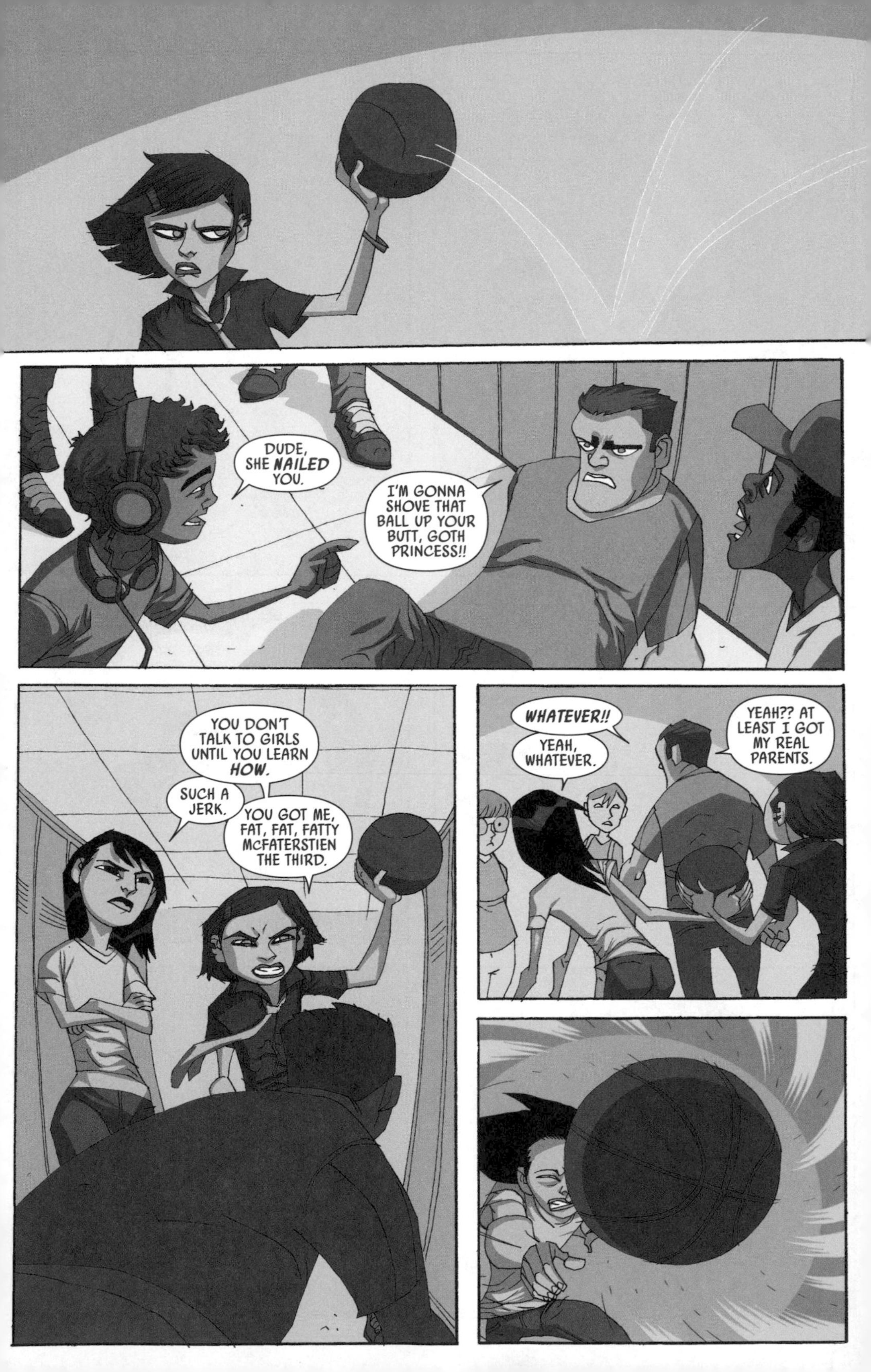
DUDE, SHE NAILED YOU.
I'M GONNA SHOVE THAT BALL UP YOUR BUTT, GOTH PRINCESS!!
YOU DON'T TALK TO GIRLS UNTIL YOU LEARN HOW.
SUCH A JERK.
YOU GOT ME, FAT, FAT, FATTY McFATERSTIEN THE THIRD.
WHATEVER!!
YEAH, WHATEVER.
YEAH?? AT LEAST I GOT MY REAL PARENTS.

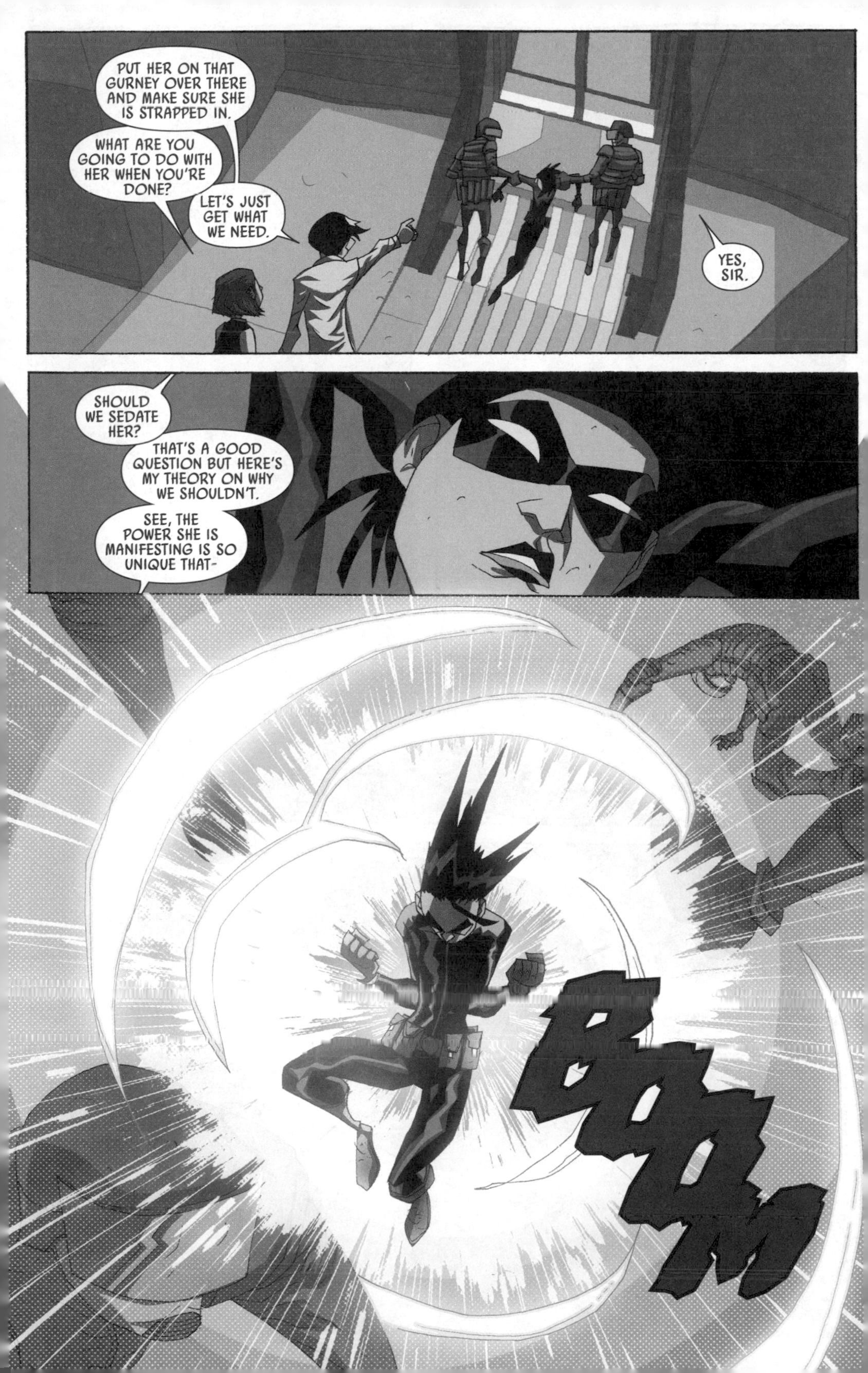
PUT HER ON THAT GURNEY OVER THERE AND MAKE SURE SHE IS STRAPPED IN.
WHAT ARE YOU GOING TO DO WITH HER WHEN YOU'RE DONE?
LET'S JUST GET WHAT WE NEED.
YES, SIR.
SHOULD WE SEDATE HER?
THAT'S A GOOD QUESTION BUT HERE'S MY THEORY ON WHY WE SHOULDN'T.
SEE, THE POWER SHE IS MANIFESTING IS SO UNIQUE THAT-
BOOM

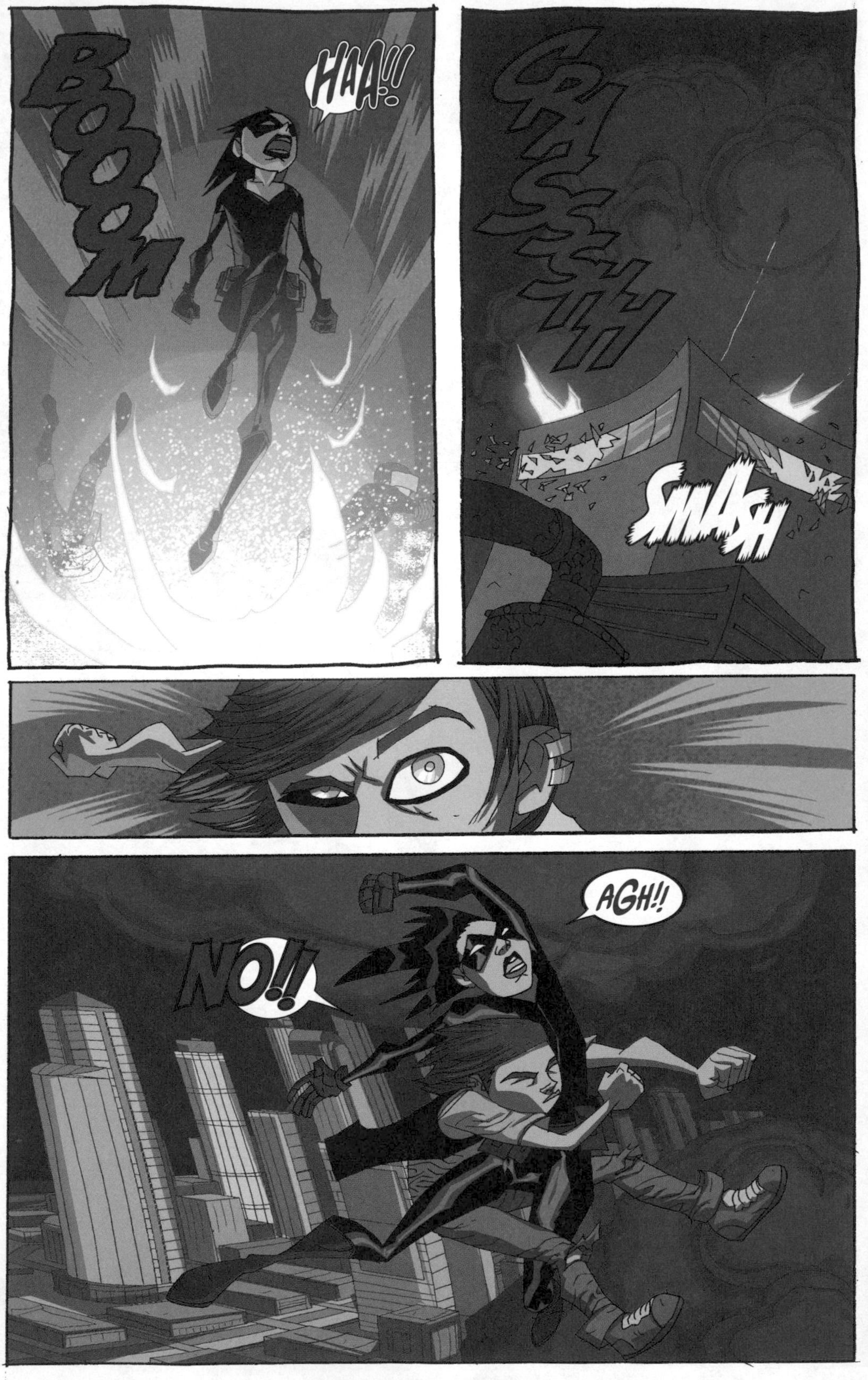
BOOOOM
HAA!!
CRASSHHH
SMASH
AGH!!
NO!!

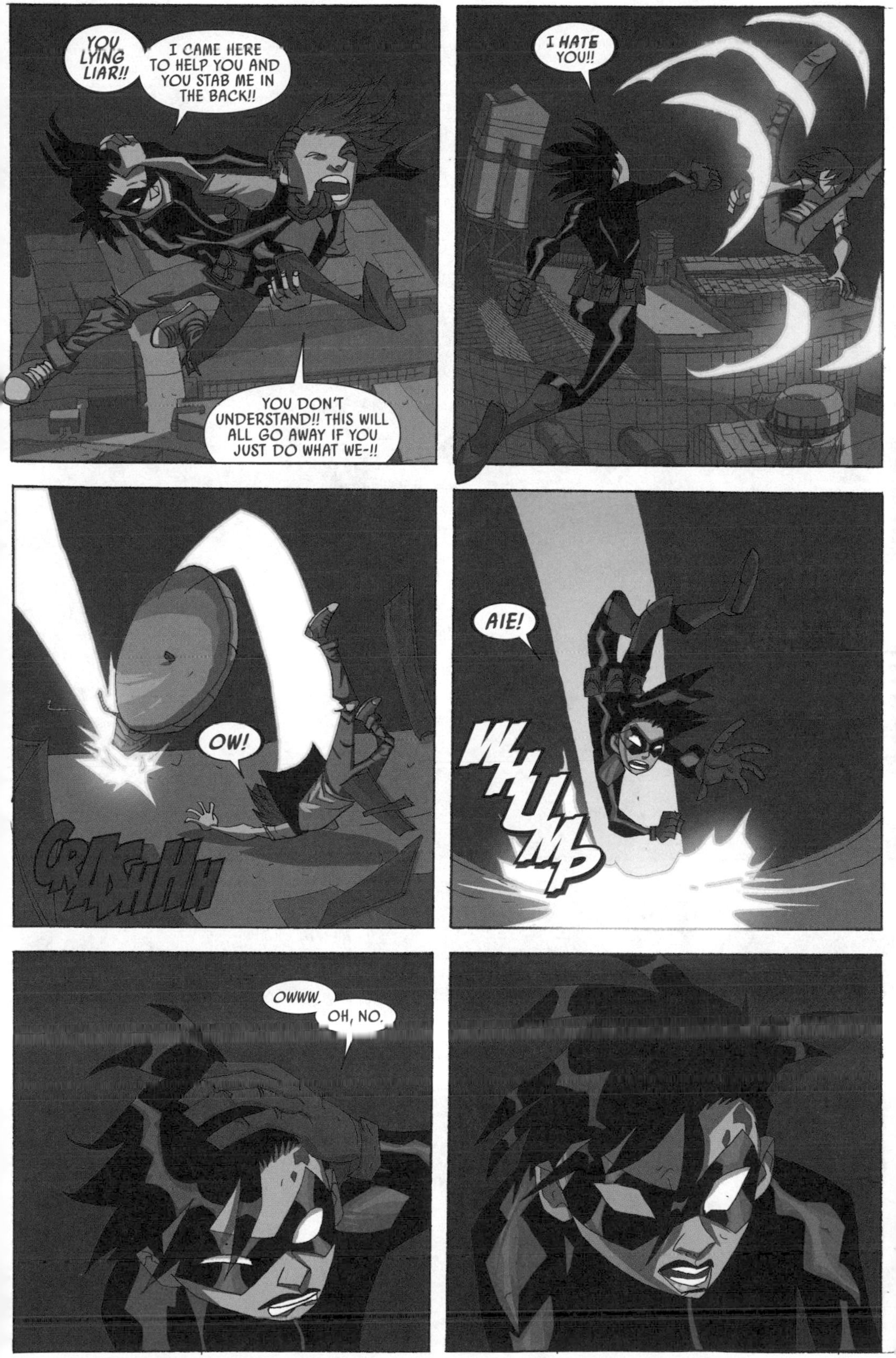
YOU LYING LIAR!!
I CAME HERE TO HELP YOU AND YOU STAB ME IN THE BACK!!
YOU DON'T UNDERSTAND!! THIS WILL ALL GO AWAY IF YOU JUST DO WHAT WE-!!
I HATE YOU!!
OW!
CRASHHH
AIE!
WHUMP
OWWW.
OH, NO.

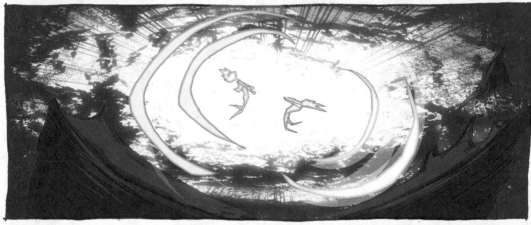

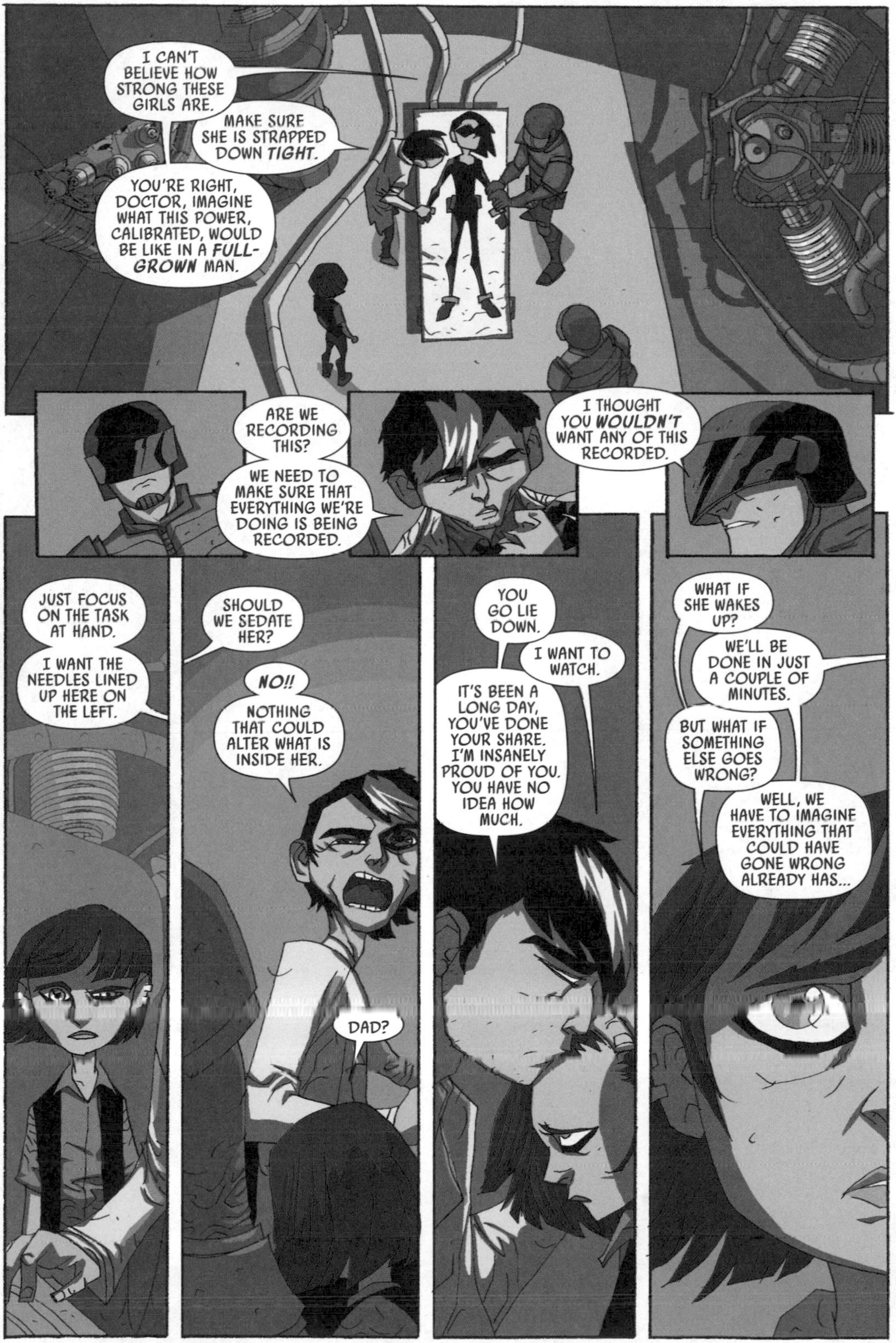
I CAN'T BELIEVE HOW STRONG THESE GIRLS ARE.
MAKE SURE SHE IS STRAPPED DOWN *TIGHT*.
YOU'RE RIGHT, DOCTOR, IMAGINE WHAT THIS POWER, CALIBRATED, WOULD BE LIKE IN A *FULL-GROWN* MAN.
ARE WE RECORDING THIS?
WE NEED TO MAKE SURE THAT EVERYTHING WE'RE DOING IS BEING RECORDED.
I THOUGHT YOU ***WOULDN'T*** WANT ANY OF THIS RECORDED.
JUST FOCUS ON THE TASK AT HAND.
I WANT THE NEEDLES LINED UP HERE ON THE LEFT.
SHOULD WE SEDATE HER?
NO!!
NOTHING THAT COULD ALTER WHAT IS INSIDE HER.
DAD?
YOU GO LIE DOWN.
I WANT TO WATCH.
IT'S BEEN A LONG DAY, YOU'VE DONE YOUR SHARE. I'M INSANELY PROUD OF YOU. YOU HAVE NO IDEA HOW MUCH.
WHAT IF SHE WAKES UP?
WE'LL BE DONE IN JUST A COUPLE OF MINUTES.
BUT WHAT IF SOMETHING ELSE GOES WRONG?
WELL, WE HAVE TO IMAGINE EVERYTHING THAT COULD HAVE GONE WRONG ALREADY HAS...

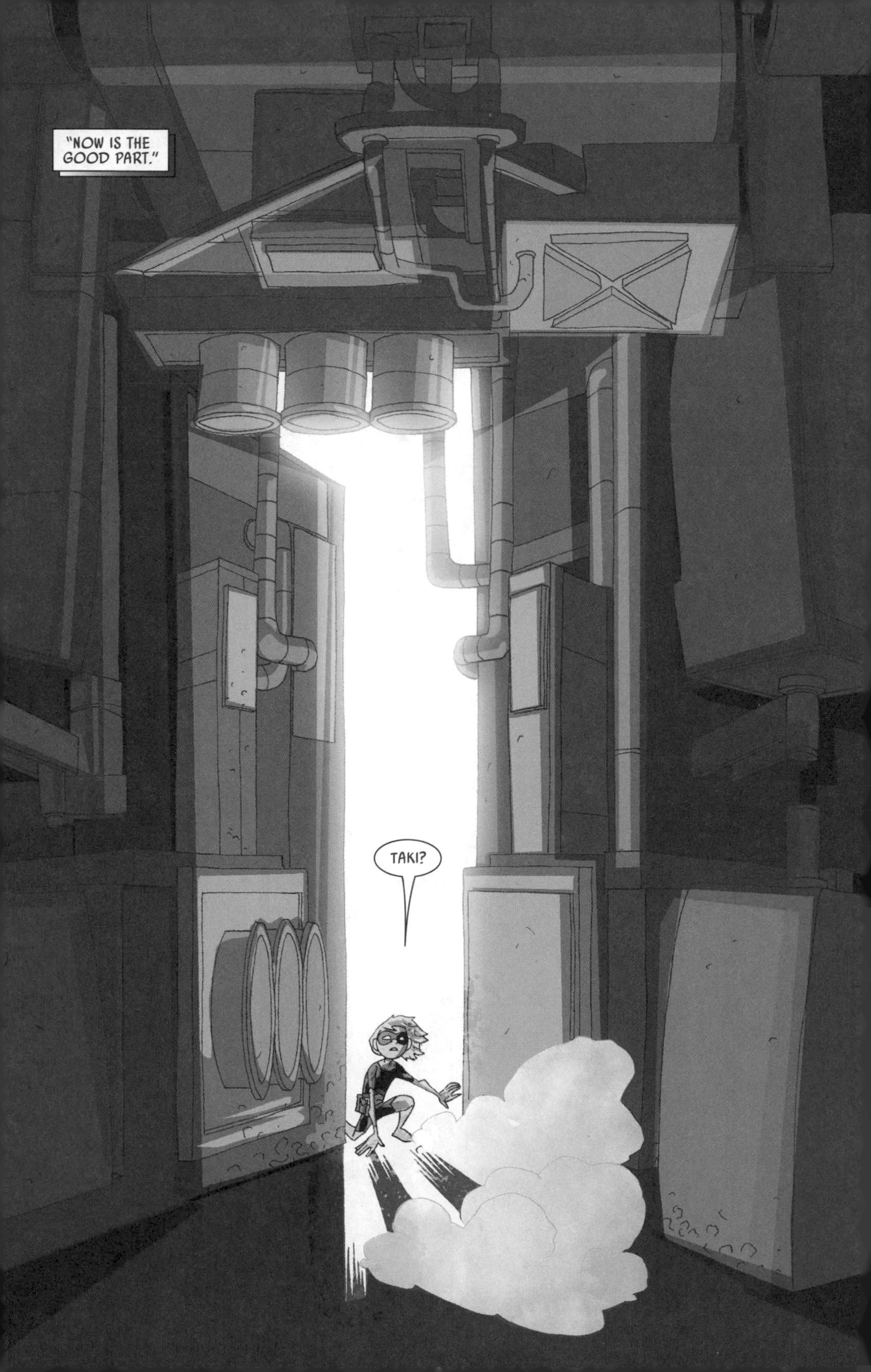
"NOW IS THE GOOD PART."
TAKI?

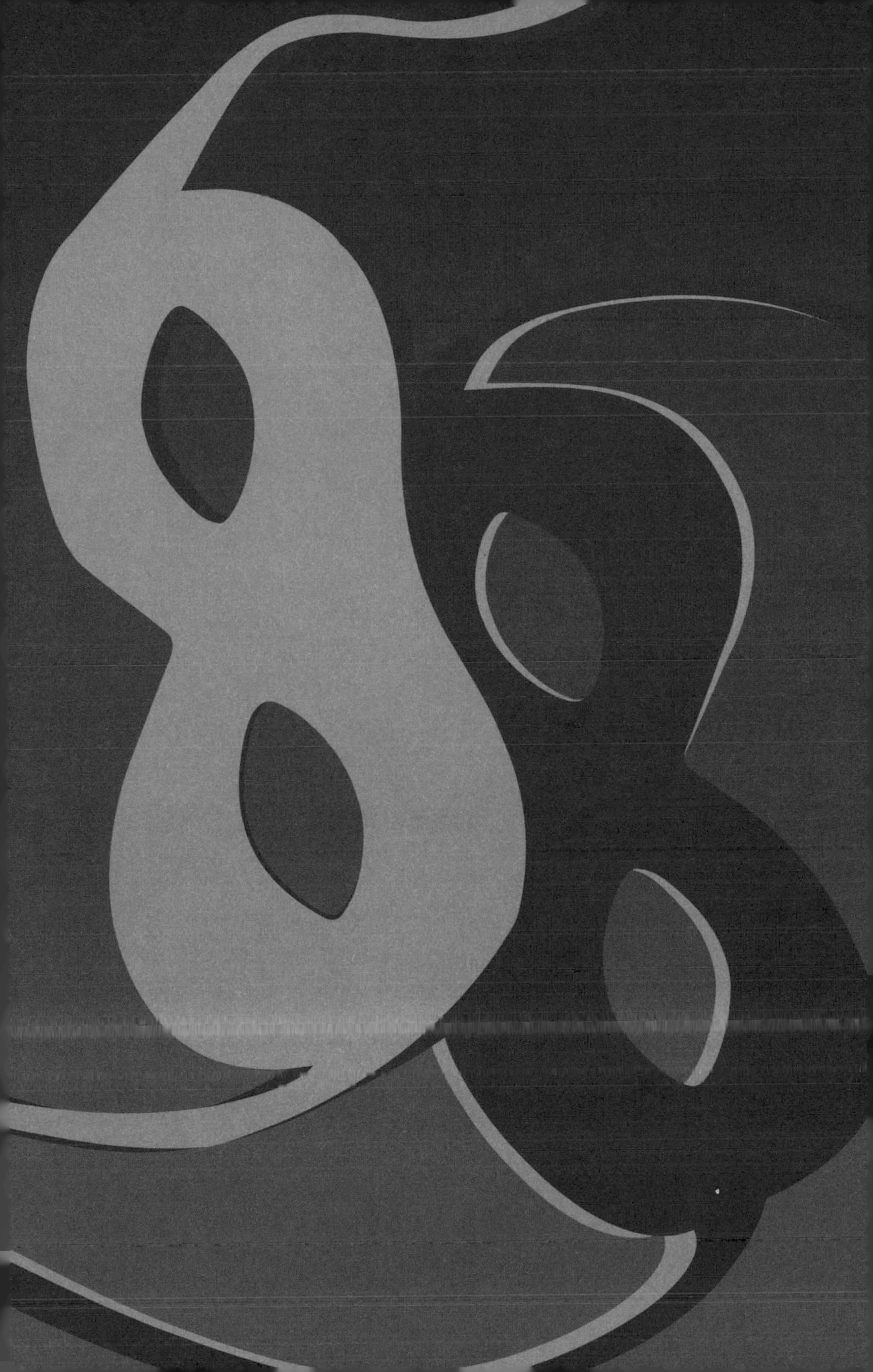

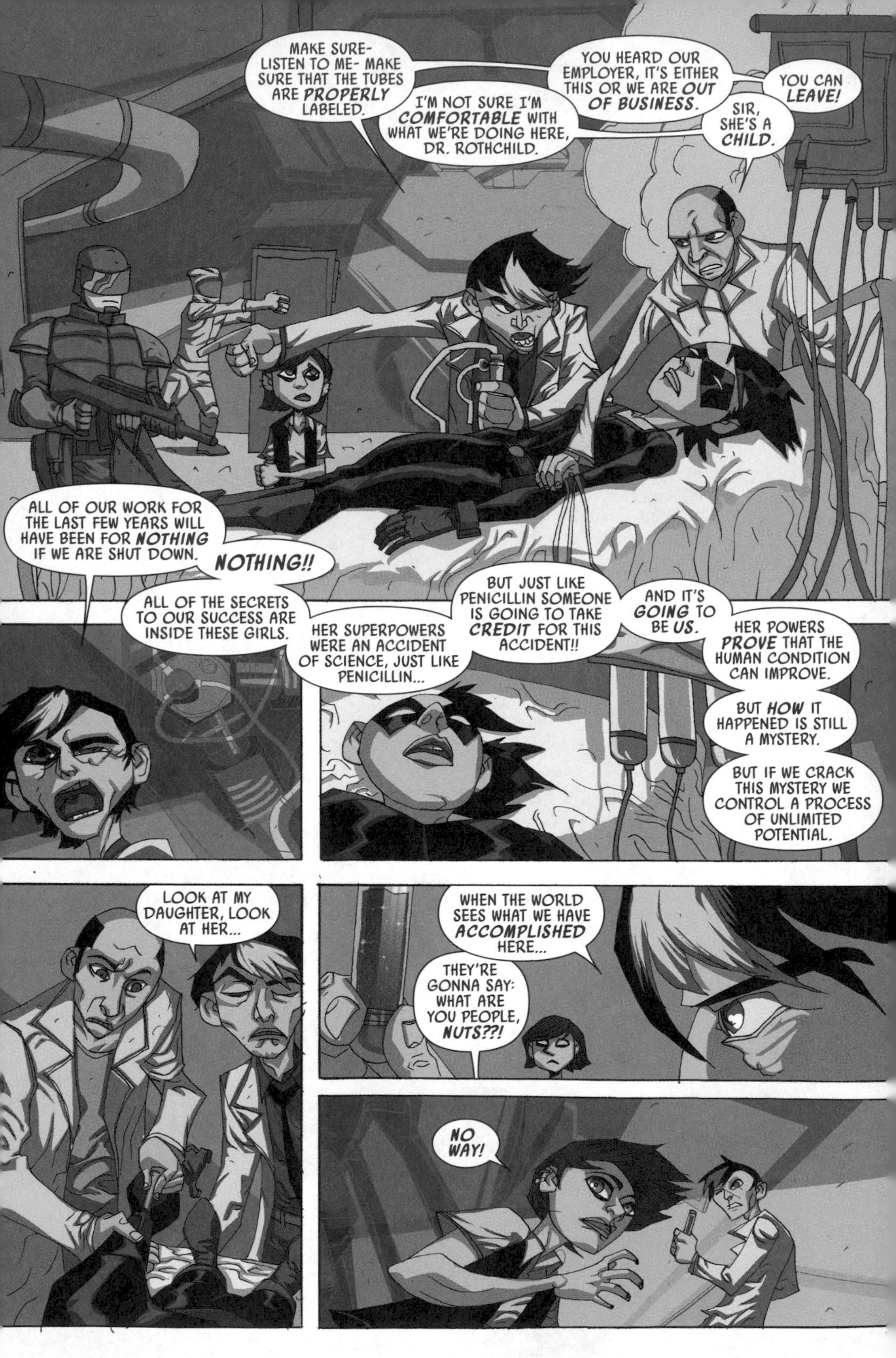

MAKE SURE- LISTEN TO ME- MAKE SURE THAT THE TUBES ARE PROPERLY LABELED.
I'M NOT SURE I'M COMFORTABLE WITH WHAT WE'RE DOING HERE, DR. ROTHCHILD.
YOU HEARD OUR EMPLOYER, IT'S EITHER THIS OR WE ARE OUT OF BUSINESS.
YOU CAN LEAVE!
SIR, SHE'S A CHILD.
ALL OF OUR WORK FOR THE LAST FEW YEARS WILL HAVE BEEN FOR NOTHING IF WE ARE SHUT DOWN.
NOTHING!!
ALL OF THE SECRETS TO OUR SUCCESS ARE INSIDE THESE GIRLS.
HER SUPERPOWERS WERE AN ACCIDENT OF SCIENCE, JUST LIKE PENICILLIN...
BUT JUST LIKE PENICILLIN SOMEONE IS GOING TO TAKE CREDIT FOR THIS ACCIDENT!!
AND IT'S GOING TO BE US.
HER POWERS PROVE THAT THE HUMAN CONDITION CAN IMPROVE.
BUT HOW IT HAPPENED IS STILL A MYSTERY.
BUT IF WE CRACK THIS MYSTERY WE CONTROL A PROCESS OF UNLIMITED POTENTIAL.
LOOK AT MY DAUGHTER, LOOK AT HER...
WHEN THE WORLD SEES WHAT WE HAVE ACCOMPLISHED HERE...
THEY'RE GONNA SAY: WHAT ARE YOU PEOPLE, NUTS??!
NO WAY!

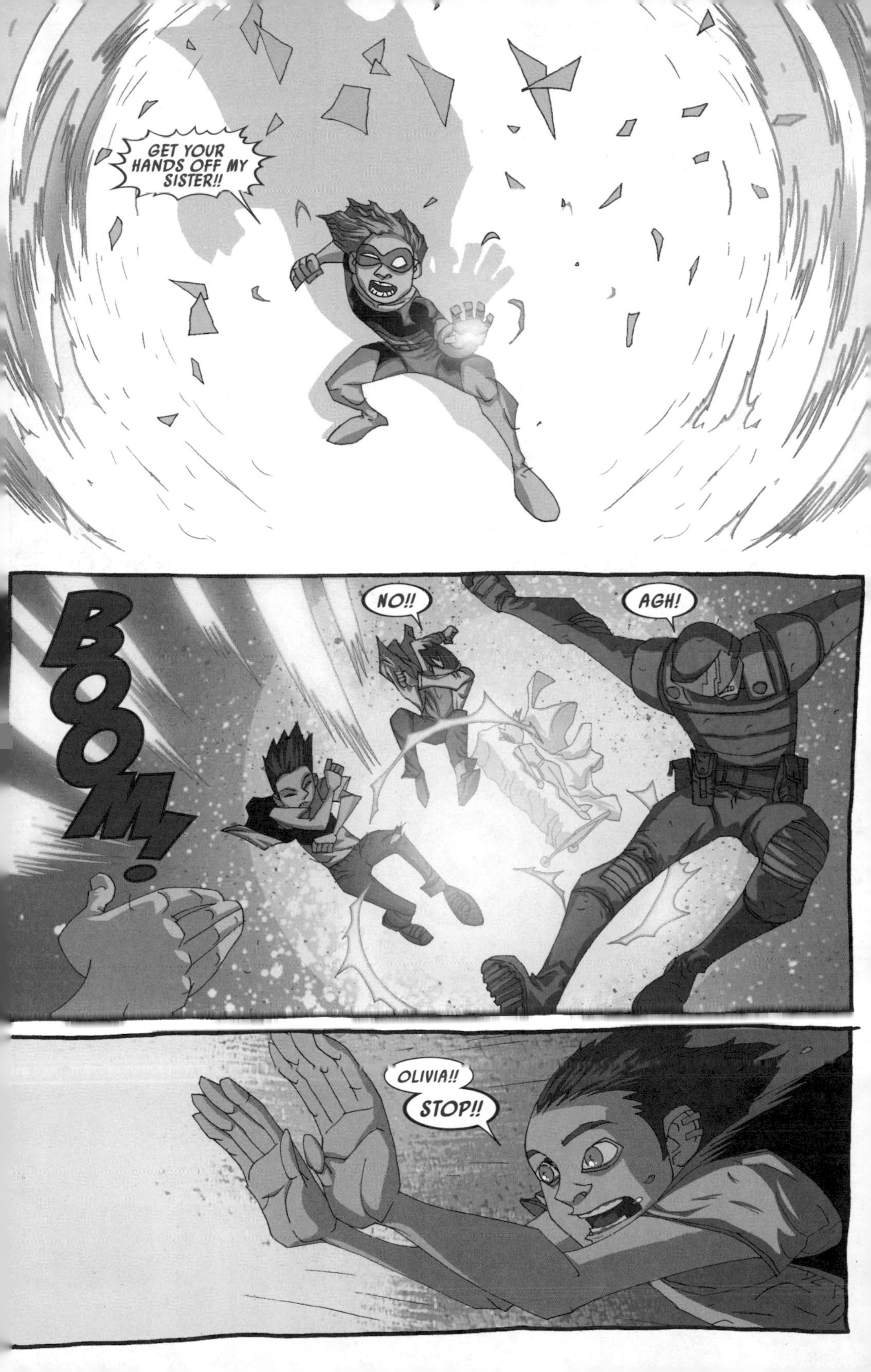
GET YOUR HANDS OFF MY SISTER!!
BOOM!
NO!!
AGH!
OLIVIA!!
STOP!!

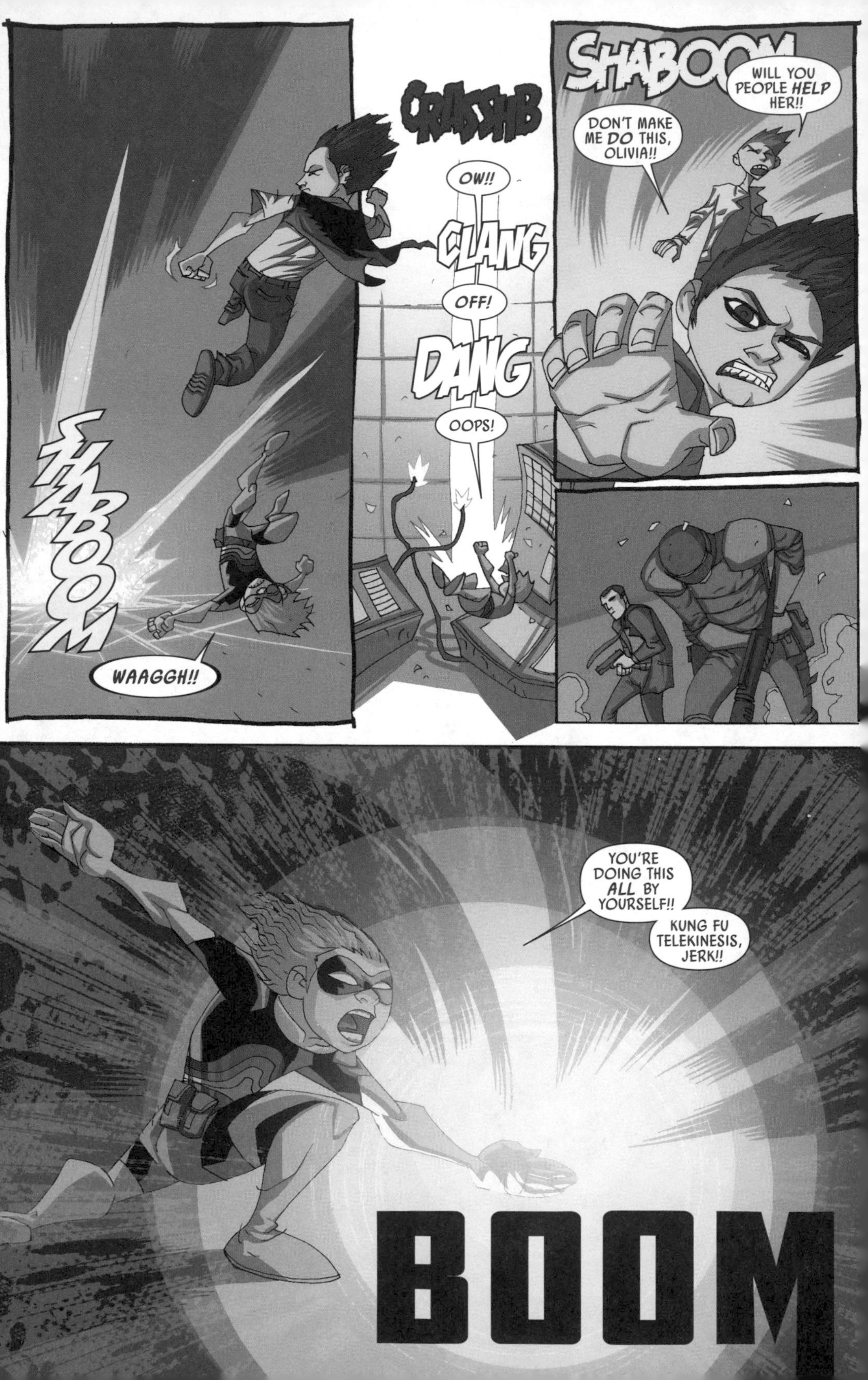
SHABOOM
WAAGGH!!
CRASSHB
OW!!
CLANG
OFF!
DANG
OOPS!
SHABOOM
DON'T MAKE ME DO THIS, OLIVIA!!
WILL YOU PEOPLE HELP HER!!
YOU'RE DOING THIS ALL BY YOURSELF!!
KUNG FU TELEKINESIS, JERK!!
BOOM

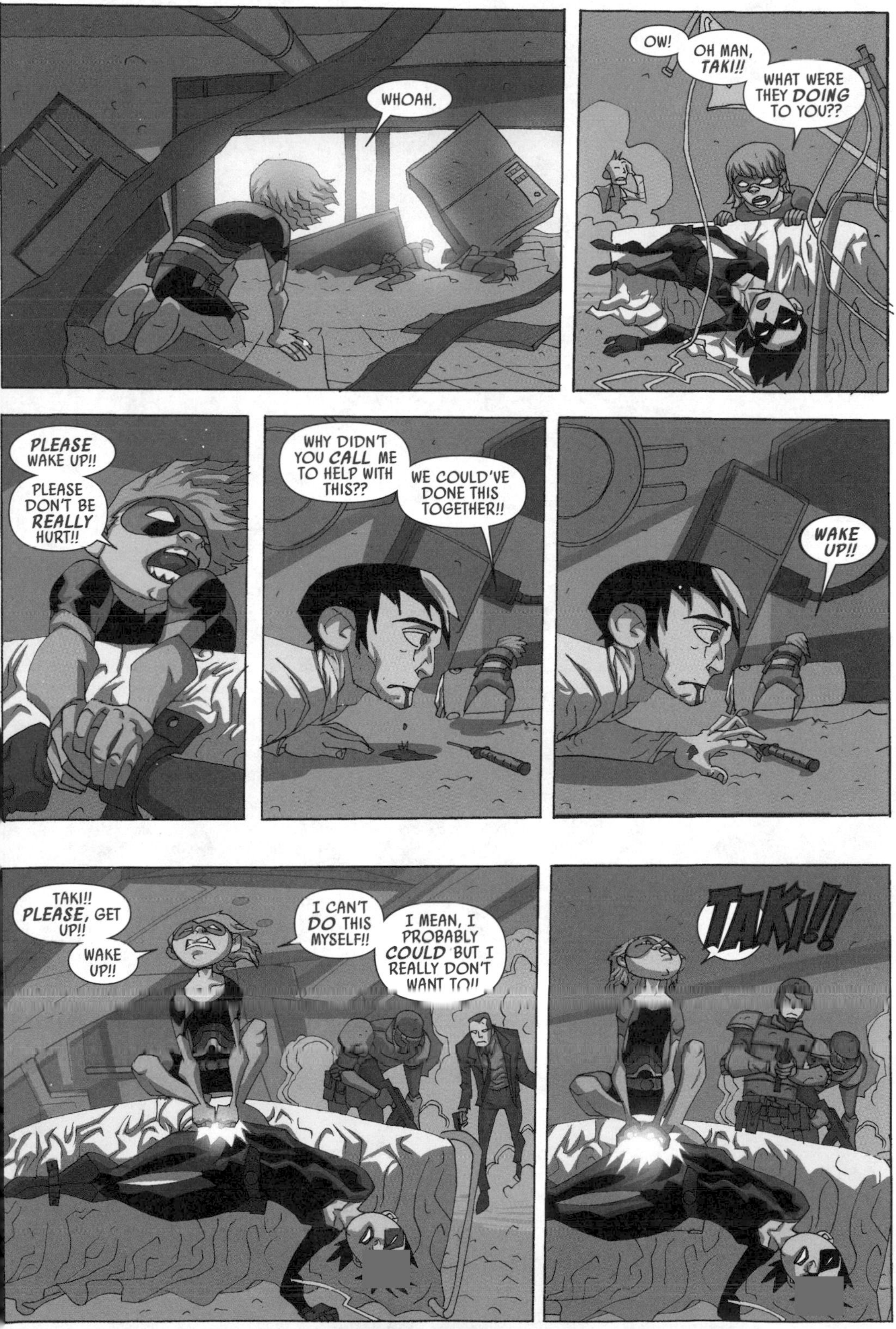
WHOAH.
OW!
OH MAN, TAKI!!
WHAT WERE THEY DOING TO YOU??
PLEASE WAKE UP!!
PLEASE DON'T BE REALLY HURT!!
WHY DIDN'T YOU CALL ME TO HELP WITH THIS??
WE COULD'VE DONE THIS TOGETHER!!
WAKE UP!!
TAKI!! PLEASE, GET UP!!
WAKE UP!!
I CAN'T DO THIS MYSELF!!
I MEAN, I PROBABLY COULD BUT I REALLY DON'T WANT TO!!
TAKI!!

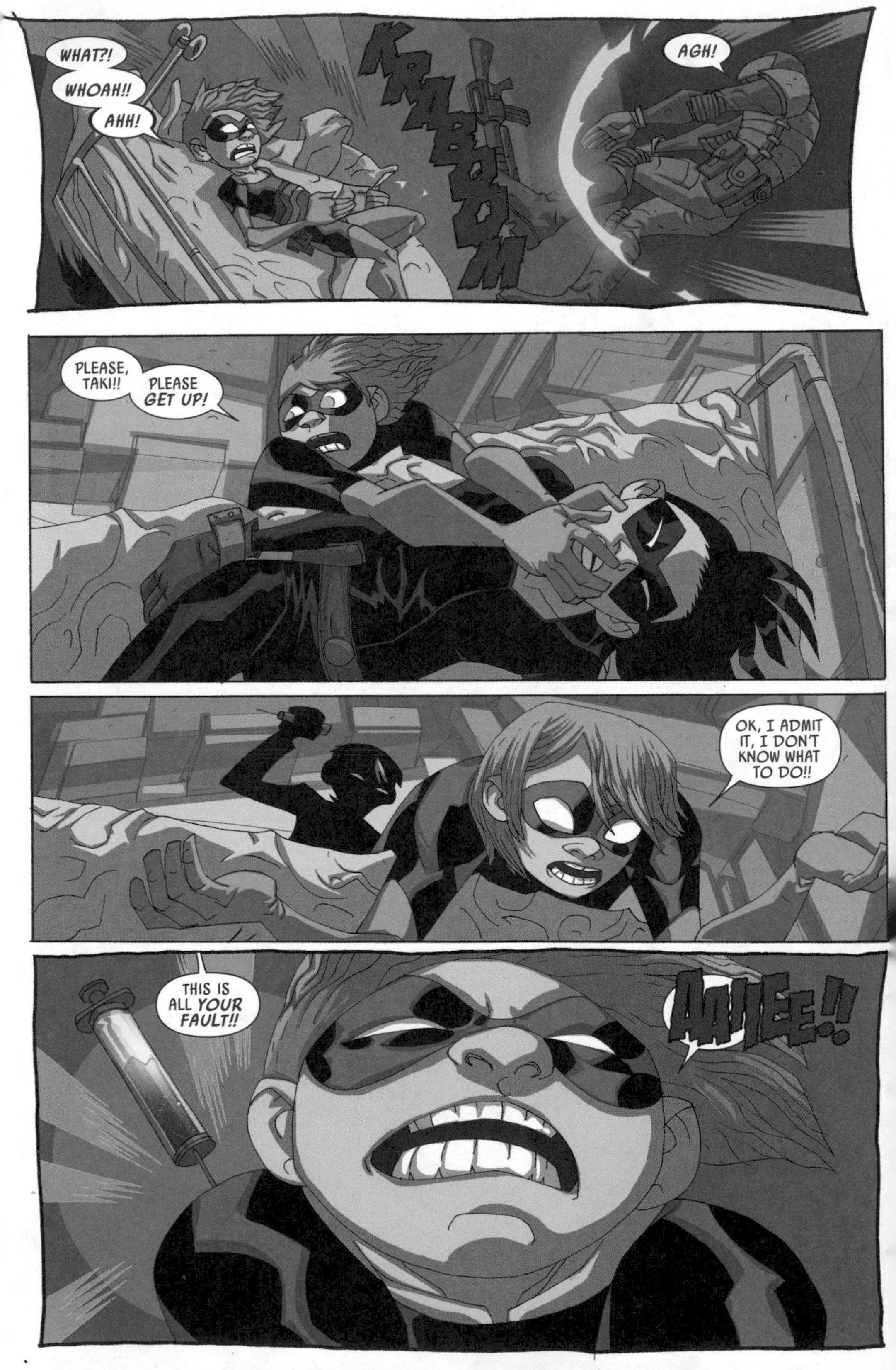
WHAT?!
WHOAH!!
AHH!
KRABOOM
AGH!
PLEASE, TAKI!!
PLEASE GET UP!
OK, I ADMIT IT, I DON'T KNOW WHAT TO DO!!
THIS IS ALL YOUR FAULT!!
AAIIEE!!

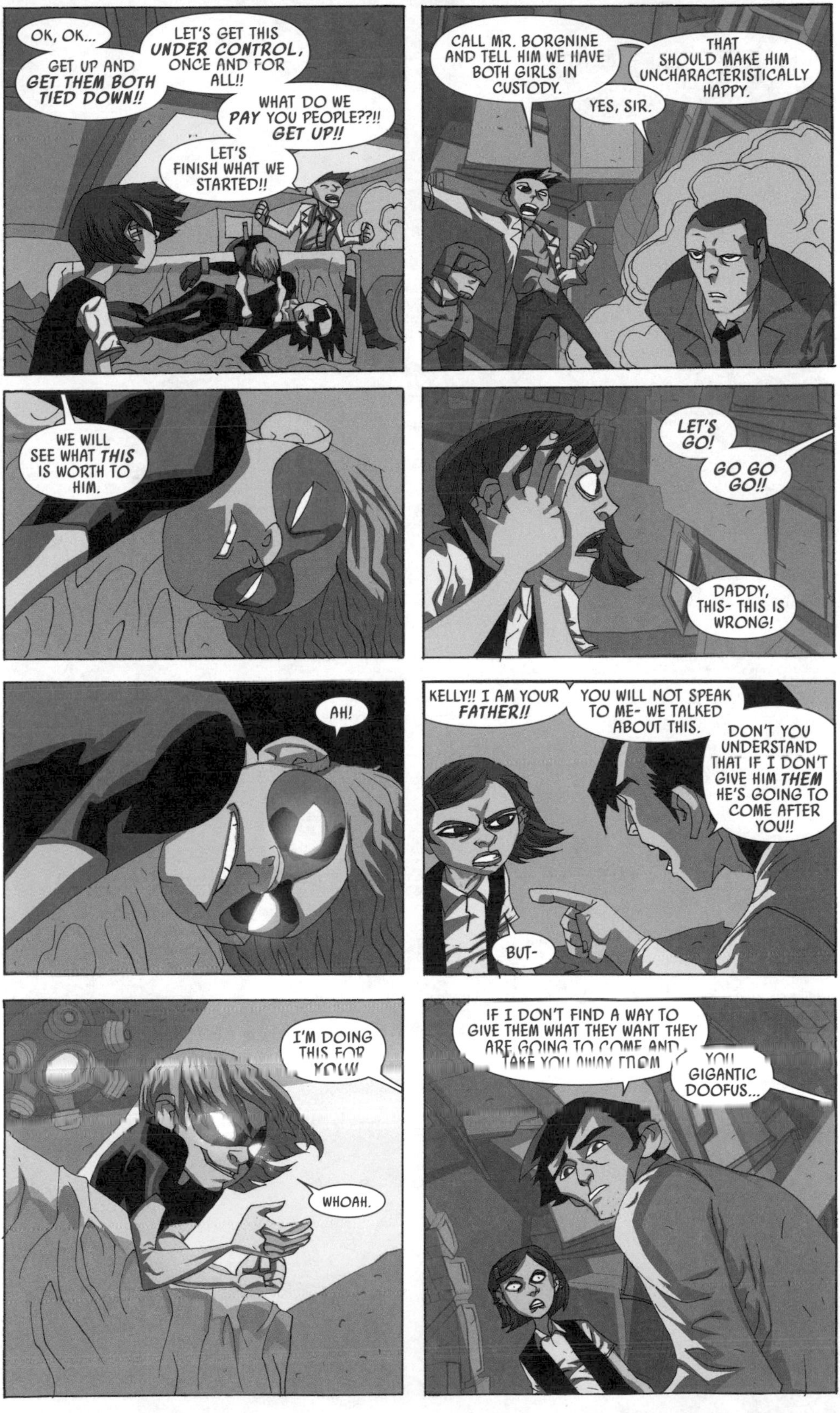
OK, OK...
GET UP AND GET THEM BOTH TIED DOWN!!
LET'S GET THIS UNDER CONTROL, ONCE AND FOR ALL!!
WHAT DO WE PAY YOU PEOPLE??!! GET UP!!
LET'S FINISH WHAT WE STARTED!!
CALL MR. BORGNINE AND TELL HIM WE HAVE BOTH GIRLS IN CUSTODY.
YES, SIR.
THAT SHOULD MAKE HIM UNCHARACTERISTICALLY HAPPY.
WE WILL SEE WHAT THIS IS WORTH TO HIM.
LET'S GO!
GO GO GO!!
DADDY, THIS- THIS IS WRONG!
AH!
KELLY!! I AM YOUR FATHER!!
YOU WILL NOT SPEAK TO ME- WE TALKED ABOUT THIS.
DON'T YOU UNDERSTAND THAT IF I DON'T GIVE HIM THEM HE'S GOING TO COME AFTER YOU!!
BUT-
I'M DOING THIS FOR
WHOAH.
IF I DON'T FIND A WAY TO GIVE THEM WHAT THEY WANT THEY
GIGANTIC DOOFUS...

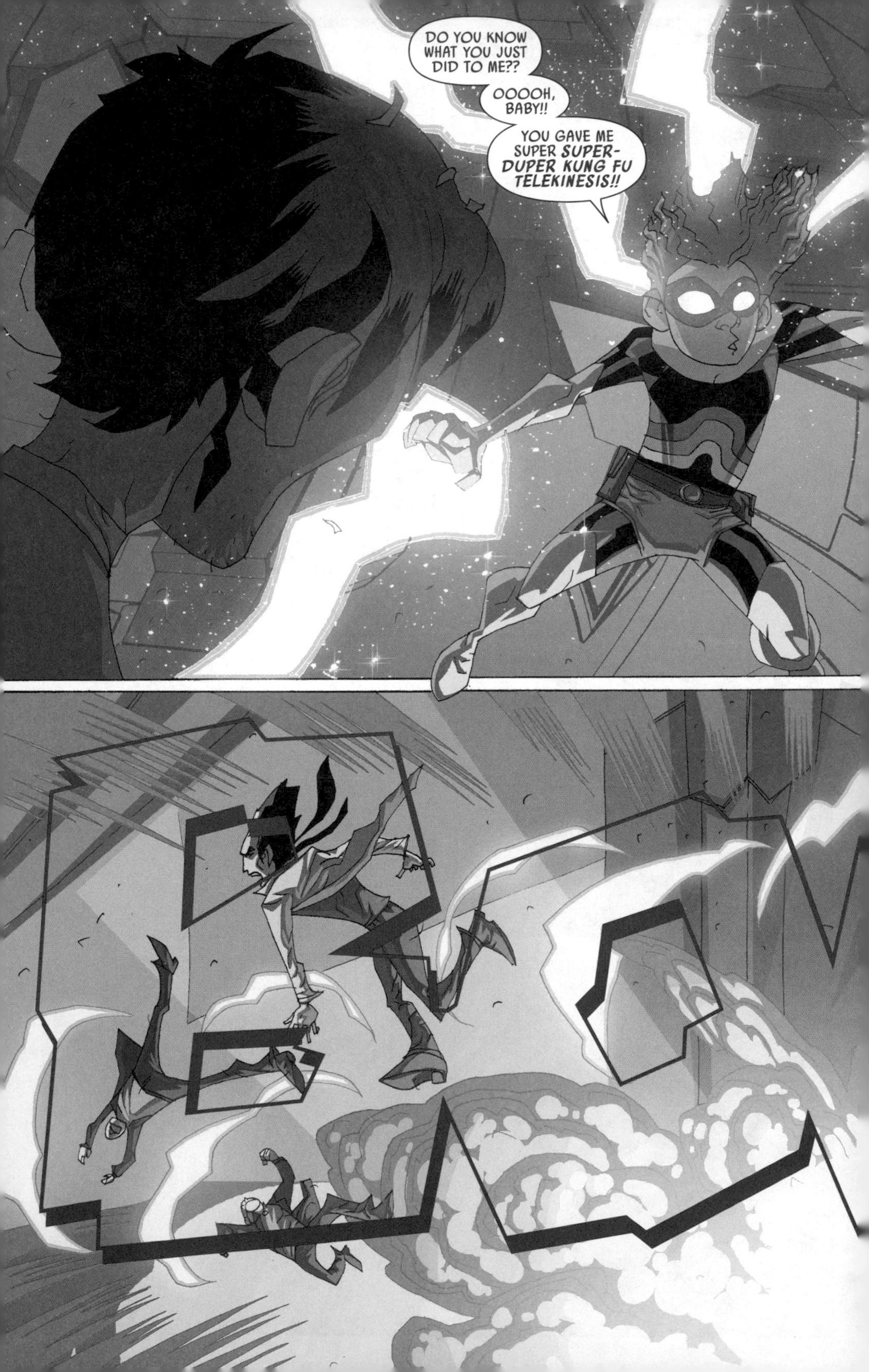
DO YOU KNOW WHAT YOU JUST DID TO ME??
OOOOH, BABY!!
YOU GAVE ME SUPER SUPER-DUPER KUNG FU TELEKINESIS!!

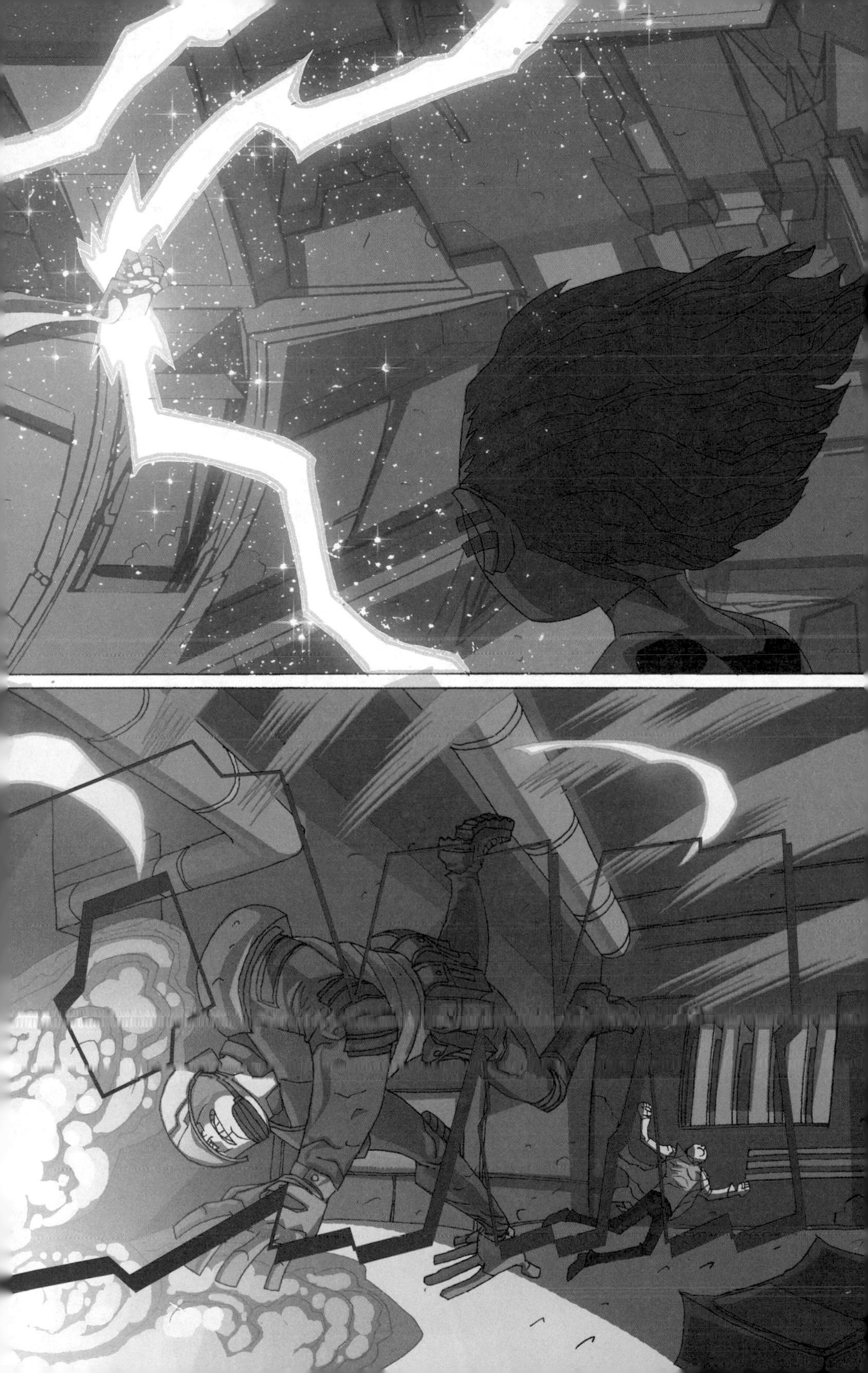

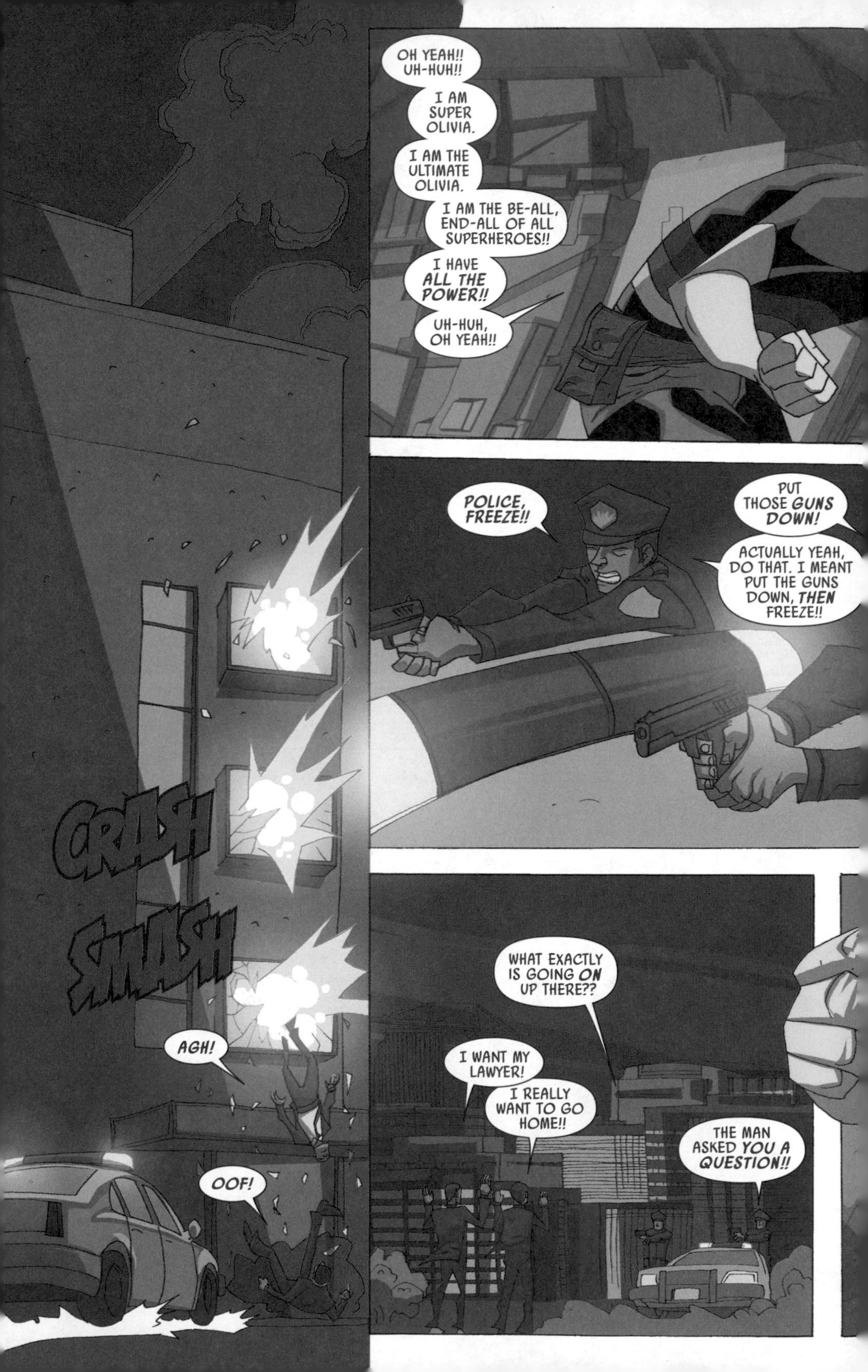
OH YEAH!! UH-HUH!!
I AM SUPER OLIVIA.
I AM THE ULTIMATE OLIVIA.
I AM THE BE-ALL, END-ALL OF ALL SUPERHEROES!!
I HAVE ALL THE POWER!!
UH-HUH, OH YEAH!!
CRASH
SMASH
AGH!
OOF!
POLICE, FREEZE!!
PUT THOSE GUNS DOWN!
ACTUALLY YEAH, DO THAT. I MEANT PUT THE GUNS DOWN, THEN FREEZE!!
WHAT EXACTLY IS GOING ON UP THERE??
I WANT MY LAWYER!
I REALLY WANT TO GO HOME!!
THE MAN ASKED YOU A QUESTION!!

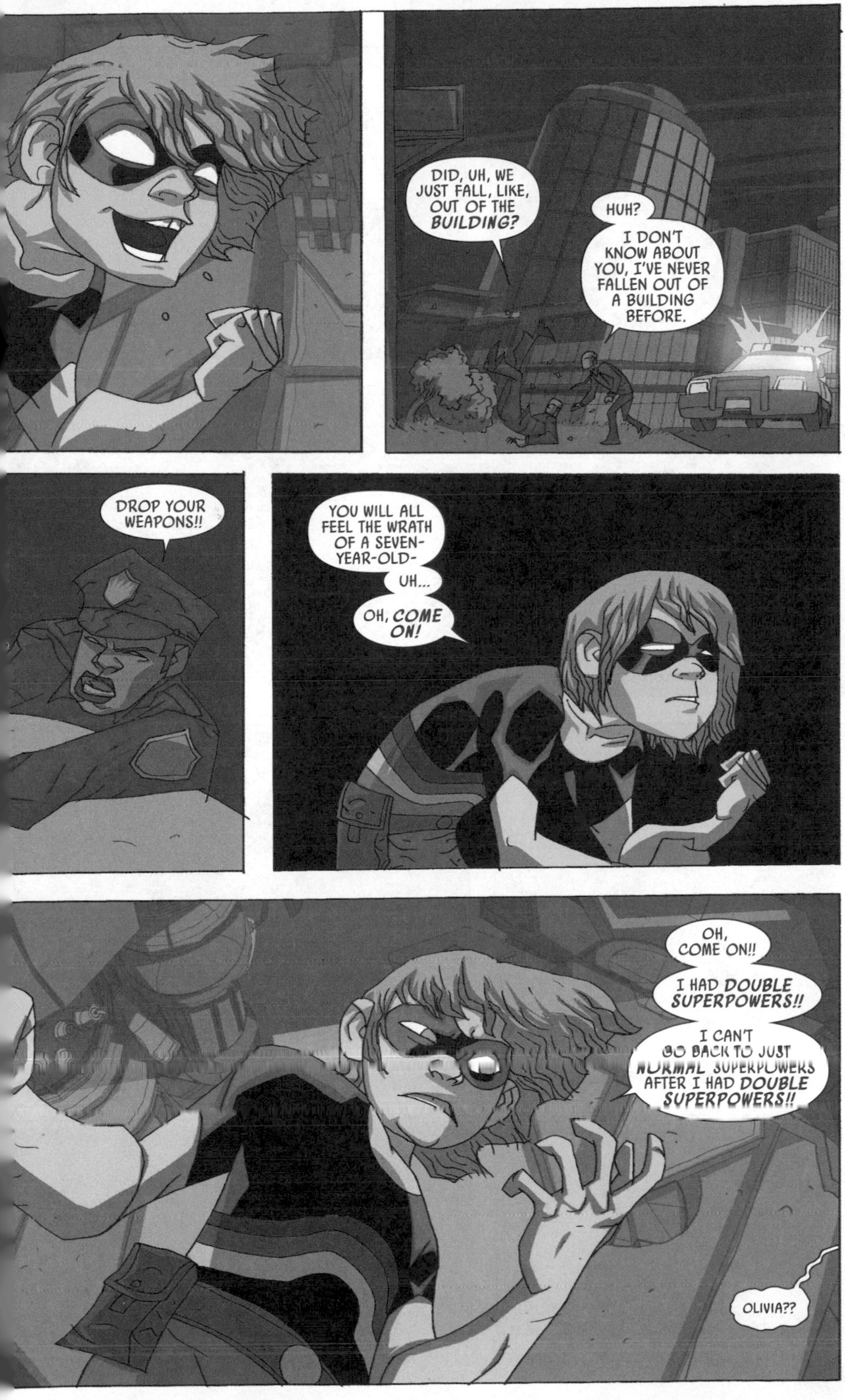
DID, UH, WE JUST FALL, LIKE, OUT OF THE BUILDING?
HUH?
I DON'T KNOW ABOUT YOU, I'VE NEVER FALLEN OUT OF A BUILDING BEFORE.
DROP YOUR WEAPONS!!
YOU WILL ALL FEEL THE WRATH OF A SEVEN-YEAR-OLD-
UH...
OH, COME ON!
OH, COME ON!!
I HAD DOUBLE SUPERPOWERS!!
I CAN'T GO BACK TO JUST NORMAL SUPERPOWERS AFTER I HAD DOUBLE SUPERPOWERS!!
OLIVIA??

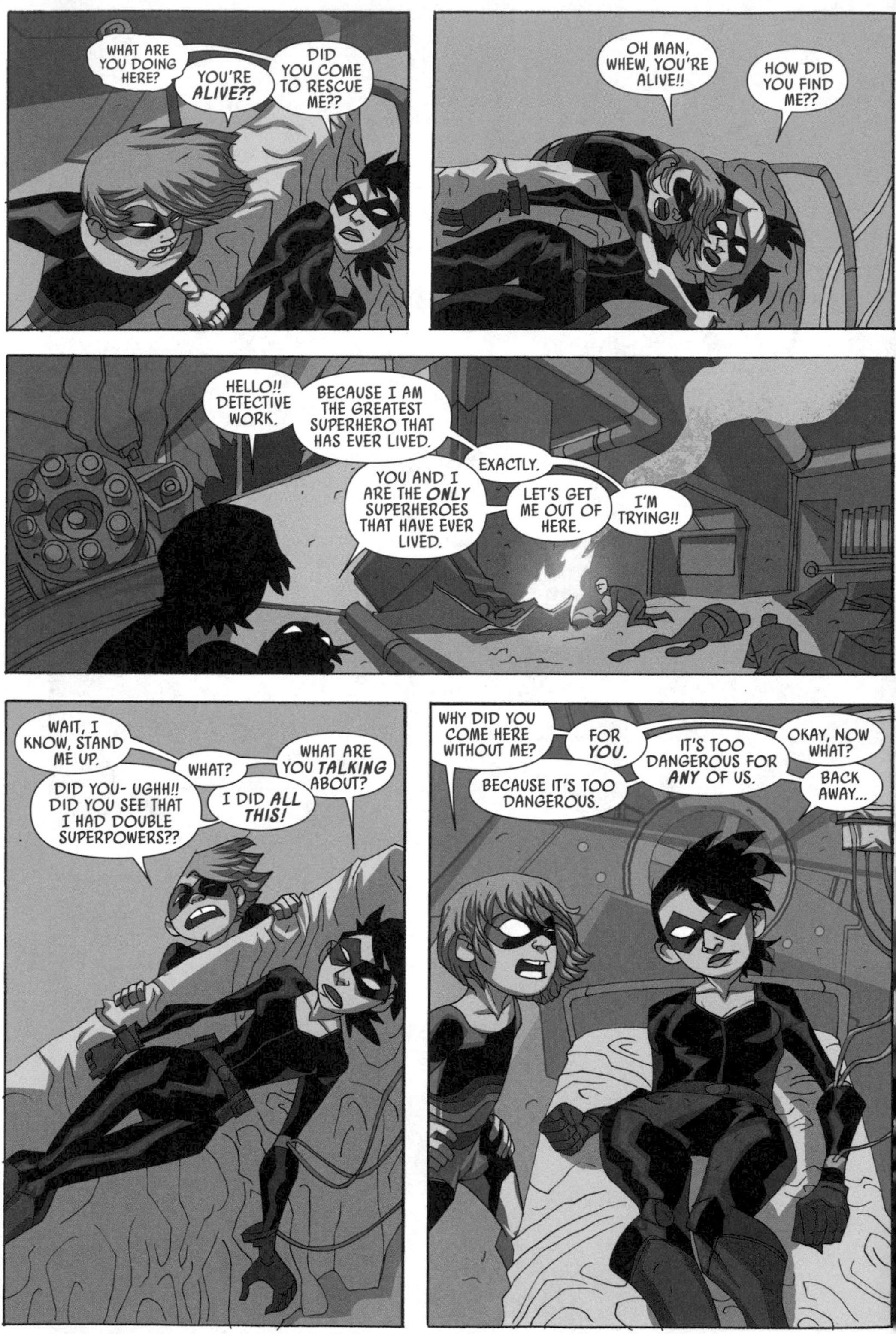

WHAT ARE YOU DOING HERE?
YOU'RE *ALIVE??*
DID YOU COME TO RESCUE ME??
OH MAN, WHEW, YOU'RE ALIVE!!
HOW DID YOU FIND ME??
HELLO!! DETECTIVE WORK.
BECAUSE I AM THE GREATEST SUPERHERO THAT HAS EVER LIVED.
EXACTLY.
YOU AND I ARE THE *ONLY* SUPERHEROES THAT HAVE EVER LIVED.
LET'S GET ME OUT OF HERE.
I'M TRYING!!
WAIT, I KNOW, STAND ME UP.
WHAT?
WHAT ARE YOU *TALKING* ABOUT?
DID YOU- UGHH!! DID YOU SEE THAT I HAD DOUBLE SUPERPOWERS??
I DID *ALL THIS!*
WHY DID YOU COME HERE WITHOUT ME?
FOR *YOU.*
BECAUSE IT'S TOO DANGEROUS.
IT'S TOO DANGEROUS FOR *ANY* OF US.
OKAY, NOW WHAT?
BACK AWAY...

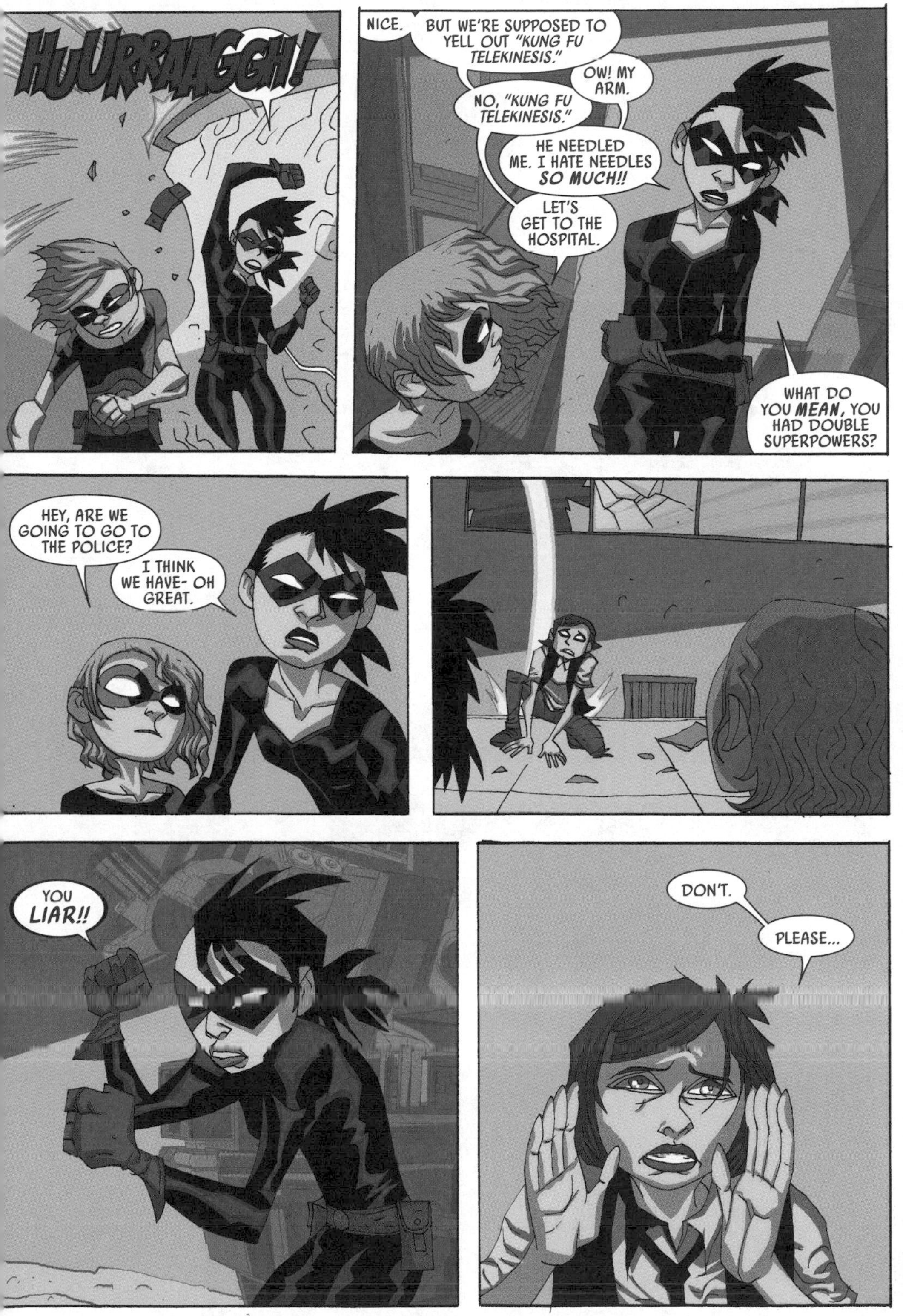
HUURRAAGGH!
NICE.
BUT WE'RE SUPPOSED TO YELL OUT "KUNG FU TELEKINESIS."
OW! MY ARM.
NO, "KUNG FU TELEKINESIS."
HE NEEDLED ME. I HATE NEEDLES SO MUCH!!
LET'S GET TO THE HOSPITAL.
WHAT DO YOU MEAN, YOU HAD DOUBLE SUPERPOWERS?
HEY, ARE WE GOING TO GO TO THE POLICE?
I THINK WE HAVE- OH GREAT.
YOU LIAR!!
DON'T.
PLEASE...

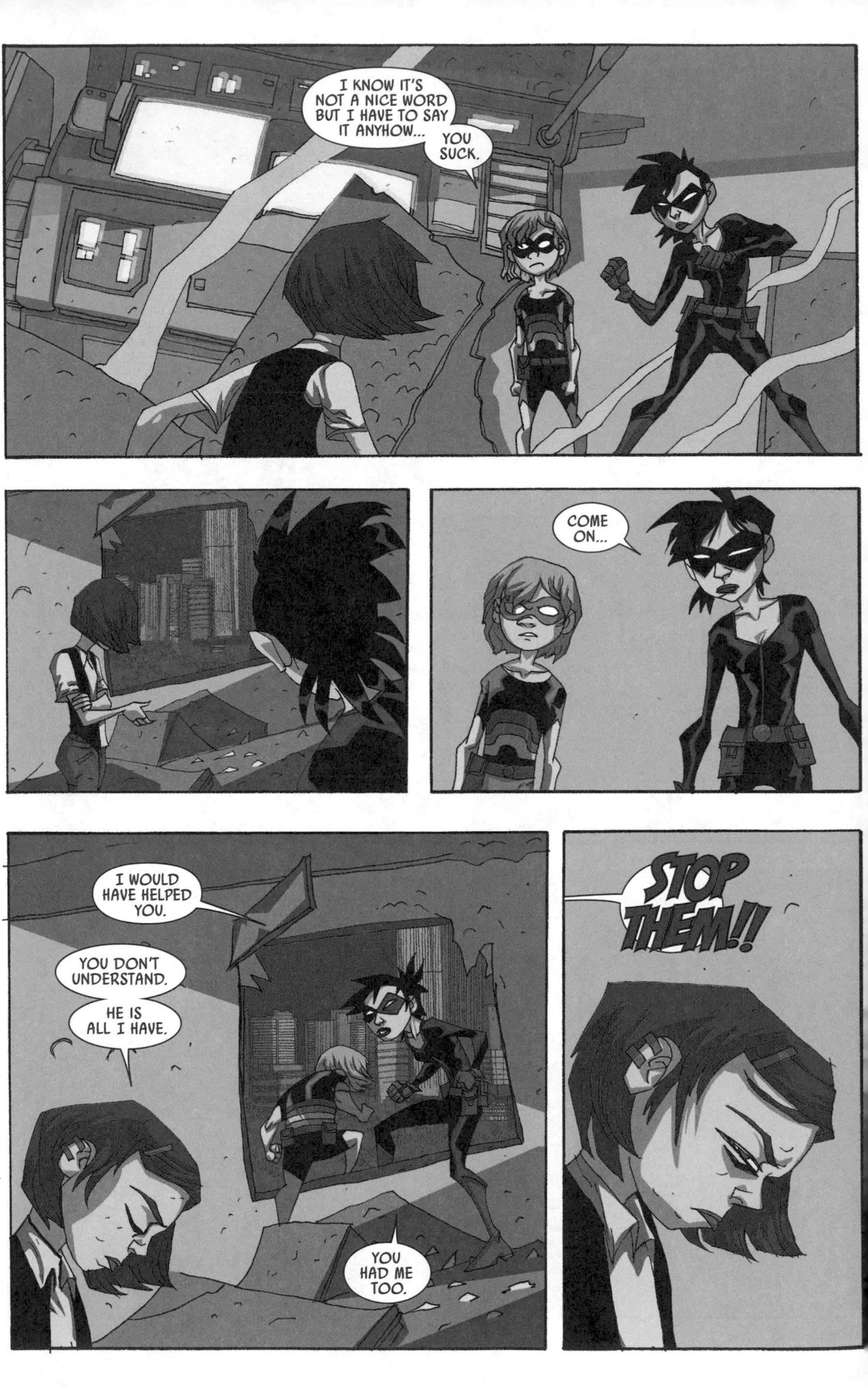
I KNOW IT'S NOT A NICE WORD BUT I HAVE TO SAY IT ANYHOW...
YOU SUCK.
COME ON...
I WOULD HAVE HELPED YOU.
YOU DON'T UNDERSTAND.
HE IS ALL I HAVE.
YOU HAD ME TOO.
STOP THEM!!

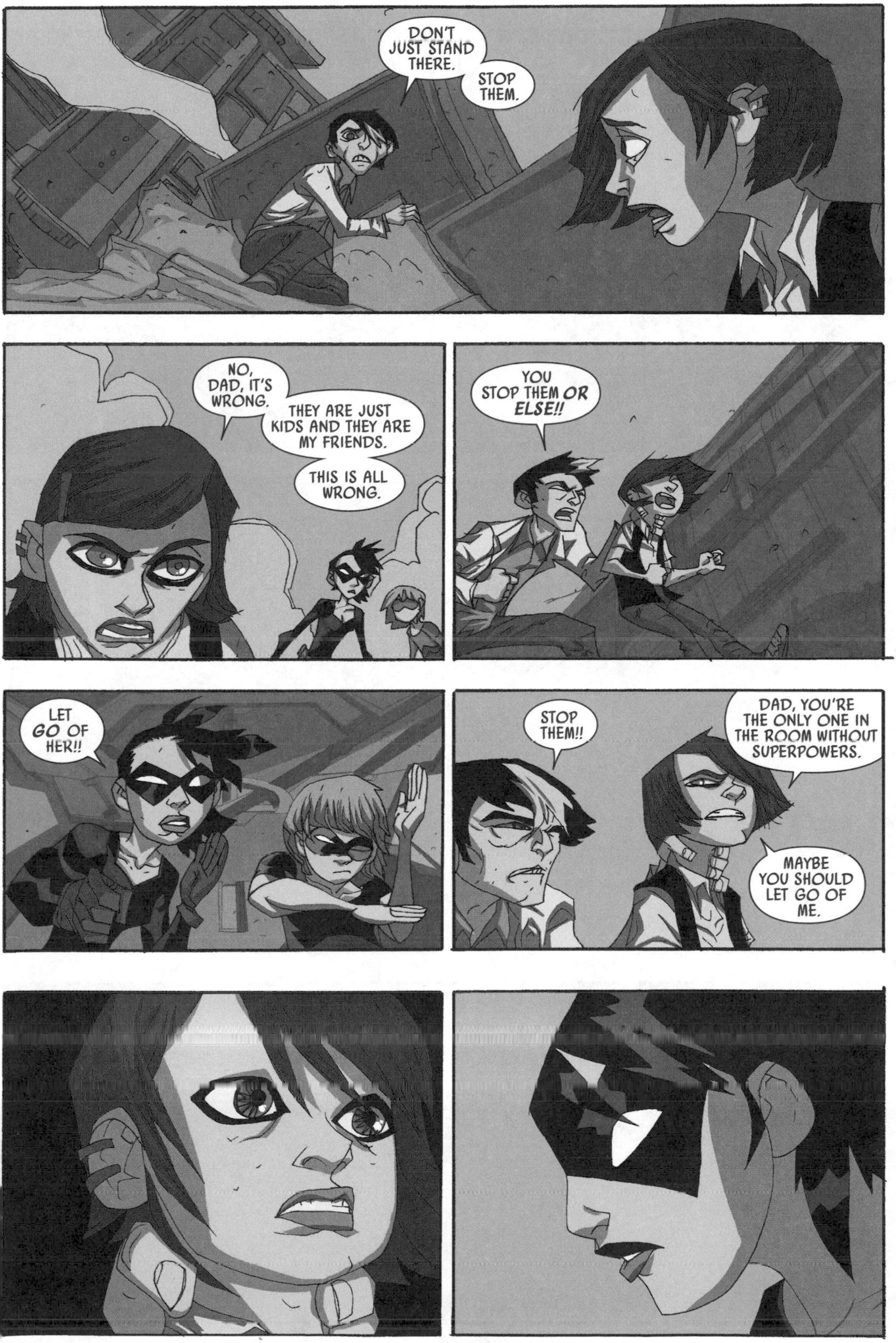
DON'T JUST STAND THERE.
STOP THEM.
NO, DAD, IT'S WRONG.
THEY ARE JUST KIDS AND THEY ARE MY FRIENDS.
THIS IS ALL WRONG.
YOU STOP THEM OR ELSE!!
LET GO OF HER!!
STOP THEM!!
DAD, YOU'RE THE ONLY ONE IN THE ROOM WITHOUT SUPERPOWERS.
MAYBE YOU SHOULD LET GO OF ME.

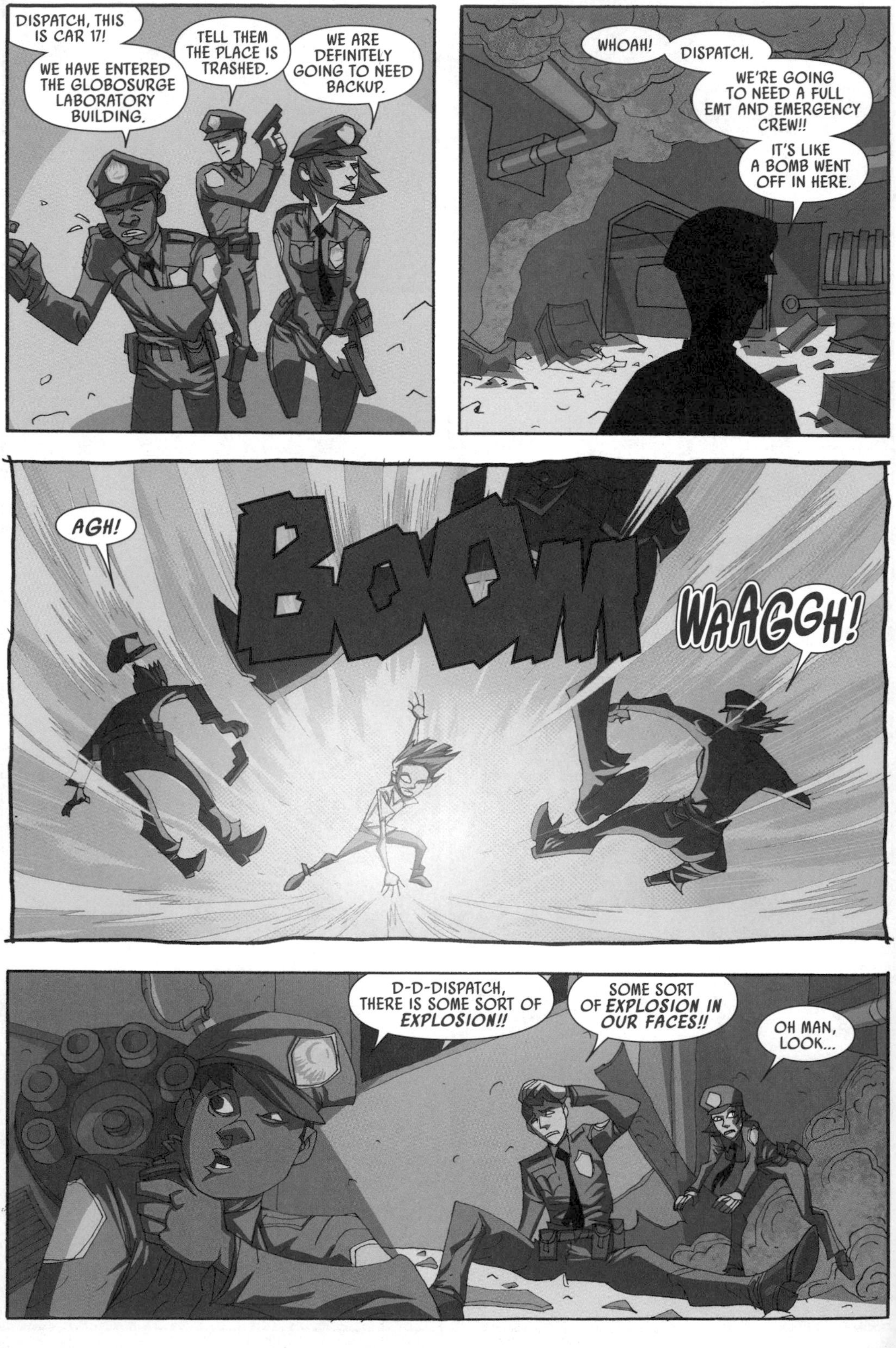

DISPATCH, THIS IS CAR 17!
WE HAVE ENTERED THE GLOBOSURGE LABORATORY BUILDING.
TELL THEM THE PLACE IS TRASHED.
WE ARE DEFINITELY GOING TO NEED BACKUP.
WHOAH!
DISPATCH.
WE'RE GOING TO NEED A FULL EMT AND EMERGENCY CREW!!
IT'S LIKE A BOMB WENT OFF IN HERE.
AGH!
BOOM
WAAGGH!
D-D-DISPATCH, THERE IS SOME SORT OF *EXPLOSION!!*
SOME SORT OF *EXPLOSION IN OUR FACES!!*
OH MAN, LOOK...

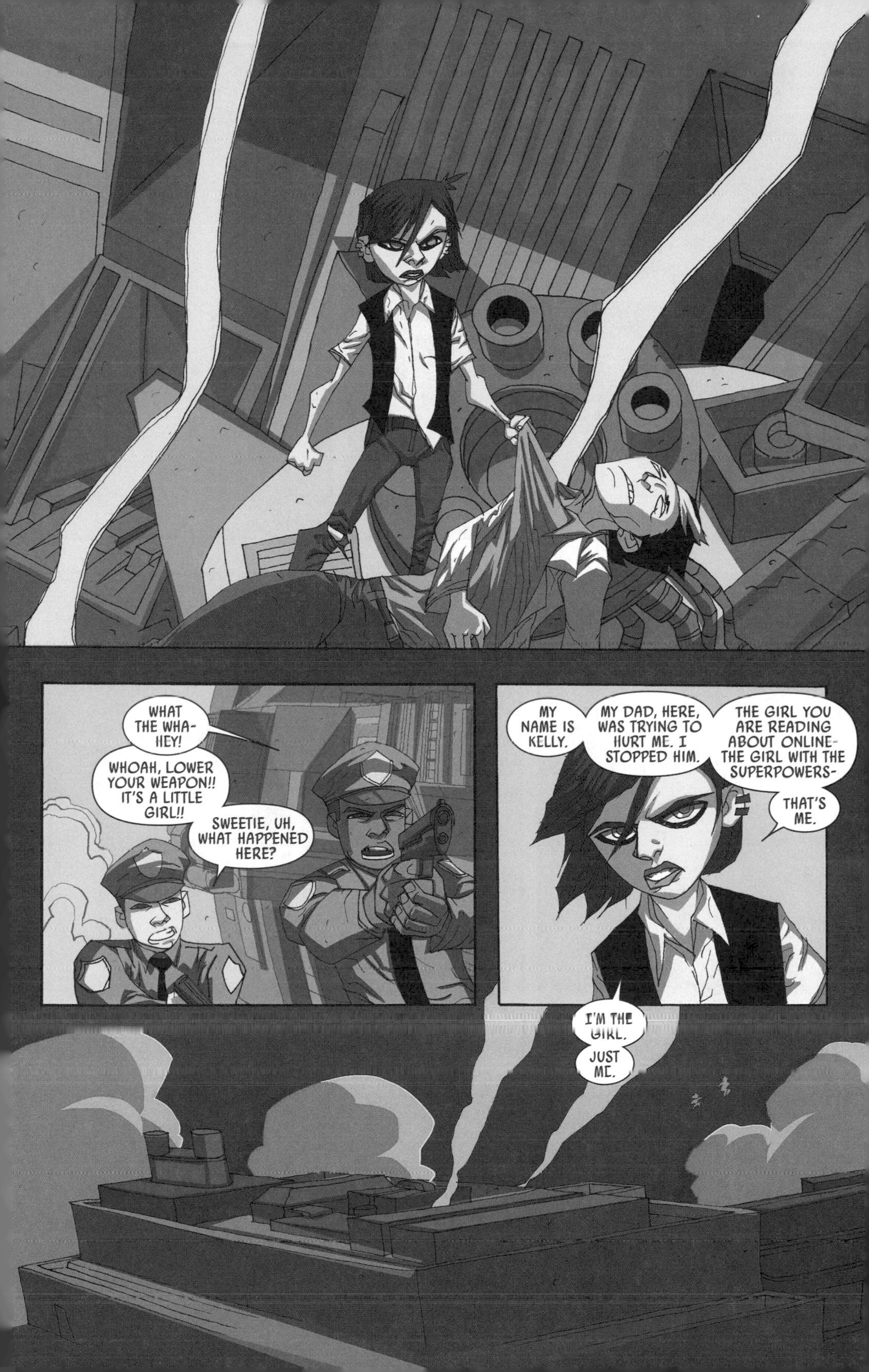
WHAT THE WHA-HEY!
WHOAH, LOWER YOUR WEAPON!! IT'S A LITTLE GIRL!!
SWEETIE, UH, WHAT HAPPENED HERE?
MY NAME IS KELLY.
MY DAD, HERE, WAS TRYING TO HURT ME. I STOPPED HIM.
THE GIRL YOU ARE READING ABOUT ONLINE- THE GIRL WITH THE SUPERPOWERS-
THAT'S ME.
I'M THE GIRL.
JUST ME.

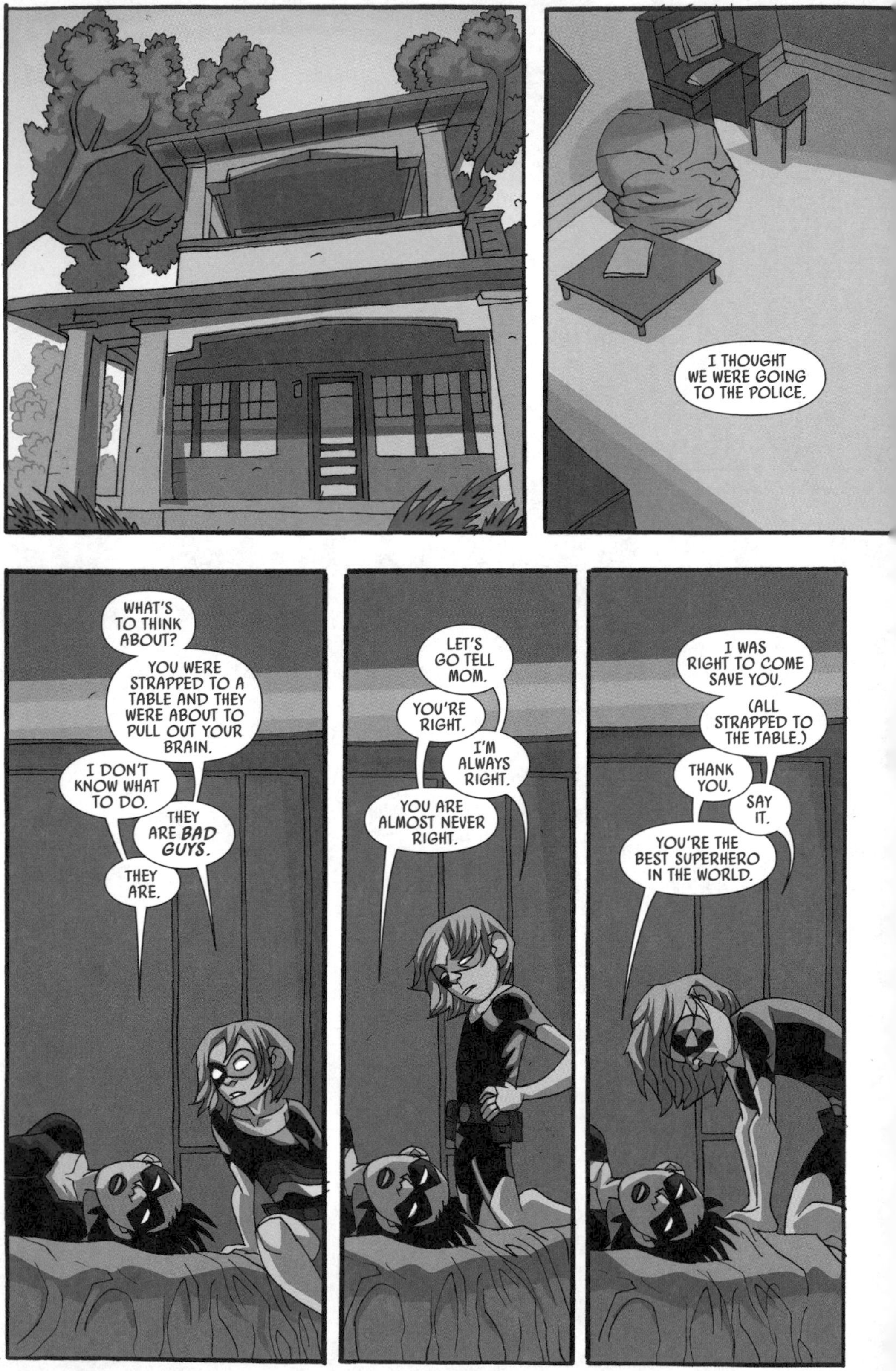
I THOUGHT WE WERE GOING TO THE POLICE.
WHAT'S TO THINK ABOUT?
YOU WERE STRAPPED TO A TABLE AND THEY WERE ABOUT TO PULL OUT YOUR BRAIN.
I DON'T KNOW WHAT TO DO.
THEY ARE *BAD GUYS*.
THEY ARE.
LET'S GO TELL MOM.
YOU'RE RIGHT.
I'M ALWAYS RIGHT.
YOU ARE ALMOST NEVER RIGHT.
I WAS RIGHT TO COME SAVE YOU.
(ALL STRAPPED TO THE TABLE.)
THANK YOU.
SAY IT.
YOU'RE THE BEST SUPERHERO IN THE WORLD.

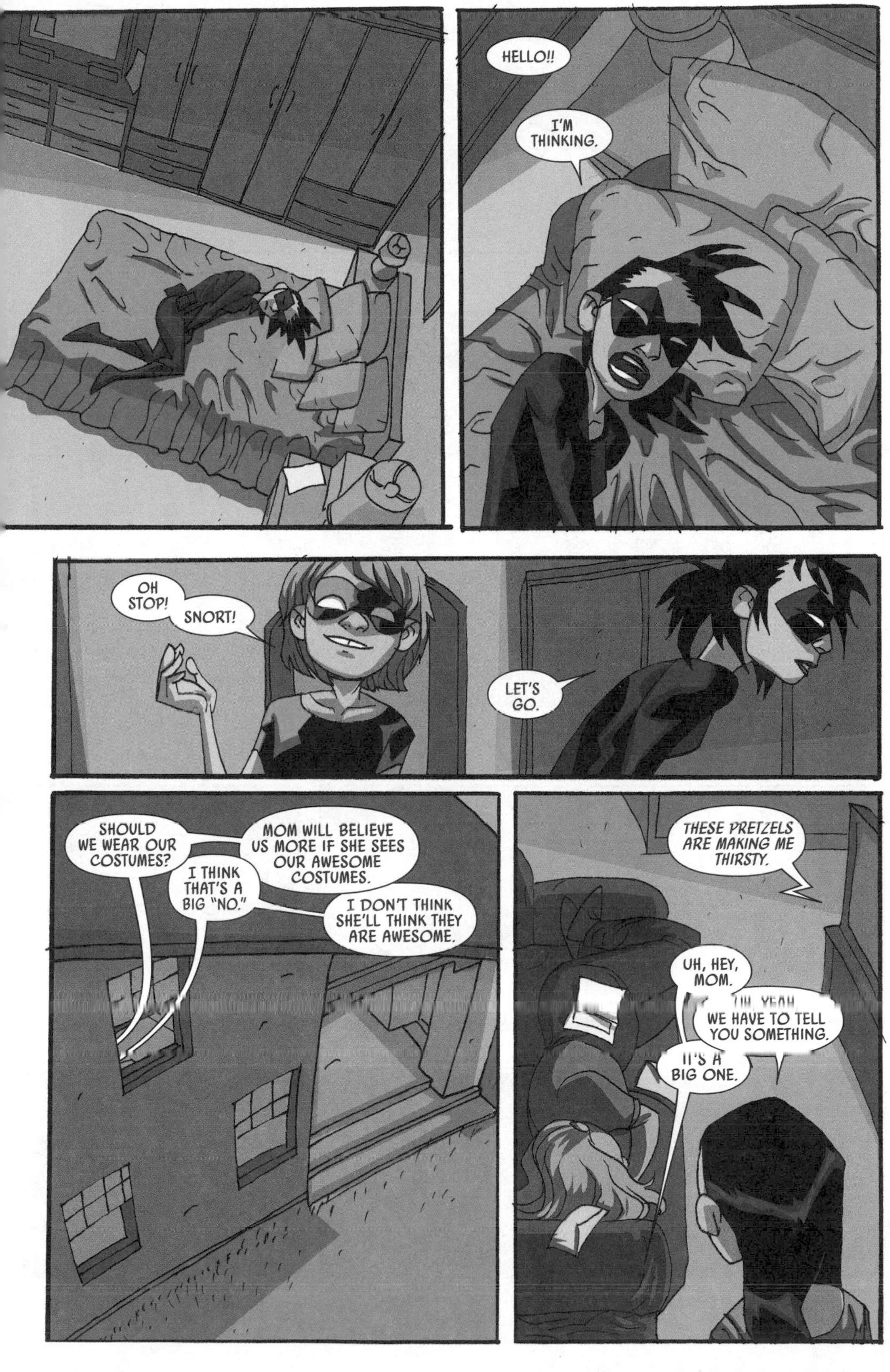
HELLO!!
I'M THINKING.
OH STOP!
SNORT!
LET'S GO.
SHOULD WE WEAR OUR COSTUMES?
MOM WILL BELIEVE US MORE IF SHE SEES OUR AWESOME COSTUMES.
I THINK THAT'S A BIG "NO."
I DON'T THINK SHE'LL THINK THEY ARE AWESOME.
THESE PRETZELS ARE MAKING ME THIRSTY.
UH, HEY, MOM.
WE HAVE TO TELL YOU SOMETHING.
IT'S A BIG ONE.

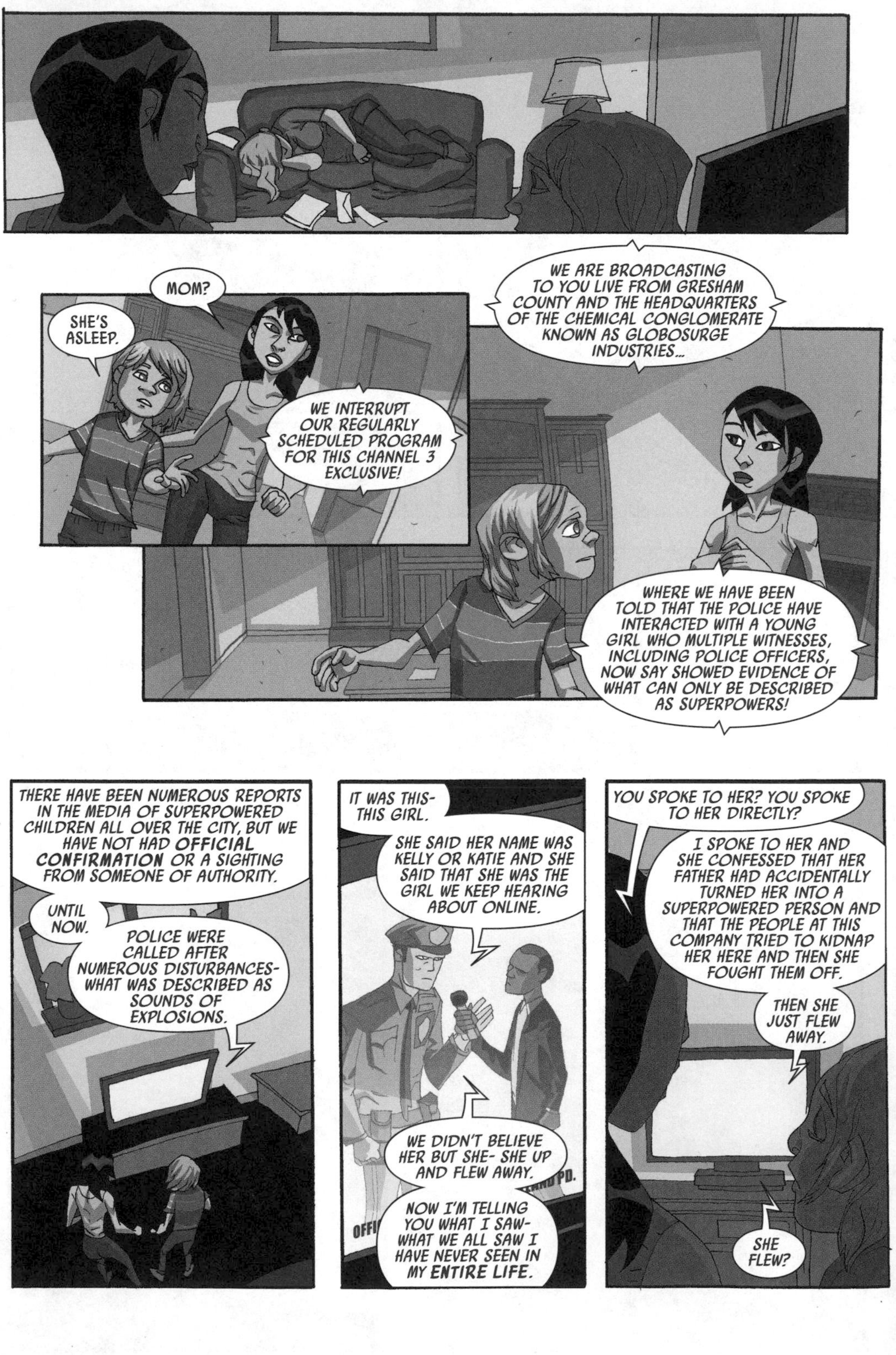

MOM?
SHE'S ASLEEP.
WE INTERRUPT OUR REGULARLY SCHEDULED PROGRAM FOR THIS CHANNEL 3 EXCLUSIVE!
WE ARE BROADCASTING TO YOU LIVE FROM GRESHAM COUNTY AND THE HEADQUARTERS OF THE CHEMICAL CONGLOMERATE KNOWN AS GLOBOSURGE INDUSTRIES...
WHERE WE HAVE BEEN TOLD THAT THE POLICE HAVE INTERACTED WITH A YOUNG GIRL WHO MULTIPLE WITNESSES, INCLUDING POLICE OFFICERS, NOW SAY SHOWED EVIDENCE OF WHAT CAN ONLY BE DESCRIBED AS SUPERPOWERS!
THERE HAVE BEEN NUMEROUS REPORTS IN THE MEDIA OF SUPERPOWERED CHILDREN ALL OVER THE CITY, BUT WE HAVE NOT HAD **OFFICIAL CONFIRMATION** OR A SIGHTING FROM SOMEONE OF AUTHORITY.
UNTIL NOW.
POLICE WERE CALLED AFTER NUMEROUS DISTURBANCES- WHAT WAS DESCRIBED AS SOUNDS OF EXPLOSIONS.
IT WAS THIS- THIS GIRL.
SHE SAID HER NAME WAS KELLY OR KATIE AND SHE SAID THAT SHE WAS THE GIRL WE KEEP HEARING ABOUT ONLINE.
WE DIDN'T BELIEVE HER BUT SHE- SHE UP AND FLEW AWAY.
NOW I'M TELLING YOU WHAT I SAW- WHAT WE ALL SAW I HAVE NEVER SEEN IN MY **ENTIRE LIFE**.
YOU SPOKE TO HER? YOU SPOKE TO HER DIRECTLY?
I SPOKE TO HER AND SHE CONFESSED THAT HER FATHER HAD ACCIDENTALLY TURNED HER INTO A SUPERPOWERED PERSON AND THAT THE PEOPLE AT THIS COMPANY TRIED TO KIDNAP HER HERE AND THEN SHE FOUGHT THEM OFF.
THEN SHE JUST FLEW AWAY.
SHE FLEW?

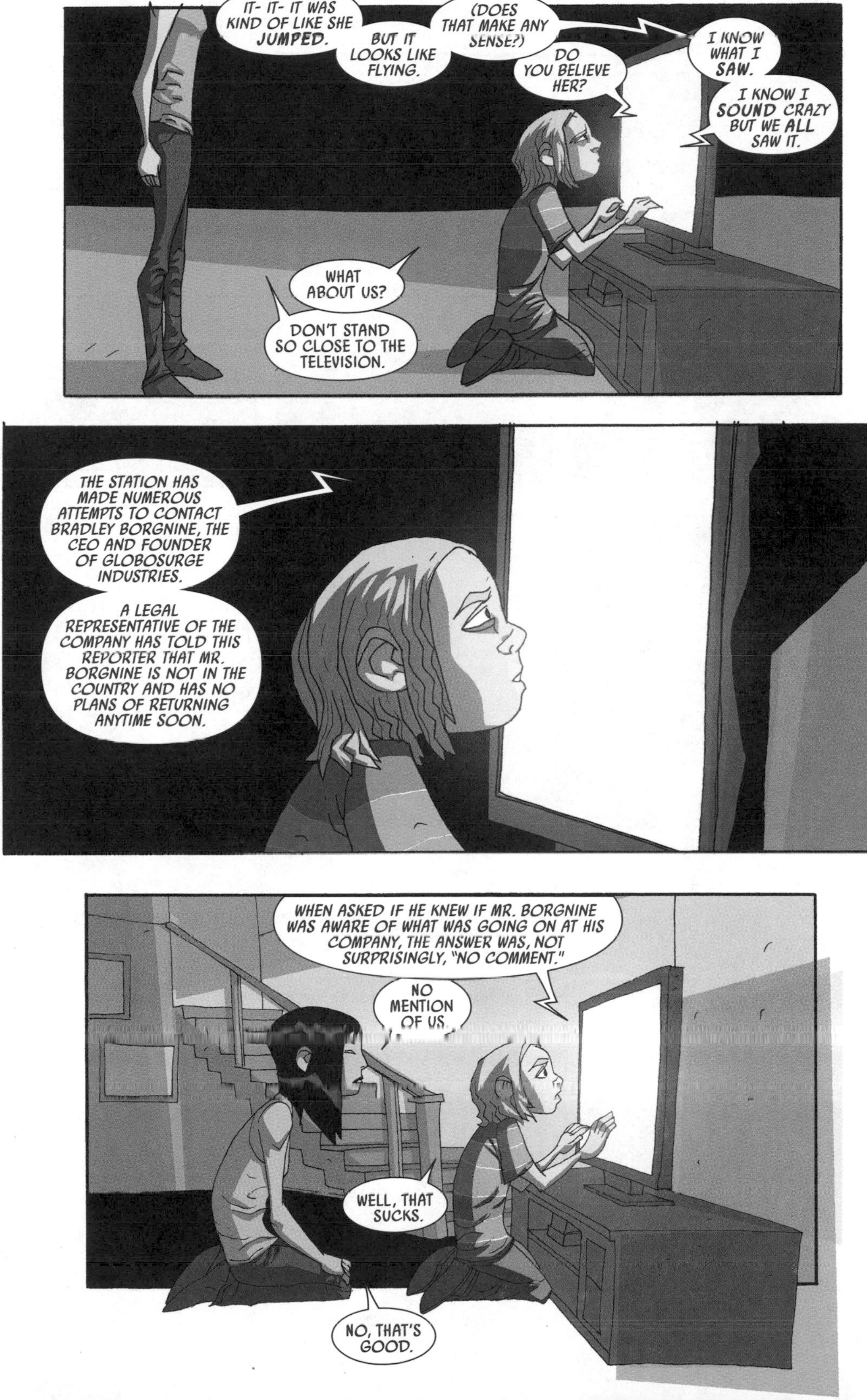
IT- IT- IT WAS KIND OF LIKE SHE JUMPED.
BUT IT LOOKS LIKE FLYING.
(DOES THAT MAKE ANY SENSE?)
DO YOU BELIEVE HER?
I KNOW WHAT I SAW.
I KNOW I SOUND CRAZY BUT WE ALL SAW IT.
WHAT ABOUT US?
DON'T STAND SO CLOSE TO THE TELEVISION.
THE STATION HAS MADE NUMEROUS ATTEMPTS TO CONTACT BRADLEY BORGNINE, THE CEO AND FOUNDER OF GLOBOSURGE INDUSTRIES.
A LEGAL REPRESENTATIVE OF THE COMPANY HAS TOLD THIS REPORTER THAT MR. BORGNINE IS NOT IN THE COUNTRY AND HAS NO PLANS OF RETURNING ANYTIME SOON.
WHEN ASKED IF HE KNEW IF MR. BORGNINE WAS AWARE OF WHAT WAS GOING ON AT HIS COMPANY, THE ANSWER WAS, NOT SURPRISINGLY, "NO COMMENT."
NO MENTION OF US.
WELL, THAT SUCKS.
NO, THAT'S GOOD.

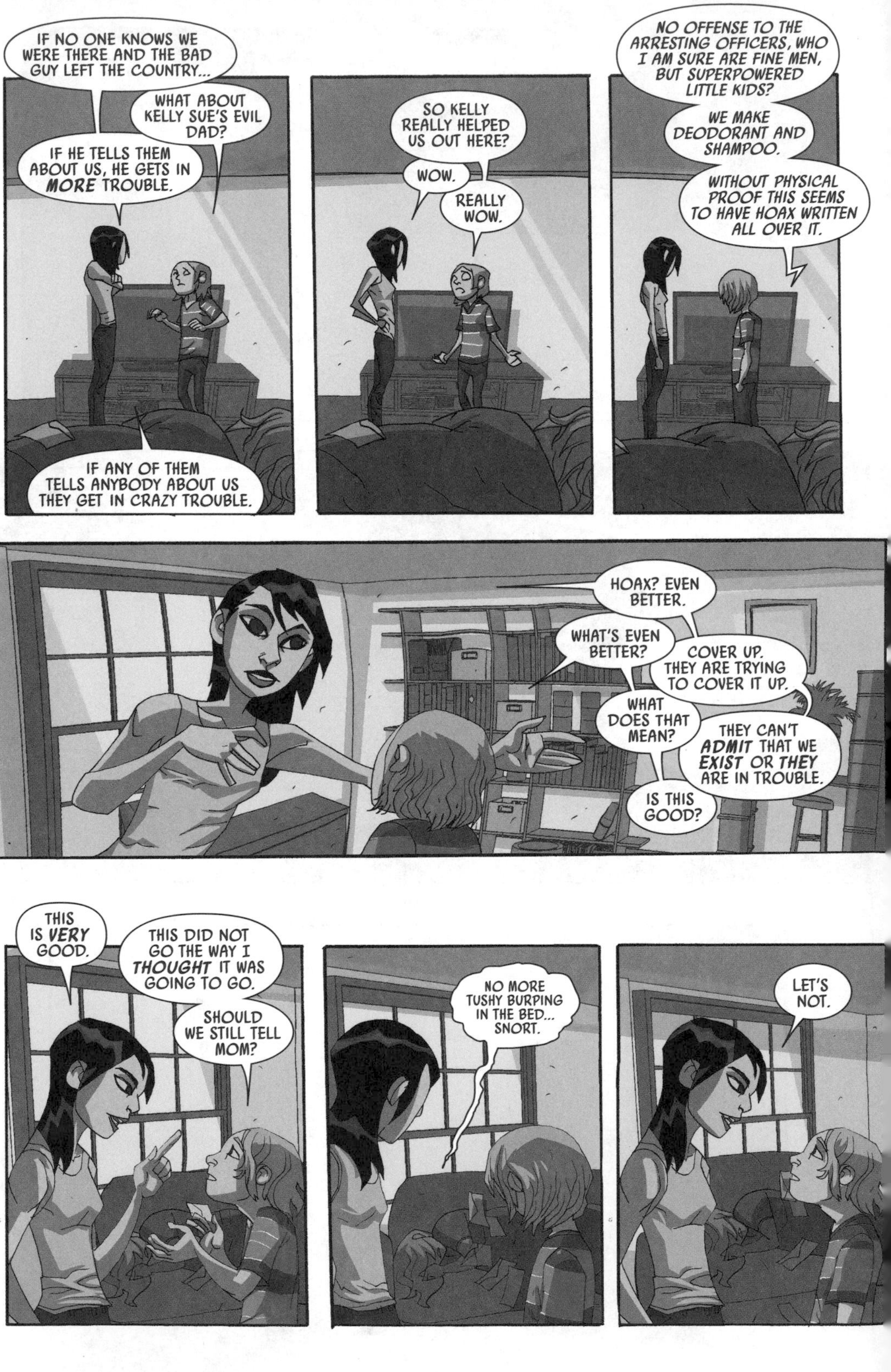
IF NO ONE KNOWS WE WERE THERE AND THE BAD GUY LEFT THE COUNTRY...
WHAT ABOUT KELLY SUE'S EVIL DAD?
IF HE TELLS THEM ABOUT US, HE GETS IN MORE TROUBLE.
IF ANY OF THEM TELLS ANYBODY ABOUT US THEY GET IN CRAZY TROUBLE.
SO KELLY REALLY HELPED US OUT HERE?
WOW.
REALLY WOW.
NO OFFENSE TO THE ARRESTING OFFICERS, WHO I AM SURE ARE FINE MEN, BUT SUPERPOWERED LITTLE KIDS?
WE MAKE DEODORANT AND SHAMPOO.
WITHOUT PHYSICAL PROOF THIS SEEMS TO HAVE HOAX WRITTEN ALL OVER IT.
HOAX? EVEN BETTER.
WHAT'S EVEN BETTER?
COVER UP. THEY ARE TRYING TO COVER IT UP.
WHAT DOES THAT MEAN?
THEY CAN'T ADMIT THAT WE EXIST OR THEY ARE IN TROUBLE.
IS THIS GOOD?
THIS IS VERY GOOD.
THIS DID NOT GO THE WAY I THOUGHT IT WAS GOING TO GO.
SHOULD WE STILL TELL MOM?
NO MORE TUSHY BURPING IN THE BED... SNORT.
LET'S NOT.

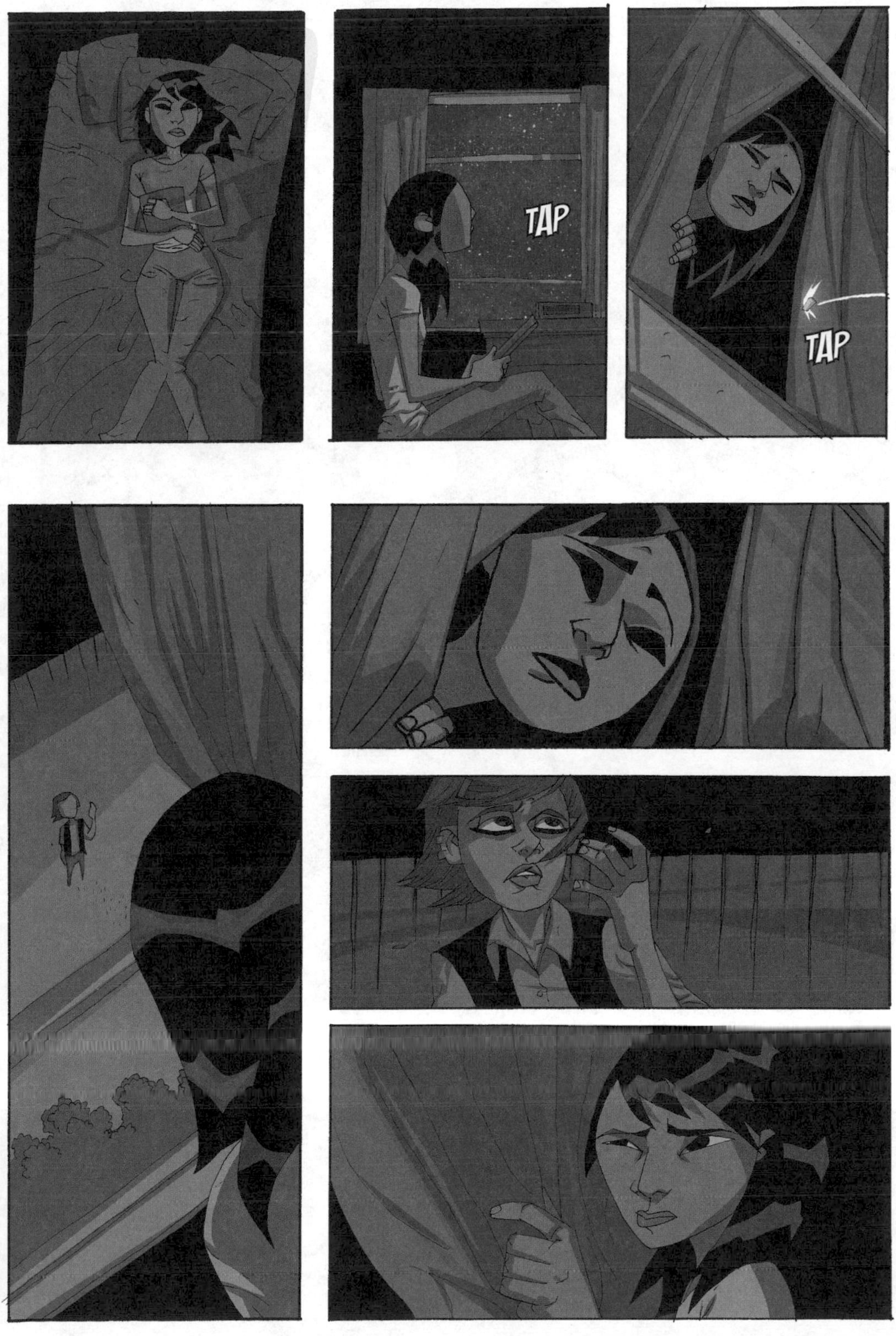
TAP
TAP

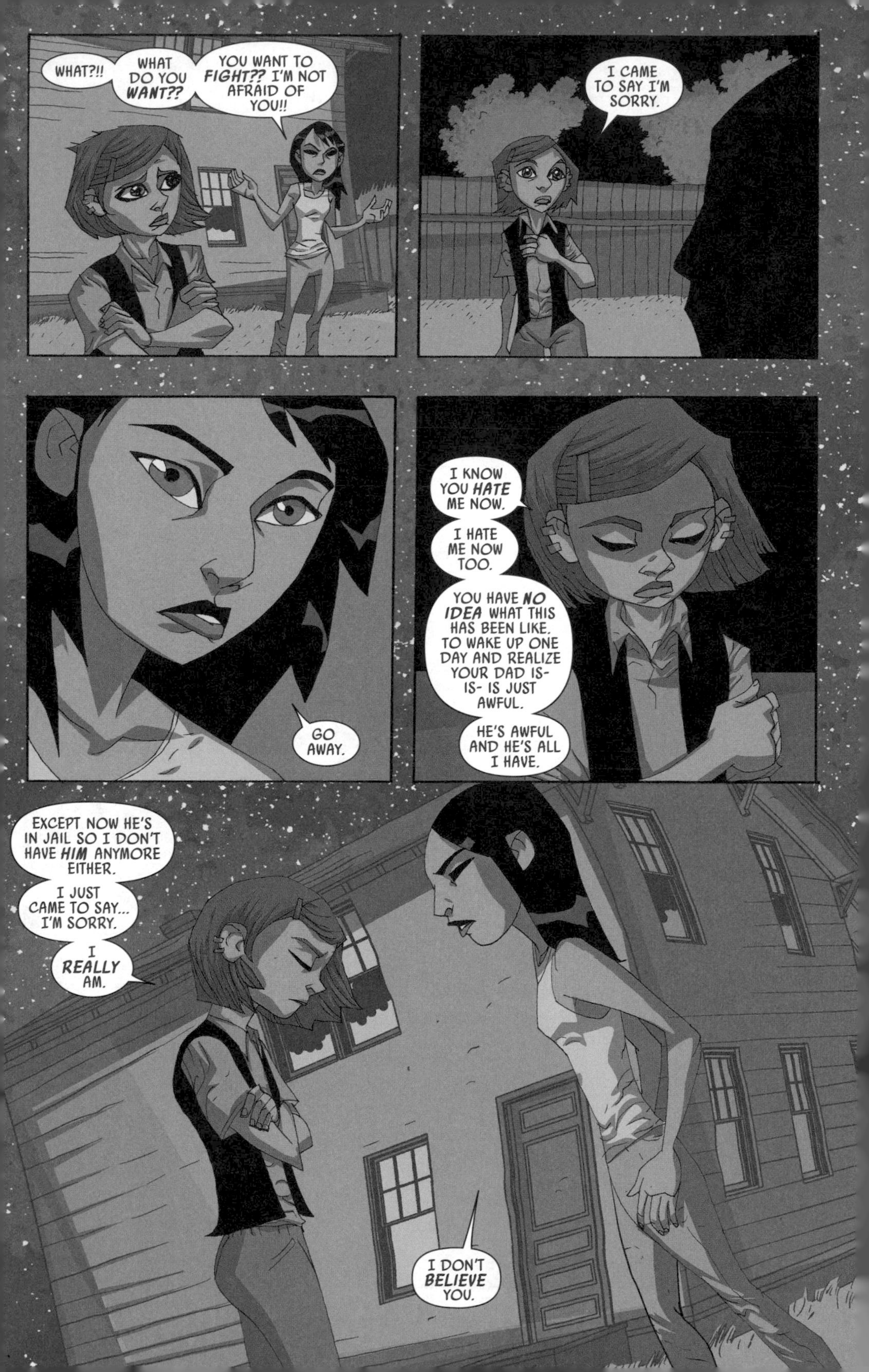
WHAT?!!
WHAT DO YOU WANT??
YOU WANT TO FIGHT?? I'M NOT AFRAID OF YOU!!
I CAME TO SAY I'M SORRY.
GO AWAY.
I KNOW YOU HATE ME NOW.
I HATE ME NOW TOO.
YOU HAVE NO IDEA WHAT THIS HAS BEEN LIKE. TO WAKE UP ONE DAY AND REALIZE YOUR DAD IS- IS- IS JUST AWFUL.
HE'S AWFUL AND HE'S ALL I HAVE.
EXCEPT NOW HE'S IN JAIL SO I DON'T HAVE HIM ANYMORE EITHER.
I JUST CAME TO SAY... I'M SORRY.
I REALLY AM.
I DON'T BELIEVE YOU.

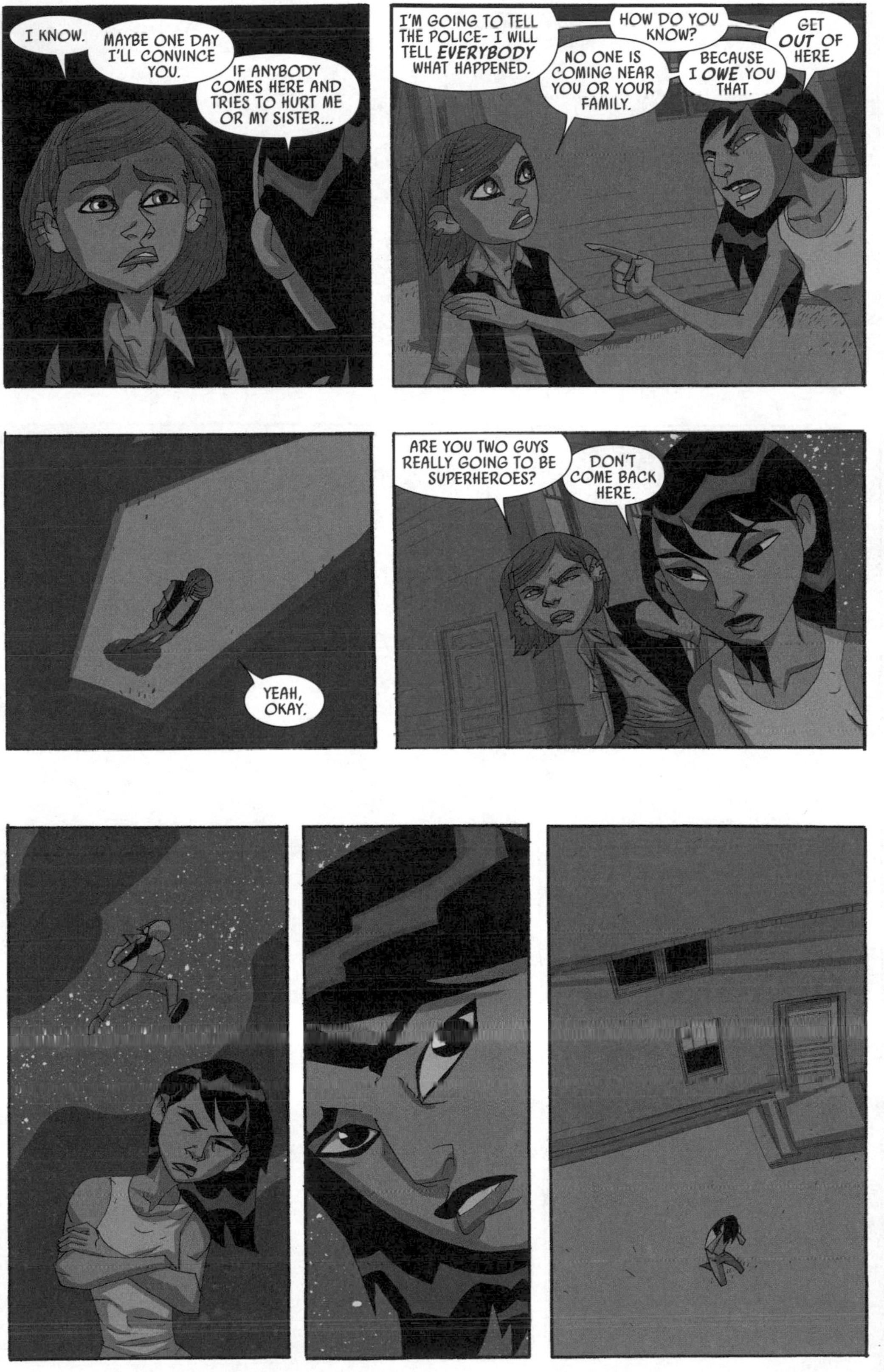
I KNOW.
MAYBE ONE DAY I'LL CONVINCE YOU.
IF ANYBODY COMES HERE AND TRIES TO HURT ME OR MY SISTER...
I'M GOING TO TELL THE POLICE- I WILL TELL EVERYBODY WHAT HAPPENED.
HOW DO YOU KNOW?
NO ONE IS COMING NEAR YOU OR YOUR FAMILY.
BECAUSE I OWE YOU THAT.
GET OUT OF HERE.
YEAH, OKAY.
ARE YOU TWO GUYS REALLY GOING TO BE SUPERHEROES?
DON'T COME BACK HERE.

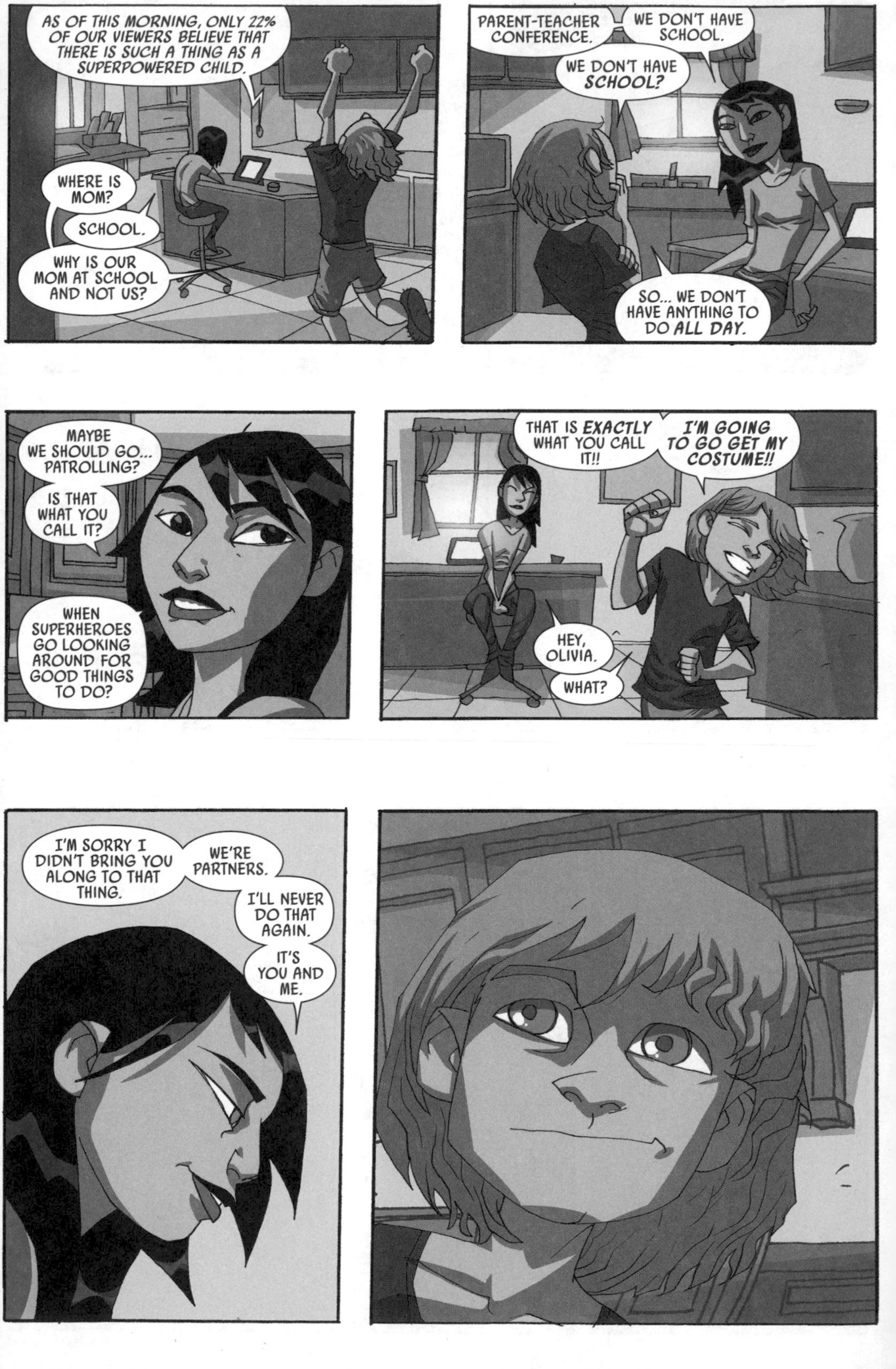
AS OF THIS MORNING, ONLY 22% OF OUR VIEWERS BELIEVE THAT THERE IS SUCH A THING AS A SUPERPOWERED CHILD.
WHERE IS MOM?
SCHOOL.
WHY IS OUR MOM AT SCHOOL AND NOT US?
PARENT-TEACHER CONFERENCE.
WE DON'T HAVE SCHOOL.
WE DON'T HAVE SCHOOL?
SO... WE DON'T HAVE ANYTHING TO DO ALL DAY.
MAYBE WE SHOULD GO... PATROLLING?
IS THAT WHAT YOU CALL IT?
WHEN SUPERHEROES GO LOOKING AROUND FOR GOOD THINGS TO DO?
THAT IS EXACTLY WHAT YOU CALL IT!!
I'M GOING TO GO GET MY COSTUME!!
HEY, OLIVIA.
WHAT?
I'M SORRY I DIDN'T BRING YOU ALONG TO THAT THING.
WE'RE PARTNERS.
I'LL NEVER DO THAT AGAIN.
IT'S YOU AND ME.

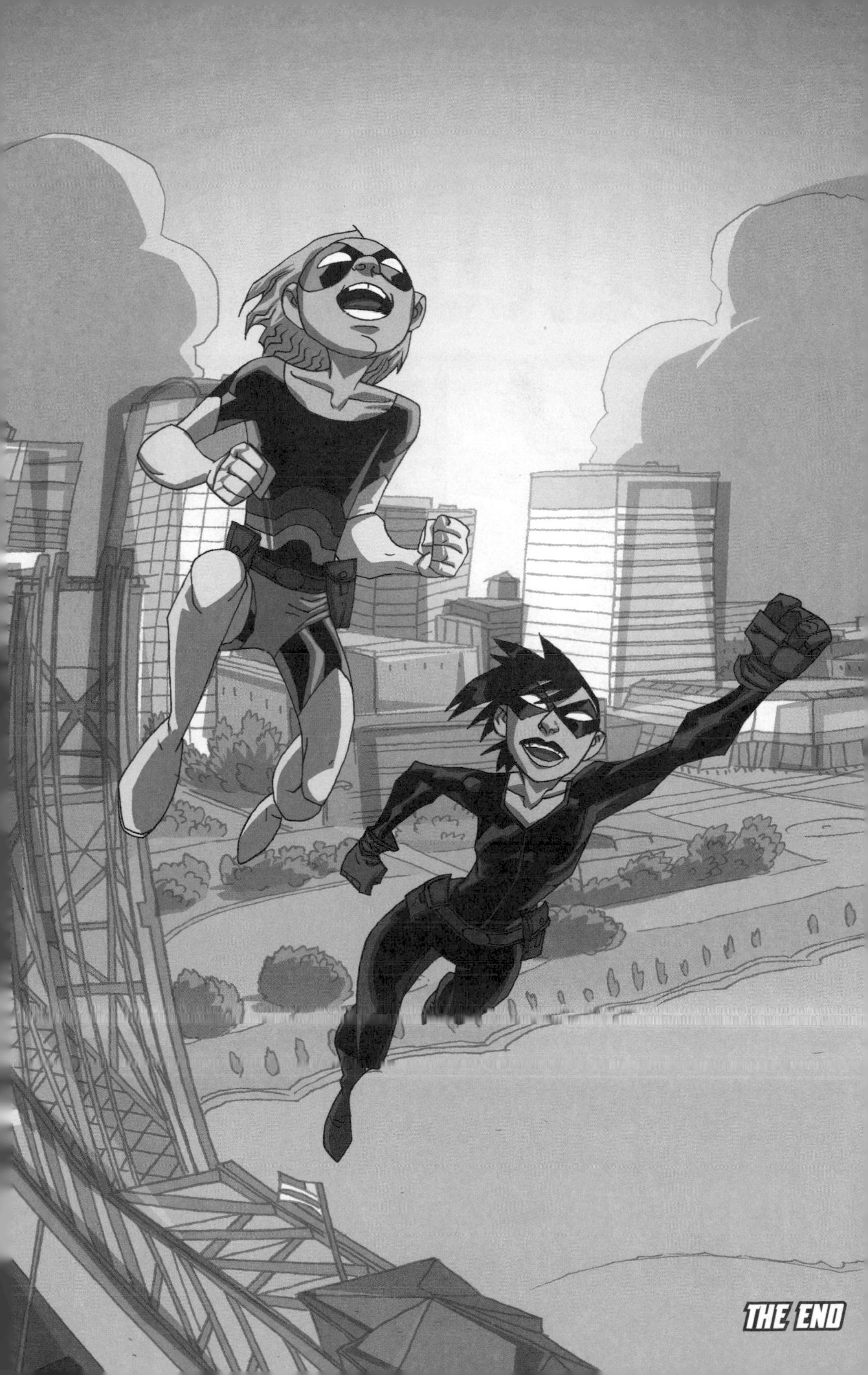
THE END

COVER GALLERY

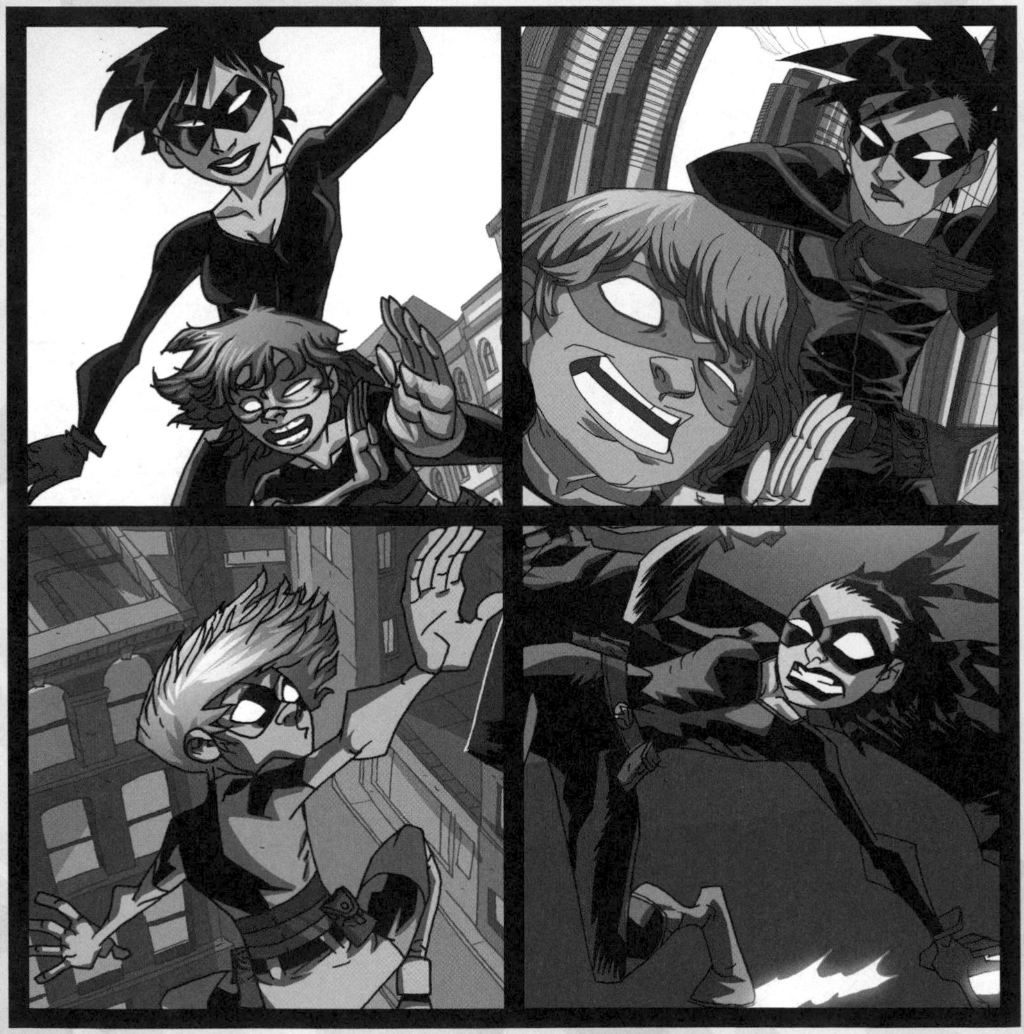

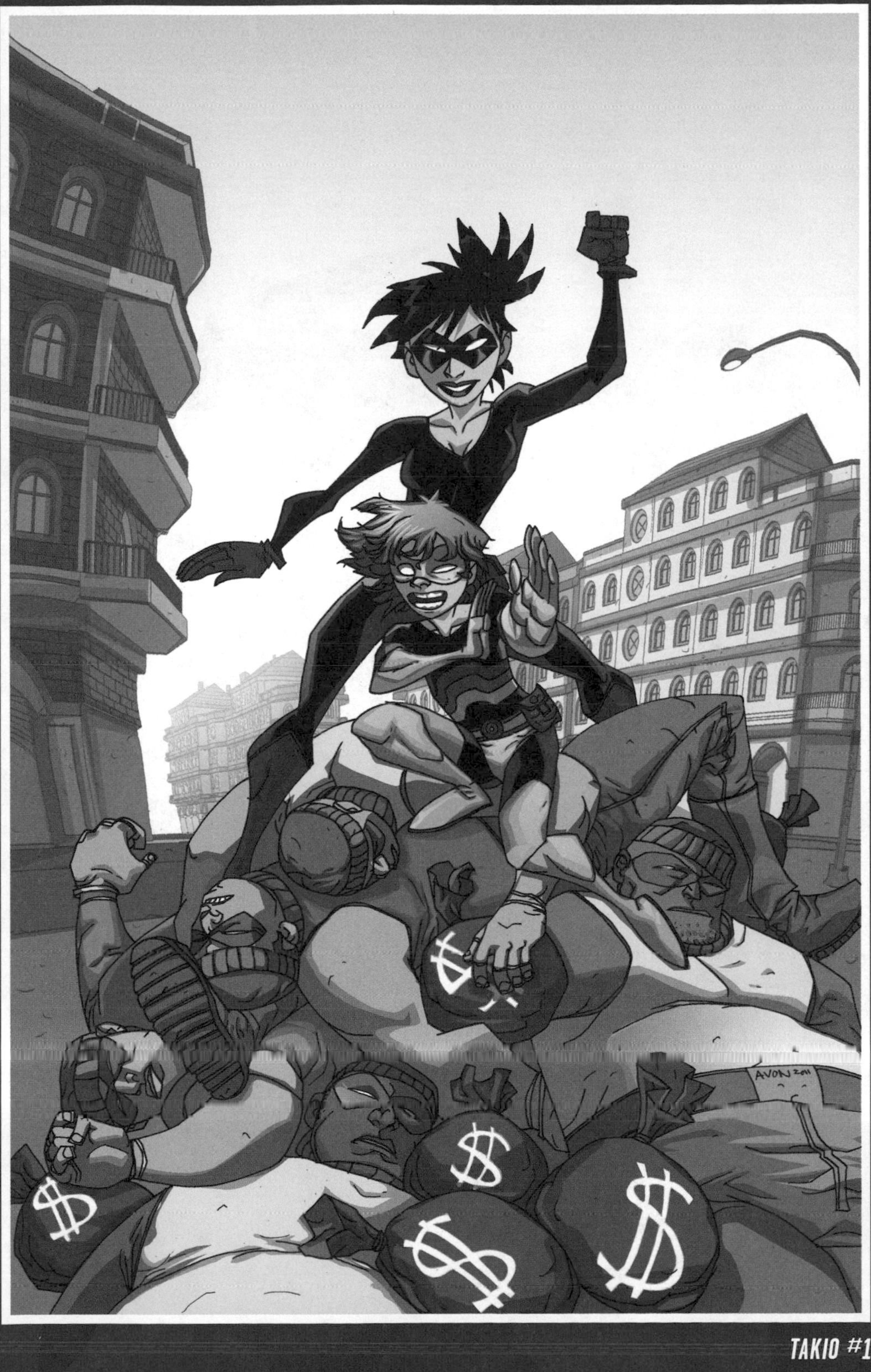

AVON 2011

TAKIO #1

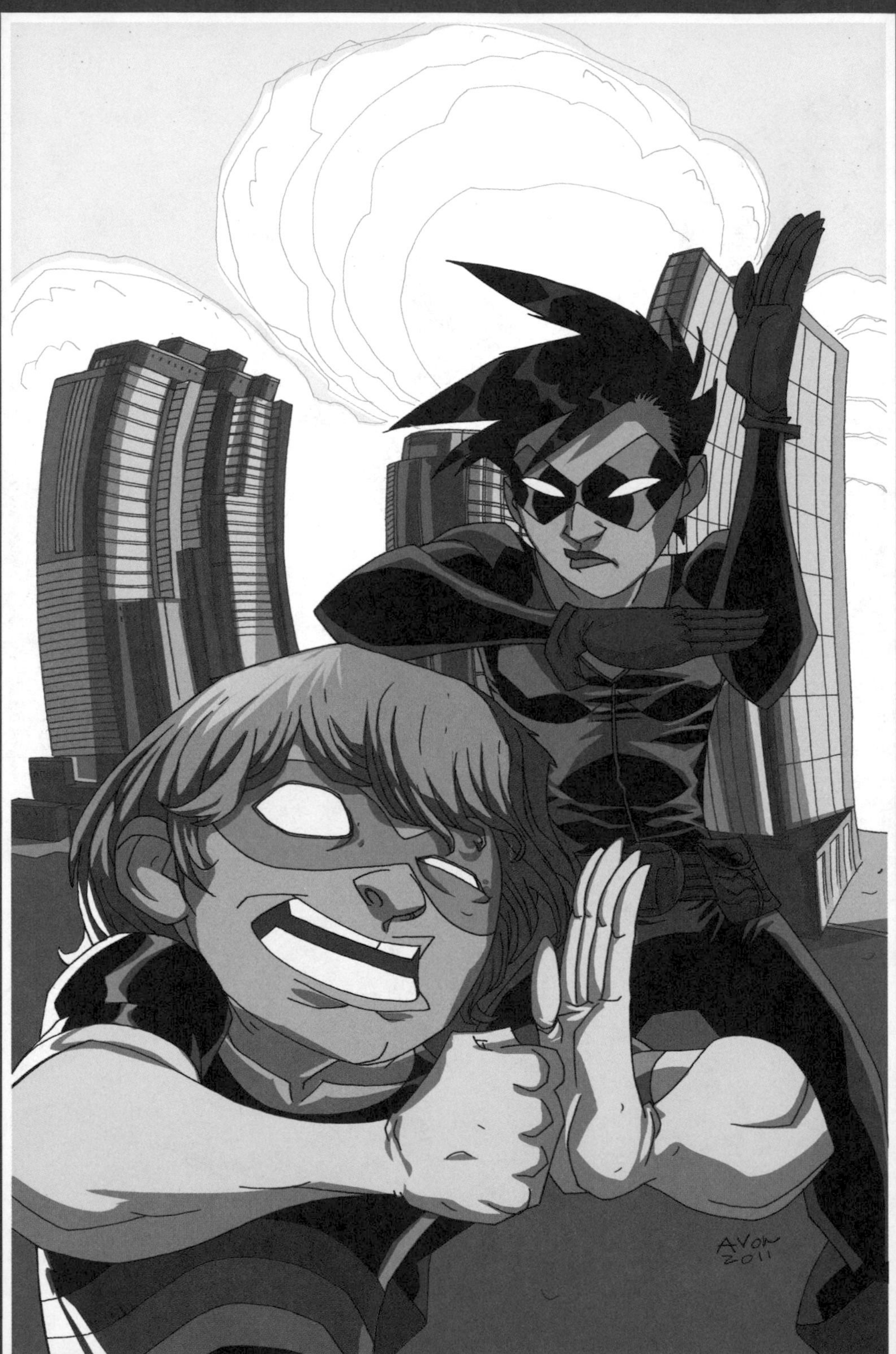
AVON
2011

TAKIO #2

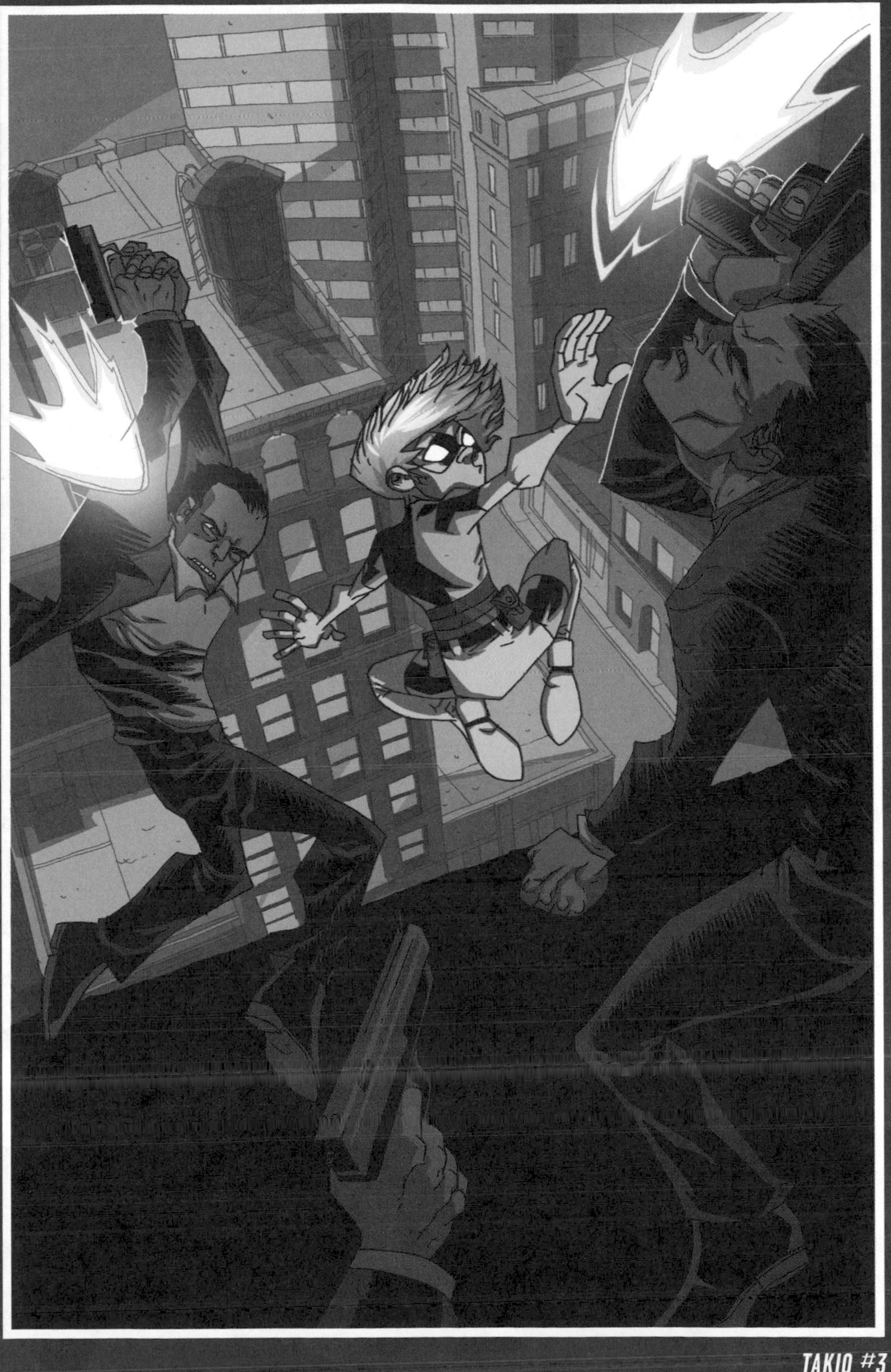

TAKIO #3

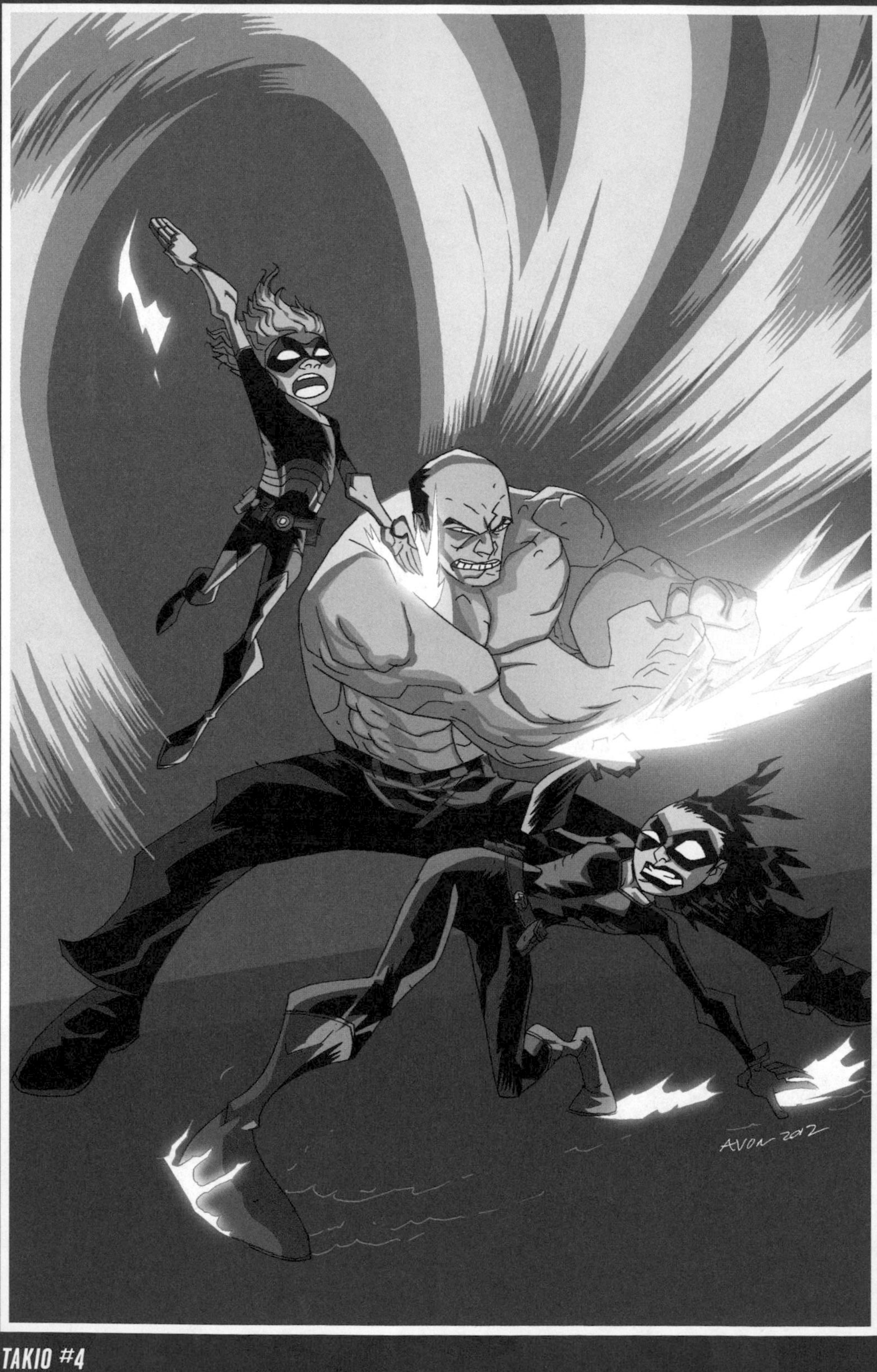
AVON 2012

TAKIO #4

SKETCH BOOK

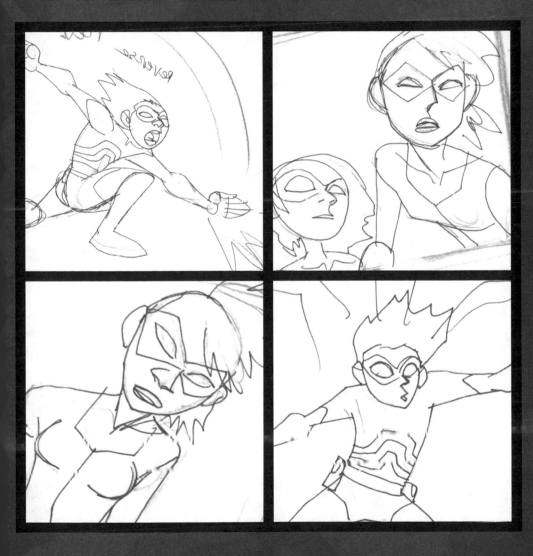

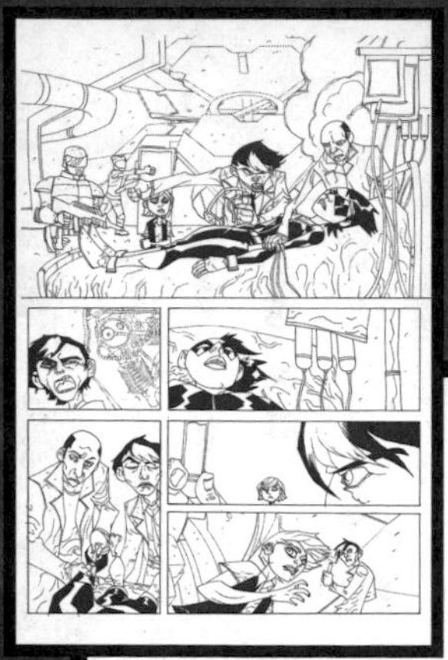

Layout & Final Art #4, Page 1

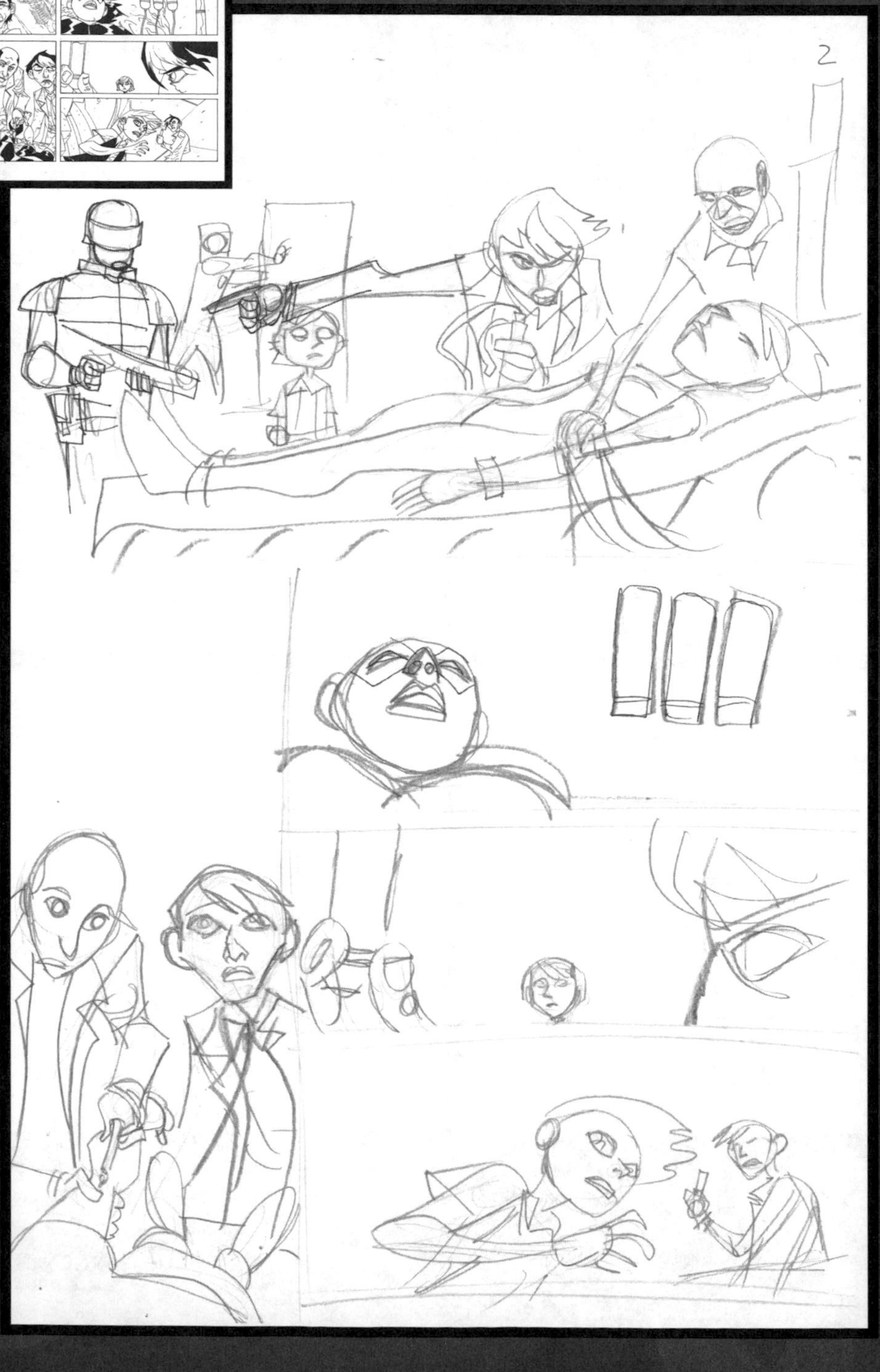

Layout & Final Art #4, Page 2

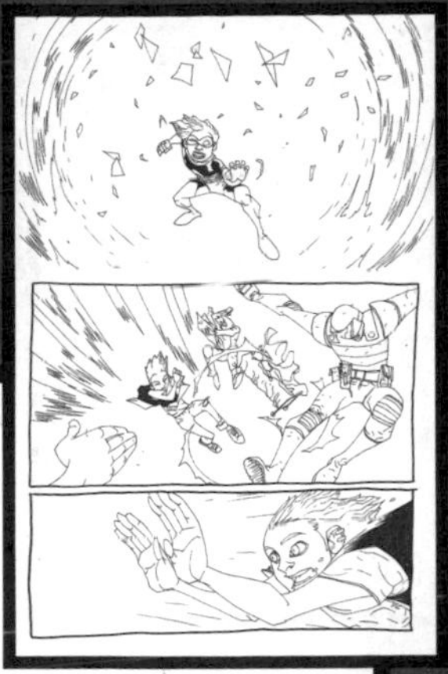

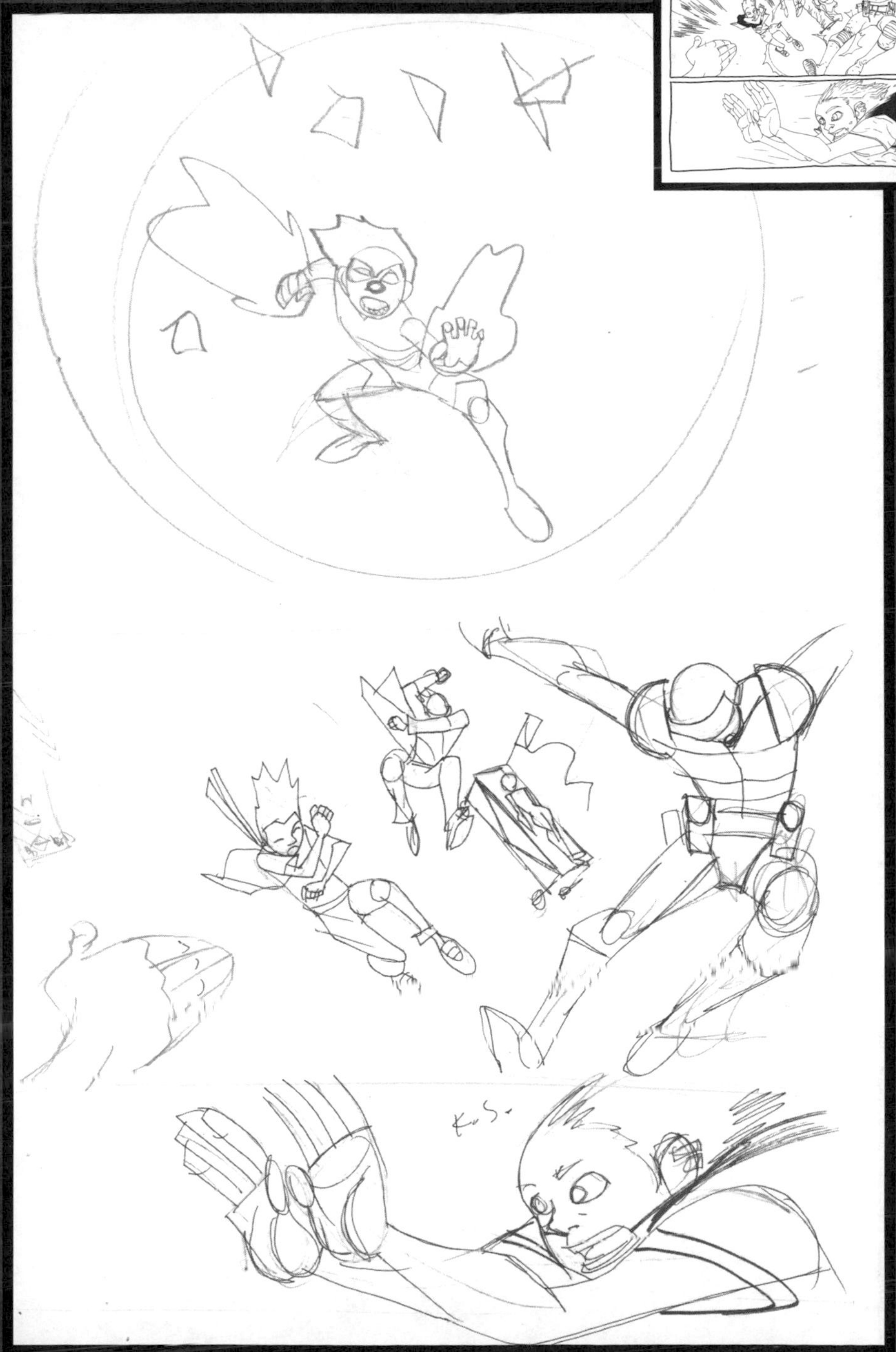

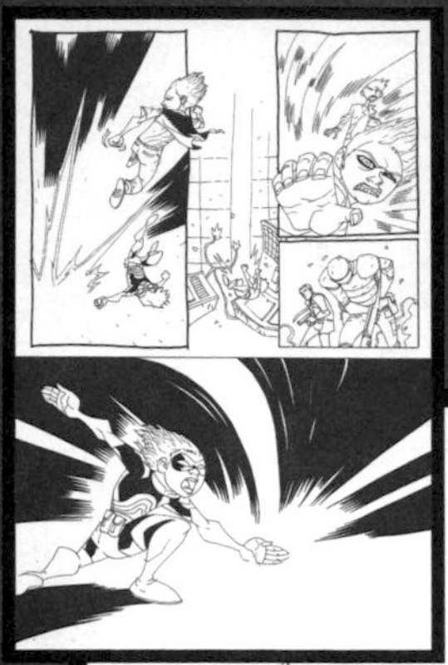

Layout & Final Art #4, Page 3

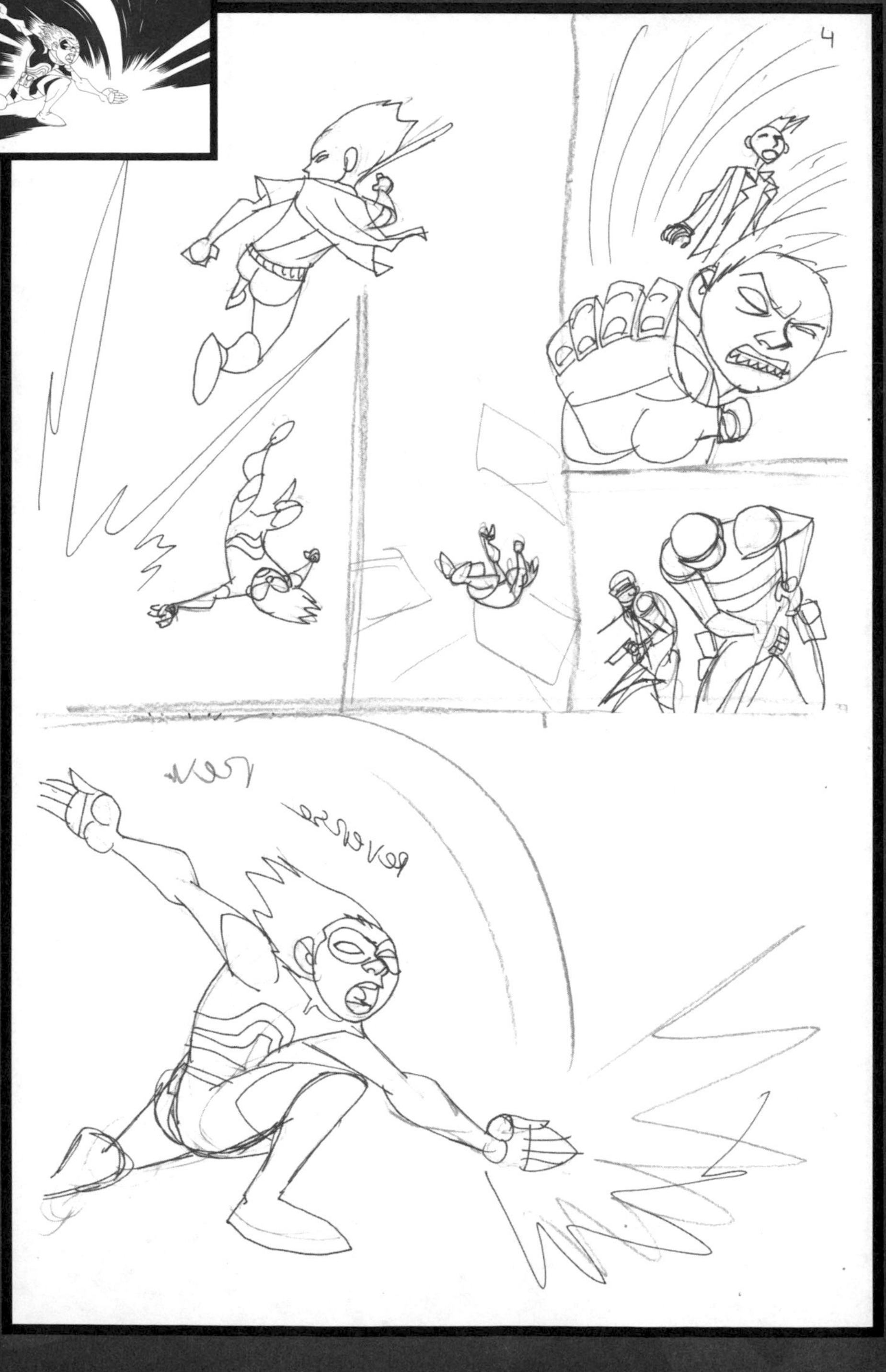

Layout & Final Art #4, Page 4

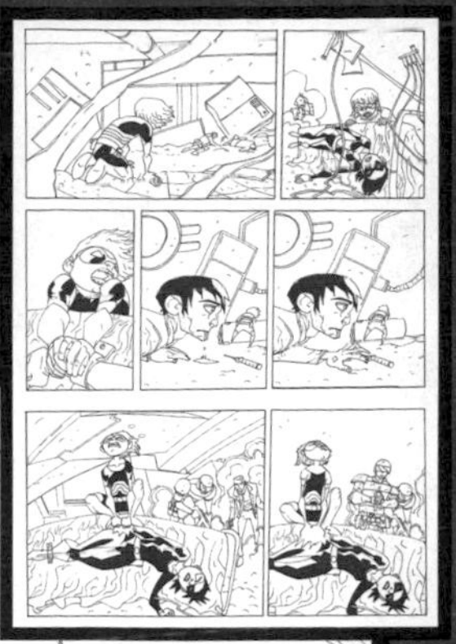

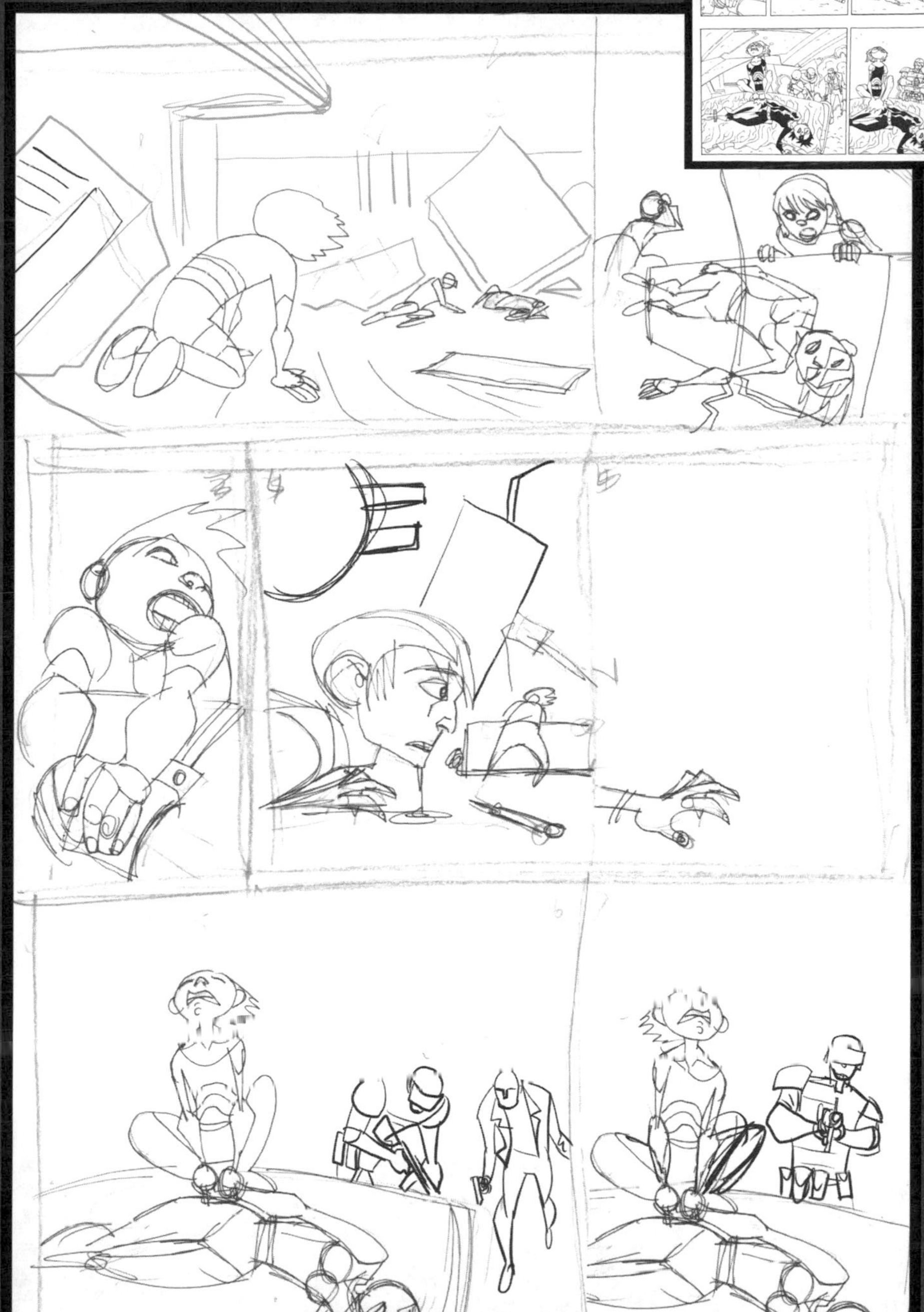

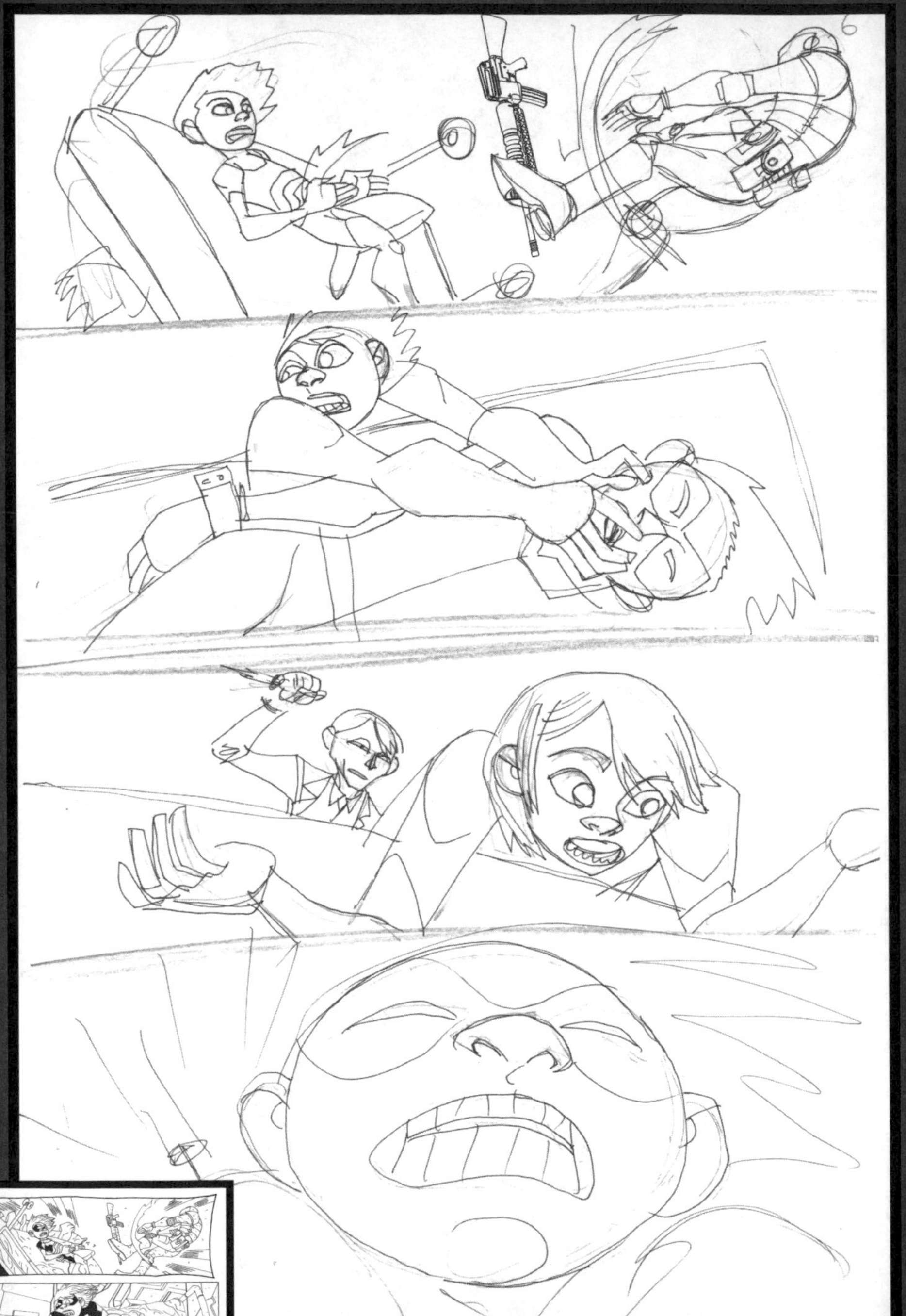

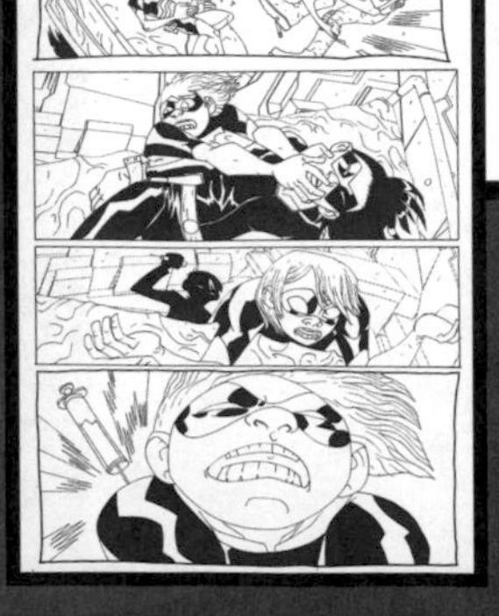

Layout & Final Art #4, Page 5

Layout & Final Art #4, Page 6

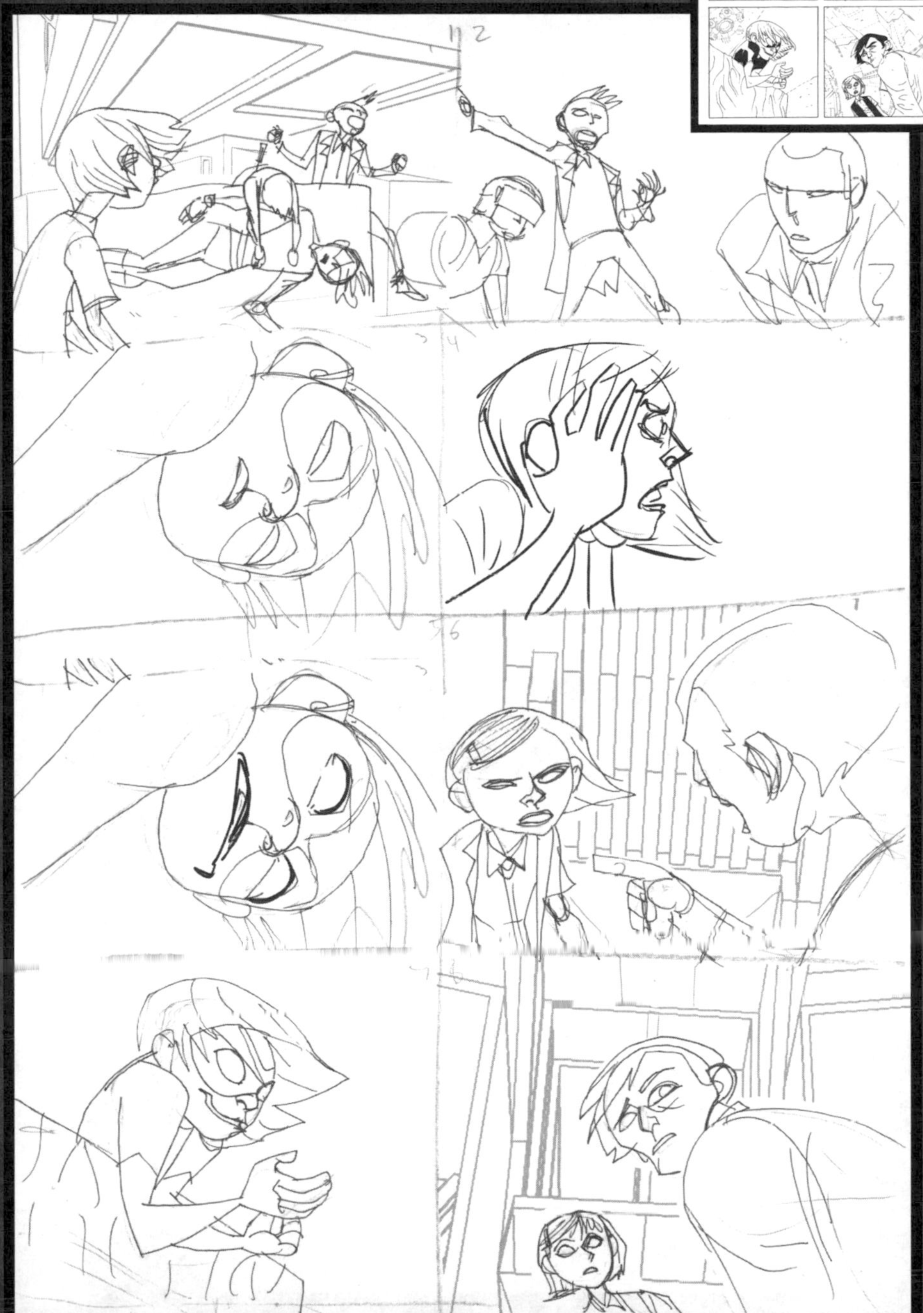

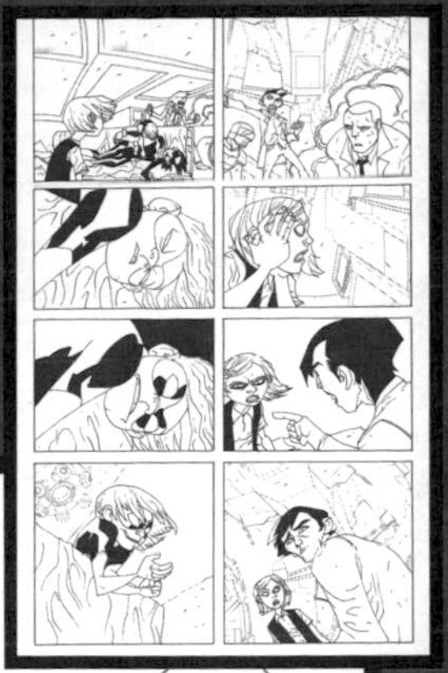

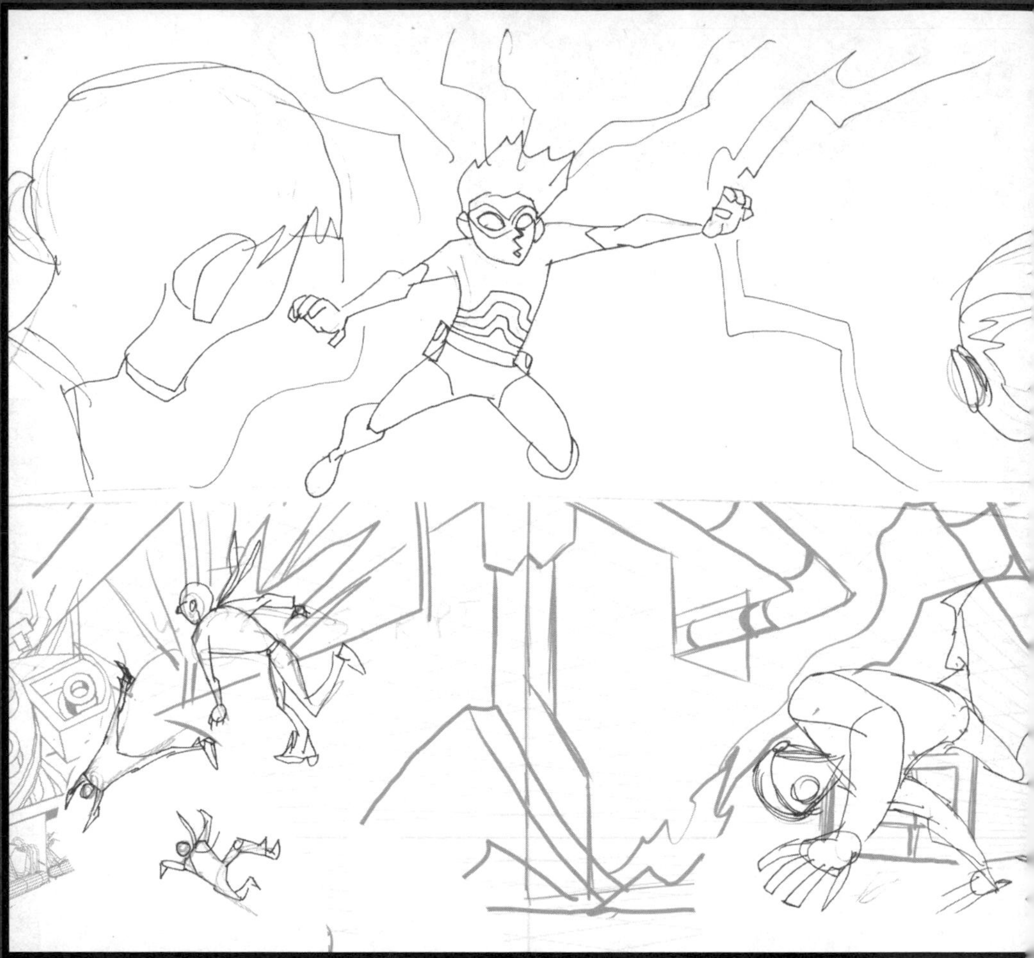

Layout & Final Art #4, Pages 7-8

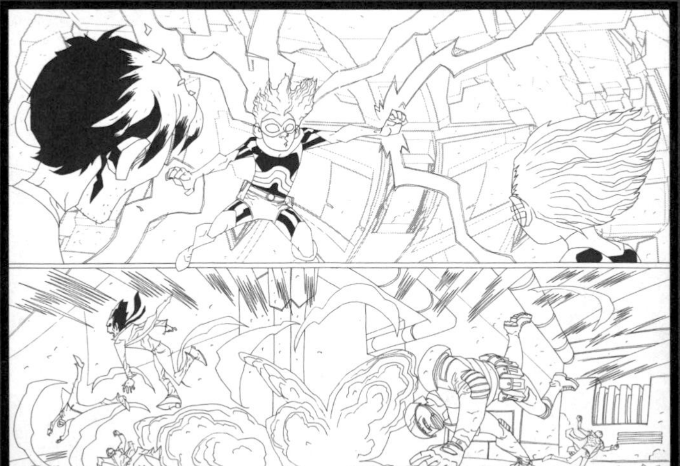

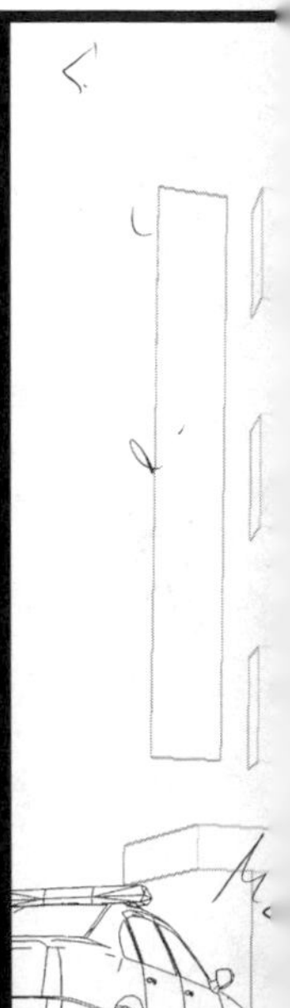

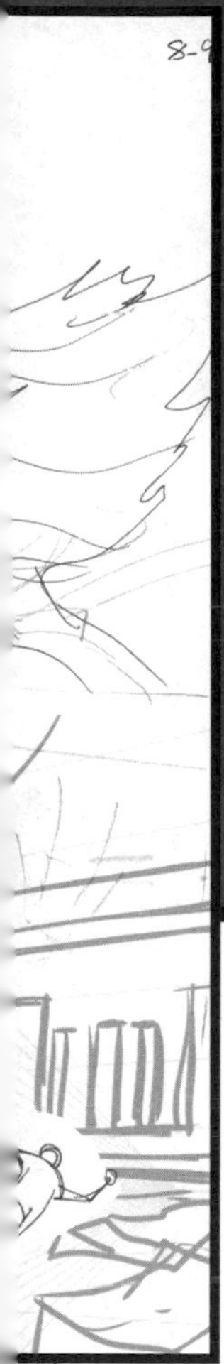

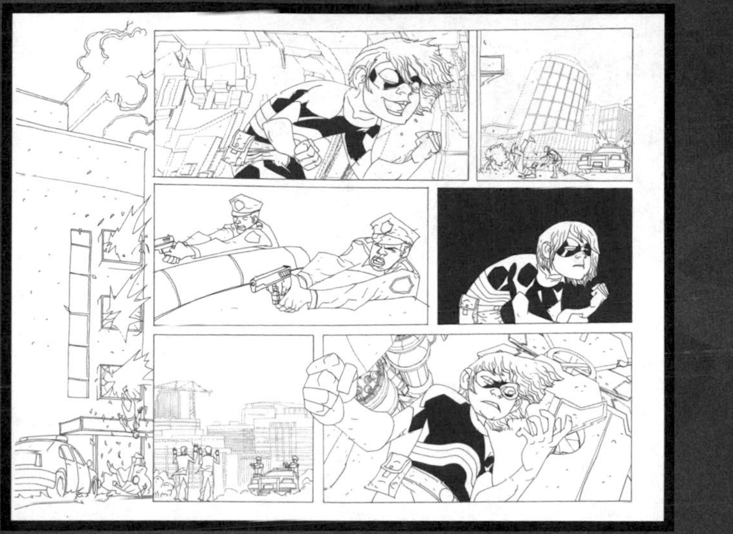

Layout & Final Art #4, Pages 9-10

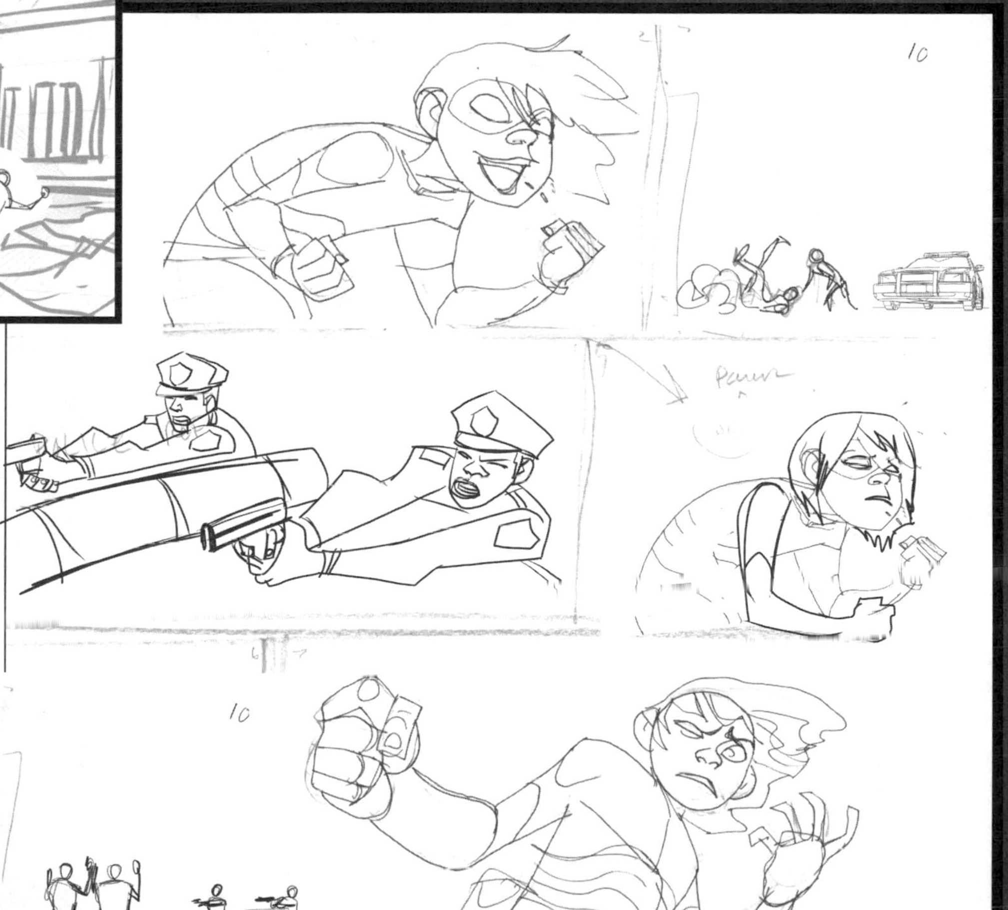

Layout & Final Art #4, Page 11

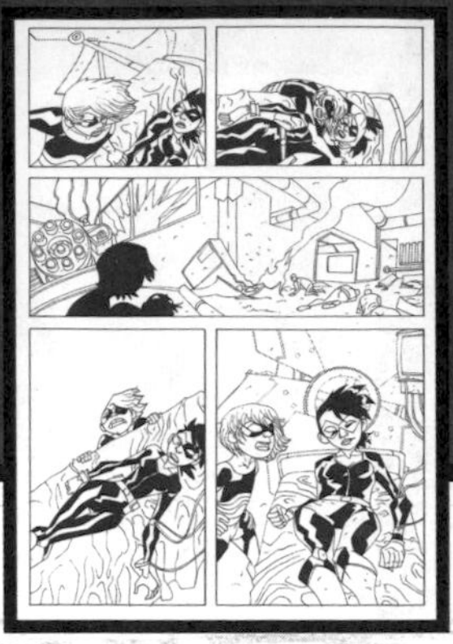

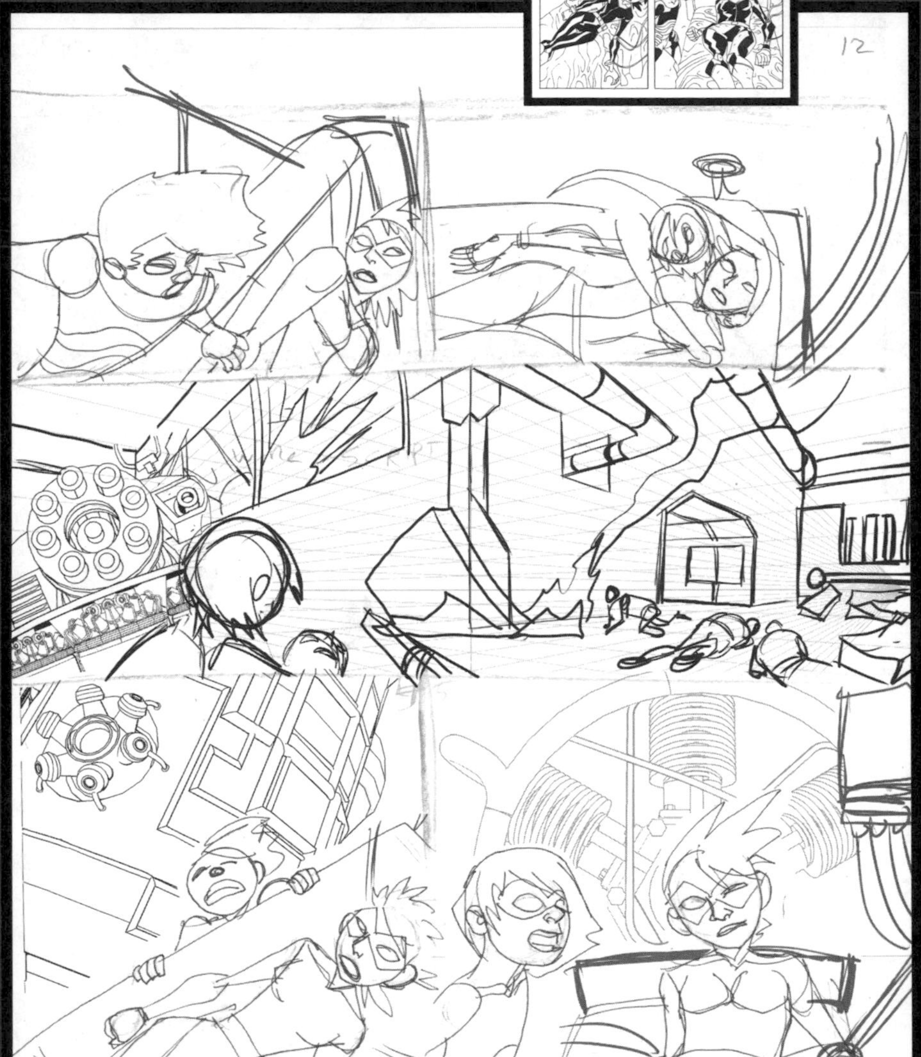
12

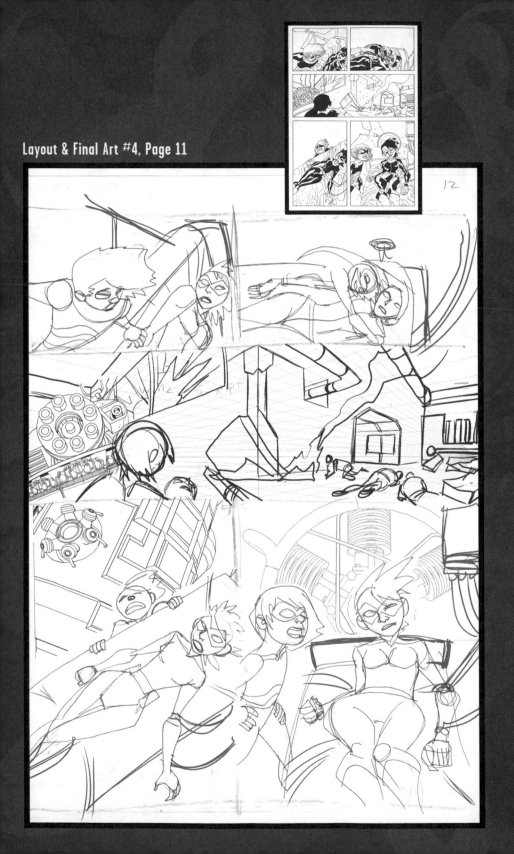